BISON
BOOKS

A Season in Purgatory

VILLANOVA AND LIFE IN COLLEGE FOOTBALL'S LOWER CLASS

TONY MOSS

UNIVERSITY OF NEBRASKA PRESS · LINCOLN & LONDON

Library of Congress Cataloging-in-Publication Data
Moss, Tony (Anthony Lyle)
A season in purgatory: Villanova and life in college football's lower class / Tony Moss.
p. cm.
ISBN-13: 978-0-8032-5959-1
(pbk.: alk. paper)
ISBN-10: 0-8032-5959-X
(pbk.: alk. paper)
1. Villanova University—Football.
I. Title.
GV958.V5M67 2007
796.332'6309748'14—dc22
2007011371

Set in Janson Text by Bob Reitz.

For my grandfather,
Mike Markowski
A good man,
and a strong man

CONTENTS

ILLUSTRATIONS

ACKNOWLEDGMENTS

A head football coach allowing a reporter full access to his program is akin to a taxpayer inviting the IRS to spend a year or so painstakingly poring over the details of his or her finances. No matter how honest you are or how firmly you believe you are doing the right thing at all times, a close enough view will no doubt reveal some irregularities.

To his great credit, Andy Talley knew this to be the reality of the situation from the very beginning of the process but explicitly told me that he believed my book would uncover more positives than negatives in his program. I believe he was 100 percent correct. Talley understands and appreciates the role of the media as well if not better than any coach I have covered at any level, and it was for this reason that I chose Villanova as the focus for this work when the seed of the idea first began to germinate in my mind in February 2005.

Talley went above and beyond the call of duty in accommodating my needs in writing this book, and for that I will be eternally grateful. As the reader has undoubtedly ascertained by this point, Villanova's 2005 season was a very difficult one for Talley, his coaches, and the players, and yet I encountered not one person involved with the program who was anything but courteous and forthright when dealing with me or in suffering my endless stream of questions.

I sensed after the season was completed that Talley was somewhat embarrassed that this book was being written. He invited me into his program because he believed I would be witnessing Villanova's return to glory, and when those expectations went unmet, I think he regretted the fact that I had been there to chronicle it. That is more than understandable, though I never felt he had much about which to be embarrassed.

I believe that Talley cares deeply about his players and coaches, and I have tremendous admiration for the way he has been able to withstand the oft-difficult political climate at Villanova.

Talley is also refreshingly outspoken concerning injustices that hurt the sport or his football team, and his candor is one of the major reasons I knew he would make a fascinating book subject. Also, lest anyone be persuaded to think differently in light of a less-than-stellar season, he is also a very good coach in a pure football sense, having won 176 games in 27 seasons. The 2006 campaign, which followed the one chronicled in this book, saw Talley guide a team to a winning record for the twentieth time in his career. (The young '06 Wildcats rebounded from a 2-5 start to finish 6-5, beating the likes of William and Mary, Richmond, James Madison, and Delaware to end the year).

I often got the sense that if Talley's assistants had been afforded the opportunity to vote on whether I be allowed to follow the program for the entire season, I would have had my Saturdays free during the fall of 2005. They didn't need the added distraction and had little to gain by my presence, so if that was indeed the prevailing mindset, than I am not offended. Let it be known that every assistant I dealt with was more than friendly in their interactions with me, and for that I am appreciative. In particular, Mark Ferrante, Sam Venuto, Mark Reardon, Brian Flinn, Sean Spencer, Brendan Daly, and Justus Galac took time out of their busy schedules to speak with me, and I very much appreciate their consideration and their honesty.

Also terrific were the players, who were willing to offer the benefit of their perspectives even if it meant they wouldn't get to dinner immediately after practice. All the players deserve acknowledgment, with special recognition going to Darrell Adams, Marvin Burroughs, Dave Dalessandro, John Dieser, Christian Gaddis, Moe Gibson, Brian Hulea, Adam James, Frank Jankowski, Joe Marcoux, DeQuese May, Russell McKittrick, J. J. Outlaw, and Matt Sherry, who helped me understand the inner workings of the program.

I am sure that the players and coaches saw things differently than I did at times, and I'm fine with that. If ninety players and ten coaches each wrote their own account of the 2005 season, there would be a hundred different stories written. Hopefully, at the end of the day, those in the program feel that, on the whole, I represented their season accurately.

Two people I must express the deepest gratitude toward are Villanova director of athletics Vince Nicastro and assistant athletic director for communications Dean Kenefick, who along with Talley green-lighted this project despite reservations about letting it move forward.

There were some difficult aspects within the world of Villanova football, and life at the I-AA level, that I had to shine a light on if I wished for my account to be honest and accurate, and Nicastro provided me with more perspective, not to mention facts and figures, than most in his position would have been compelled to do. When he couldn't answer my questions, Nicastro helped set me up with those who could, and his efforts on my behalf were not taken for granted, rest assured.

Dealing with Dean Kenefick is like having recess in the midst of a long school day and was absolutely one of the most fun parts of this process. Sports information directors are a strange breed, and I should know, because I used to be one. Some that I have dealt with over the years are absolutely convinced that they are part of the coaching staff, and some others are stat-heads who are impossible to communicate with as human beings. Kenefick espouses none of these qualities. His job is to be a liaison between the media and the athletic department, and like all good media relations people, he does so without any hint of bias toward either side. You would not be reading this book without a sizeable amount of help from Kenefick. As SIDs go, he is the cream of the crop, though I make no apologies for the fact that he roots for the Pittsburgh Pirates.

I would not expect Rev. Edmund J. Dobbin, OSA, to rank this book as amongst his favorites—first, since he admitted to me that he is not much of a football fan, and second, because it deals with some topics about which he will undoubtedly take issue. Regardless, I do appreciate Father Dobbin's consent to being interviewed for the book, and he should be heartened to know that everyone I spoke to, including those who disagreed with his perspectives on the I-A study, believed that he was on the whole a good president who served Villanova with tremendous leadership and class in that role for eighteen years.

Other members of the Villanova family who were of assistance include senior associate athletic director Bob Steitz, a true professional and longtime friend and confidante; director of football recruiting Ryan McNamee, who equipped me with important contact numbers and made sure I wasn't late for practice; director of football operations Joan McGuckin, who looked after me like a mother on the road and along with partner in crime Rosemary Mazzotta always provided a much-needed smiling face; associate athletic director and team chaplain Rev. Robert Hagan, OSA, a good and kind man for whom I have much admiration; football equipment manager Tom Dunphy, a friend to talk to on the sideline and someone who helped me at least dress like I was part of the team; football trainer Dan "Tiger" Jarvis, who showed patience in helping me comprehend the complicated world of football injuries; and Dr. Ray Heitzmann, who helped relay a faculty point of view as part of his perspective on the game. Thanks to my two roommates on the road—Ryan Fannon, Villanova's radio color man, and John Simpson, the head coach's longtime friend and an ardent Wildcat football supporter—who both offered much-needed encouragement when my head was spinning. Arlene Talley, the head coach's wife, also provided kind words and offered her interesting perspective at various points during the season.

Former Villanova assistants Dave Clawson and Joe Trainer were frank and forthcoming with their thoughts and reminiscences about the program, and Clawson and Lehigh head coach Pete Lembo lent valuable voices to the section regarding the Patriot League. Thanks are also due to Jason Honsel, formerly of the Lehigh admissions office, for helping me to understand certain administrative details regarding the Patriot League dynamic.

At the Atlantic 10 Conference, Stephen Haug was a great friend and a terrific sounding board throughout this process, and Ray Cella, who gave me my start in sports, was tremendous as always.

Among the media, Mike Kern and Pat McLoone of the *Philadelphia Daily News* are owed a debt of gratitude for allowing me to play the role of devil's advocate in my interviews with them. Villanova beat writers Terry Toohey, of the *Delaware County Times*, and Mike Jensen, of the *Philadelphia Inquirer*, were accommodating and supportive throughout the season. Donald Hunt, a sportswriter at the *Philadelphia Tribune* and an author in his own right, is a quality person who helped answer some book-related questions for me.

Tony Randazzo and Bob Mulcahy provided voices to this book that were absolutely essential in explaining the political climate at Villanova. As distinguished alumni of the university, both had much to lose by speaking to me, and yet they were earnest in assisting my pursuit of the truth surrounding the I-A feasibility study. I cannot thank them enough.

Bob Capone and Dick Bedesem Jr. were kind enough to recount the circumstances around the dropping of football at Villanova in 1981. The decision to drop the sport and the details of the I-A feasibility study were subjects that probably warranted their own books, and I regret that for the sake of being concise and remaining true to the theme of the book, I couldn't chronicle those events in a bit more thorough fashion.

My original idea had been to interview a large sampling of students and alumni, but Bill Nolan at Vusports.com did such an evenhanded and eloquent job of encapsulating the thoughts and feelings of so many different Villanova constituents in regard to football at the university that I felt that the book didn't require another such spokesman. Any bias that I might have harbored about the motives of those who run message boards was washed completely away after I spoke with Nolan, who was very professional and offered fresh nuances about football at Villanova that I had not considered.

You would not be holding this book in your hands had it not been for the two main champions of this project: Rob Taylor at the University of Nebraska Press and my agent, Uwe Stender, at TriadaUS. Thanks for believing in me, guys. Your enthusiasm was a major reason that I made it to the finish line. Gratitude is also due Ann Baker, my project editor at UNP, and Stephen Barnett, who did a brilliant job of copyediting.

Much appreciation goes to Phil Sokol and Mickey Charles at The Sports Network for allowing me to work on this project, as well as to Matt Dougherty, who helped me figure out was going on in I-AA.

Thanks to the friends and family who either looked over my work, offered advice, or both: Jim Brighters, Justin Cifra, Chris Cortina, Kevin Daly, Paul DeCrette, Dan Di Sciullo, Otto Fad, Christine Gazurian, Francis Green, Sean Hargadon, Heather Moss, and Alex and Ellen Schugsta.

And last, and most significantly, thanks to my wife, Bridget, who put up with my hectic schedule during football season and was always understanding and supportive. I love you, angel.

A Season in Purgatory

PROLOGUE

Moe Gibson stood alone, facing his locker, bawling like a baby. He had already removed his shoulder pads and the navy blue jersey emblazoned on both sides with No. 22, the one with his surname printed in large capital letters on the reverse and "Villanova," in smaller type, along the front.

Gibson, by now the only person remaining in the university's spacious football locker room, cried for the name on the back of the jersey, and he cried for the name on the front. For four years the kid who was known by his given name, Martin, to just about no one, had returned kicks and played running back for the Villanova football team. On this crisp late-November afternoon, Gibson had made his last run and had also run out of time.

Villanova had been manhandled by its archrival, the University of Delaware, in its season finale, which was also the last game for Gibson and his fellow seniors. It was a fitting end to an uneven, disappointing year, one that had included flashes of joy and triumph as well as extended periods of misery.

Gibson, clinging in vain to his last moments as a college football player, wept in honor of the journey's end and in honor of the personal journey he had faced. A street kid who had been raised in a rough neighborhood in southeast D.C. and an only slightly less mean section of nearby Prince George's County, Maryland, Gibson had spent his last four years in the archetypal suburban utopia, far from the daily realities faced by his friends back home. The friends that were still alive, anyway. Three of his old neighborhood running mates had been gunned down since Gibson started at Villanova, victims of the pervasive drug and gun culture in the bitter end of the nation's capital he had managed to escape.

As his career died, Gibson's football past flashed before his eyes. The encouragement he had received from his uncle, Ira Hackett, the only strong male role model he had after his father had died when Gibson was two. The support from his mother, Letitia, who raised six kids on a government worker's salary. The star-studded performances for Central High School. The year in prep school spent when his chosen college, Lafayette, decided he needed to brush up academically, and the ensuing heartbreak when Lafayette determined that he still wasn't admissible. A Villanova assistant coach, Mark Ferrante, rescuing Gibson from his despair and awarding him a scholarship. The electrifying kickoff return for a touchdown in the playoffs during his freshman year. The frustration of never getting the ball with the frequency he wanted or felt he deserved. The endless practices and workouts, hours upon hours devoted to remaining at the top of his game.

And for all that he had endured, Gibson found himself alone in the locker room, feeling as empty as he had in his twenty-two years. He knew that few of his classmates at Villanova would ever be able to relate to the way he was feeling. Most of the university's students had stayed far away from the Delaware game, with the season going nowhere and the temperature in the thirties by the time the teams left the field.

As Gibson's emotions burst forth, the mostly white and privileged student body was warm in their dorm rooms, pondering which of the taverns just off campus they would seek admission to on the final Saturday night prior to Thanksgiving break.

Basketball, now in season, was king at Villanova, a fact with which the students, including Gibson, had long ago come to terms. Football, meanwhile, was but a minion. Basketball kept the school's name on TV and in the paper, football was but an occasional distraction until hoops tipped off. Men's basketball was the moneymaker for the school, while football was a financial drain.

In four years at Villanova, Gibson was one of roughly sixty full-scholarship players who would receive an education annually valued at more than $38,000 by 2005. Seeking a tangible, black-and-white return on the university's investment in Gibson or any of his teammates would be a mostly futile effort for anyone who tried to crunch the numbers.

The need for Villanova's commitment to people like Moe Gibson and to the pursuit of football in general were linchpins in a discussion to be casually trotted out in some faculty dining room or at a university board meeting somewhere on campus.

But as his tears mixed with eyeblack and sweat and fell to the navy blue carpet of the Villanova locker room, the fact that Gibson had represented the university with every ounce of determination, passion, and work ethic he had to give was not subject to debate.

1

HUDDLING

By 7 a.m. on Thursday, April 7, 2005, the temperature on Philadelphia's historic Main Line had already risen past sixty degrees. At midday the mercury reached seventy-five, the kind of perfect early-spring day that can trick a northeasterner into prematurely placing the heavy coat into mothballs. Many would play hooky from work and school that afternoon, the lure of a Phillies–Nationals matinee in south Philly proving too irresistible a temptation.

As the warmth of the morning sun intensified, the traffic began to pick up along Lancaster Avenue, the thoroughfare that cuts through the heart of the picturesque campus of Villanova University. The well-to-do Main Liners of surrounding communities like Bryn Mawr, Ardmore, and Wynnewood drove their luxury cars west past Villanova to Interstate 476 (commonly known as the "Blue Route" due to its color designation on a 1958 Pennsylvania Department of Highways proposal) before hopping on the Schuylkill Expressway to begin the painfully slow procession to workplaces in Center City Philadelphia. The trek of less than twenty miles could take more than ninety minutes, an exercise in patience undertaken daily by thousands of commuters.

Work had yet to begin for the denizens of the Main Line and indeed most of the populace of the United States, but Lancaster Avenue travelers could peer to the right as they passed Villanova Stadium and glimpse a flurry of activity taking place on the University's synthetic athletic surface. Villanova had begun spring football practice that morning.

The first of the Wildcats' fifteen formal April training sessions would not be front-page, back-page, or even agate-type news in either of the city's two main newspapers—the *Philadelphia Inquirer* and the *Philadelphia Daily News*—nor would any of the local television outlets find their way to Philly's western suburbs to issue a report. This was not the University of Florida, where both *Sports Illustrated* and ESPN *SportsCenter* had covered the school's preseason gridiron happenings days earlier, nor was it the University of Nebraska, at which 63,416 people attended an intrasquad scrimmage nine days later. At power schools in the Southeast and parts of the Midwest, as the saying goes, there are two sports worth following: football and spring football. At Villanova, the major sports topic on this unseasonably warm day was the men's basketball team's recently completed run to the "Sweet 16," and the buzz from that somewhat unexpected journey would last until well after the spring semester ended in early May and most students had departed campus.

Not that this seeming ambivalence toward football was anything new. For the past twenty years, Villanova's gridiron program had been labeled as a member of Division I-AA, an emblem that often resembled a scarlet letter for the university and most of the 120-plus institutions of its ilk. The NCAA had split Division I football into two groups in the mid-1970s in an effort to curb the arms race taking place in the sport at the time (which continues to this day), allowing institutions that were having trouble meeting escalating financial demands to play football at a more cost-feasible level while remaining Division I across the board. Villanova, which had participated at the highest level of Division I before controversially dropping football in 1981, had been born again in 1984 as a I-AA entity. And despite a couple of efforts of varying success to move football either up or down within the Division I hierarchy in the two decades since, I-AA is where the program remained.

On paper, the major difference in 2005 between I-A and I-AA was scholarships. While the big boys up the road at Penn State could offer eighty-five football scholarships per year, Villanova could award just sixty-three. Though the $3 million that most I-AAs spent on football each season would yield a high level of play and ultimately turn out a number of NFL stars, somewhere in the previous quarter century, the mainstream media and average fan had determined that as essentially a minor league, I-AA was scarcely worth noticing. The wane in interest nearly coincided with the rise of what is now known as the Bowl Championship Series (BCS), a conglomerate of the nation's six premiere football conferences (ACC, Big East, Big Ten, Big 12, Pac-10, SEC) that controlled and allocated the millions of dollars in bowl game payouts and television rights fees that major corporations and networks were shelling out with increased willingness. Enhanced financial profiles for BCS schools spelled even bigger stadiums, better practice facilities, and limitless budgets to recruit the best players from all over the nation.

When the quality of play spiked, so did the popularity of college football. Television networks noticed, and in place of the I-AA national championship, which had always been on one of the three majors, there was a BCS conference title game or major rivalry of some sort. I-AA got kicked to cable, and by the end of the 1990s, prior to the emergence of fringe networks like CSTV and ESPN University, the ESPN-broadcast title game and the Bayou Classic, between traditional black powers Grambling and Southern, were I-AA's only nationally televised games.

The print media soon followed TV's lead. In preseason publications like *The Sporting News*, I-AA coverage was reduced from twelve or fourteen pages to a single-page spread. *USA Today* scaled back its usual detailed I-AA national overview in favor of greater coverage for I-A, particularly the BCS schools and conferences.

Other Division I colleges and universities saw how quickly the BCS gravy train had pulled out of the station, and many gave chase. Though most programs in lower-profile I-A leagues like the Western Athletic Conference and Mid-American Conference, and later Conference USA and the Mountain West, had a fraction of the financial wherewithal of the generally larger BCS schools, their mere membership in I-A and association with the nation's best programs had given them a boost of cachet in the eyes of those who studied box scores rather than budgets.

Meanwhile, with attention for I-AA on the decline and the lure of "big-time" money floating like a mirage in the distance, a number of I-AA universities suddenly determined that fiscal responsibility was less important than the status and potential dollars that came with the elimination of an "A", and made the jump. Some, especially those that already had sizeable fan bases, achieved modest success (including the University of Connecticut, Marshall, and Boise State), but most (including the University of Buffalo, the University of Idaho, and most of what is now the Sun Belt Conference) failed, married to a dubious "if we build it, they will come" mentality that ultimately spelled a sea of red ink, major defeats on the football field, and a loss-fueled erosion of whatever fan support may have initially existed for the program. Without sizeable TV contracts, generous bowl game tie-ins, or adequate ticket sales, and with twenty-two more scholarships to fund along with the facilities upgrades necessary to be competitive in recruiting, a good number of these universities were spending $7 million per season on football before they made back their first million. On the field, few were getting any closer to the behemoth BCS programs, but ego and stigma prevented them from cutting their losses and playing at the more cost-conscious I-AA level. In reality, the top third of I-AA and most of I-A's non-BCS institutions were strikingly similar in resources and talent level as 2005 began, though the seemingly outdated Division I dividing line continued to segregate the two in the hearts and minds of most casual fans and the media. Villanova was one of those sitting at the rear of the Division I football bus.

Despite the lack of attention for the Wildcats' present football activities, the fifty-eight players and ten coaches who took the stadium field just after dawn on April 7 radiated an intensity that was quiet but palpable. Though VU was more than five months from its first game of the 2005 season, there was an eagerness to begin anew, to erase what had undoubtedly been one of the darkest periods in program history. The preceding eighteen months had been marked by equal measures of disappointment, heartbreak, and tragedy, casting a dark cloud over a team that had finished in the top five at its level as recently as 2002.

The 2002 team went 11-4 and reached the semifinals of the I-AA playoffs, the furthest Villanova had ever advanced in the sixteen-team tournament. In 2003 the Wildcats started the preseason ranked twelfth and began the campaign 6-0, including a dramatic 23–20 overtime win over Big East member Temple in the first college football game played at Lincoln Financial Field, home of the NFL Philadelphia Eagles. By mid-October, Villanova had risen to No. 2 on the I-AA charts. But in game number seven, against UMass, sophomore quarterback Joe Casamento was sidelined by a hard shot to the passing shoulder. His replacement, raw but talented freshman Marvin Burroughs, looked to be on the way to guiding VU to a narrow 14–13 victory, until the team watched its nightmare scenario play out. With two minutes left, Burroughs mishandled the snap from center, and in an effort to reclaim the football, kicked it directly to UMass cornerback Shannon James, who scooped it up and trotted 39 yards in the other direction for a touchdown. Massachusetts, 19, Villanova 14. Since the date of that game—October 20, 2003—to this spring day a year and a half later, little had gone well for head coach Andy Talley and the Wildcats.

After the UMass debacle, in which All-American tight end Matt Chila was lost for the season with a knee injury so gruesome that few who witnessed it could stomach recounting the tale a full year after Chila had graduated, Villanova went into a full-fledged tailspin. The Cats would lose three of their final four in 2003, dropping close road games to a lowly Hofstra club (34–32), to the University of Maine in frigid conditions (14–10), and finally to archrival Delaware (20–17) at home. Following that finale, seventy-eight-year-old team chaplain Father Bernard Lazor was exiting the Villanova Stadium parking lot when his foot somehow became entangled in his car's accelerator. Lazor plowed through a group of Delaware supporters who had assembled outside the visiting locker room before a bystander managed to track down the Augustinian priest's moving car, open the driver's side door, and cut the ignition. Blue Hen long snapper Brett Wharton and his mother, Bonnie, who was knocked unconscious and suffered a concussion, were among the four people injured in the bizarre incident. All recovered, but Lazor, who was not charged by police, was quietly asked to relinquish his duties as chaplain by an embarrassed Villanova administration.

Teams rarely advanced to the I-AA playoffs with a record worse than 8-3, and the 2003 season would reflect that trend. Talley and company finished with a thud at 7-4, watched from afar as hated Delaware rolled to its first I-AA national championship, and receded into the cruel Philadelphia winter to ponder what might have been.

The worst was yet to come.

On January 25, Lou Ferry, a Villanova player in the 1940s and football coach at his alma mater since the seventies, including two separate stints as head coach, died at seventy-six of heart failure. Ferry, the only remaining coach from Talley's first Villanova staff, was beloved by the players and an icon at the school. His dedication to the university was such that when Talley first met him upon being named head coach in 1984, Ferry was spending his nights sleeping on a training table in an unheated locker room beneath the stadium. Talley noted, "Lou was always the most popular coach on our staff. In the true sense of the word, he was really from the old school—I mean the Vince Lombardi, Woody Hayes school. But the sweetest guy in the world. The kids loved him, and he was a character. Chewed tobacco, spitting all the time, talked to himself, said funny things to the kids. And he always thought of the kids first. After every game he went through the locker room and shook everybody's hand. He crossed over to o-linemen, running backs, wide receivers. . . . They just liked him because he was a nice man and he had no agenda. He had no political agenda, he had no personal agenda. He was a consummate football coach who thought only of football and of the players, 24/7."

Ferry's death was a blow, but it had rallied the team in the spring of 2004. A promising group led by All-American free safety and senior Ray Ventrone was considered a Top 10 unit in I-AA circles, and as the team broke for the summer, a trip back to the postseason loomed as a realistic goal.

Two weeks before fall preparations were to begin, amid the positive buzz, the unthinkable occurred.

On July 25, David Reid, a rising senior offensive lineman who had impressed coaches in the spring's final scrimmage just three months before, attended a graduation party along with his parents at the home of a neighbor in his native Medford, New Jersey. As the festivities progressed into the late evening, Reid and some friends retreated to the pool area, where they engaged in a contest based on who could hold their breath the longest. Reid was beneath the surface of the water for a long period before a member of the group realized that something wasn't quite right. By the time the 6-foot-4, 260-pound athlete was pulled from the water, he had ceased breathing. Vigorous resuscitation efforts were ultimately ineffective. At twenty years old, just like that, with a promising senior year and a more promising future ahead of him, David Reid was dead.

For Talley, who was forced to break the news to a disbelieving group of players on an otherwise tranquil summer Sunday afternoon, the death of a current team member was a first. Talley had been a head coach for the previous twenty-six years and had dealt with a score of difficulties among the nearly one thousand young men he had tutored—drug and alcohol problems, unplanned pregnancies of players' girlfriends, a rare sexual harassment accusation, occasional academic shortcomings, and a host of other day-to-day problems that come with the territory for all college football head coaches good enough to remain in the oft-demanding profession for an extended period of time. Talley had even dealt with a prominent player who confessed his homosexuality to the coach just prior to his senior season, a potentially volatile locker room situation (Talley welcomed the player, who kept his sexual preference a secret from the others, to remain on the team, and he had a productive senior year). But nothing prepared the sixty-one-year-old head coach for the cruelty of a player's untimely death, and when he eulogized Reid at a heart-wrenching funeral service days later, the usually well-spoken Talley struggled to find the right words.

"It was very hard as a head coach because I really had to keep our team together—we had a bus to take the players down, had it all planned out, what we were going to do, we had a set itinerary for everybody so everybody could be a part of it. It was a lot of preparation. So when I got to the mass, I wanted to crawl into the woodwork, sort of sit in the back, put my head down and do my sorrowful cry, and at that point just let the kid go. And his aunt came up to me just before communion and said to me, 'We'd like you to speak.' I wanted to say something to help our team, I wanted to say something to help the family, and something that would be a tribute to David. And I honestly only asked for one thing at that point, because I had about five minutes to put my thoughts together. And all I said was, 'God, just don't let me break down.'

"He was a guy that crossed over with every group on our team. He had good friends in the freshman class, he had phenomenal friends in the senior class, he was personable with the African American kids on our team. He was one of those extremely well-liked and respected players, and a player that you never really realized had the kind of impact that he had on the team. That came out in a lot of the eulogies afterward, and also just the outpouring of sorrow during the wake and funeral. That's when I realized we had lost a very important part of our football team. It had an immense effect on us."

For the grief-stricken teammates, each of whom attended the funeral, football became a footnote.

"We just pretty much went into shock," said receiver John Dieser, one of Reid's roommates and best friends on the team. "You come back to a house where he was every day, and he's not there. He was the guy that was out on the field every day, working hard every snap, and suddenly he's not. It's something that you can't prepare yourself for. We weren't even thinking about football at that stage."

With heavy hearts over the loss of Ferry and Reid, Villanova did its best to pull it together in time for the 2004 season. Dazed but hungry to honor their fallen comrades, the Cats started the year 2-0, holding off a late rally by Bucknell and winning, 20–14, before erasing a double-digit halftime deficit to beat Lehigh, 22–16. The victories, both over slightly inferior opponents from the Patriot League, moved VU to No. 5 in the I-AA poll prior to a Week 3 meeting with a talented James Madison club at Villanova Stadium. JMU easily disposed of the Cats,

17–0, on a wind- and rain-soaked day that saw Hurricane Ivan pass through the mid-Atlantic region. The game marked the first time Villanova had been shut out at home since 1973. There was optimism that the team would be able to turn it around against local rival Penn the following Saturday, and when Talley's crew jumped ahead, 16–0, on a touchdown run by Burroughs late in the third quarter, that hope looked to be well founded.

But moments later, the Cats would suffer their sharpest blow since the news of Reid's death permeated a tearful locker room less than two months prior. Ventrone, the emotional leader of the Villanova defense, a player who had been nicknamed "The Eraser" after knocking three of his own teammates out of spring practice months earlier, moved to make a tackle on a Penn ball carrier and heard a snap in his lower leg. As the notoriously tough as nails Pittsburgh native screamed and writhed in pain on the Franklin Field Astroturf, the familiar feeling of dread hit Ventrone's teammates yet again. Ventrone, who had suffered a broken right fibula, had just played his last snap as a collegian. A shaken group of Wildcats managed to focus and hold on for a 16–13 win. But they were never the same.

"I don't think our staff truly understood the amount of impact that one player had on a team," said Talley. "Any mistake that seemed to be made would be erased by his play. A hole would open up, a guy would look like he was going to break into the open, and all of a sudden he would be tackled for a 3-yard gain. The intensity that the kid brought to the field and the leadership that he exhibited on the field was greatly missed when we lost him. Everyone thought he was indestructible. The defense never recovered."

Whether anyone wished to admit it, the Wildcats were done without Ventrone, even at 3-1. In addition to serving as the heart and soul of the team, Ventrone just happened to be the most skilled and athletic player on Villanova's roster, and in I-AA, where personnel depth is a constant issue, the loss of so fine a player was impossible to overcome. (After rehabilitating his mangled leg, Ventrone would run a 4.42 40-yard dash the following spring and be signed as a free agent by the NFL New England Patriots.)

A defense that was the unquestioned strength of the team for the first month of 2004 immediately crumbled, giving up a total of 85 points in subsequent losses to New Hampshire (51-40) and Northeastern (34-30). A mini-winning streak against lesser Atlantic 10 lights Richmond, Towson, and Rhode Island moved the Cats to 6–3 and raised hopes briefly, but the bruised and battered defense would fall again to superior William and Mary (37-29) and Delaware (41-35) to end the season. Five Villanova opponents—Lehigh, James Madison, New Hampshire, Delaware, and William and Mary—would end up in the I-AA playoffs. JMU would win the whole shebang. Villanova, once again, would wait until next year.

For the Wildcat seniors, next year, mercifully, was here. Sort of.

One of Villanova's three 2005 captains, defensive end Darrell Adams, would be a cheerleader during the spring, the result of a left knee sprain that required surgery. The start was an inauspicious one for the jovial Adams, the member of the VU squad with the most realistic expectation to play at the next level. The team would miss the Long Islander's energy level during April practice, and his absence would only add to the concern for a defense that again looked like it would be an Achilles heel.

Another of the captains, linebacker Brian Hulea, was in uniform, though at times his mind would be 350 miles away in Canfield, Ohio, with his mother, Nancy, who had been diagnosed with breast cancer in the winter. Hulea was as reserved as they came even on his most jubilant day, and his mother's illness had pushed him further within his shell. At a time when most college seniors were looking expectantly toward the future, the 6-foot-1, 235-pound Hulea wore the weight of the world on his substantial shoulders, and football would take an indefinite back seat to his mother's ordeal.

On the offensive side of the ball, where the Wildcats were expected to thrive, there were concerns as well. Receiver J. J. Outlaw, an All-Conference performer and arguably the team's most electrifying player, was mostly absent from contact drills. Nagging hamstring problems were the official reason for Outlaw's new-found role as a spectator, though some associated with the program seemed to question the Baltimore native's degree of toughness.

At one of Villanova's early practices, the question "What's wrong with J. J.?" was posed by an observer to Wildcat football trainer Dan "Tiger" Jarvis.

"J. J.'s a fucking pussy," Jarvis shot back, and the trainer's frustration with the talented receiver was hardly a unique viewpoint. Outlaw was a terrific player when the bell rang during the regular season, and had earned the nickname "Hollywood" due to his affinity for the spotlight and easygoing way with any media that dropped by to cover the club. But when it came to toughness, the 5-foot-9, 185-pound Outlaw readily admitted, "I don't like to get hit." And so Outlaw would remain out of harm's way throughout most of April, preserving himself for a time in September when the curtain was lifted and a more suitable audience would be present.

Before the spring ended, Outlaw would have plenty of company on the sideline. Offensive lineman Alex Suder, who was struggling with academic problems, would spend the better part of April with a parachute tied to his waist, running up and down one side of the track as punishment for his failings in the classroom. Academic shortcomings were not taken lightly by Talley, who had graduated all but a handful of his scholarship players in twenty-one seasons on the Main Line.

Promising receiver Anton Ridley, who had looked like the team's next star early in the spring, wouldn't make it to the second week of practices. Unbeknownst to the training staff, Ridley had fractured a rib while roughhousing with his brother in the winter, and when the wideout had a sore shoulder checked out following a particularly physical practice, Jarvis spotted the bum rib.

Tight end Matt Sherry, who had a history of injury problems while at Villanova, would be the next to fall. During the first of what was supposed to be three ninety-play scrimmages during the spring, Sherry landed awkwardly on his shoulder and suffered a separation. The following Sunday, at scrimmage number two, backup running back Aaron Jones sustained a torn ACL in his left knee.

With his players dropping like flies, Talley would cancel the third scrimmage, refusing to gamble that another key to his club's 2005 fortunes would be damaged. Villanova would make it through spring practice without much in the way of further drama, a welcome change for a team that had more than its fair share over the past year and a half.

Despite the injuries, the buzz coming from the players and coaches was one of cautious optimism, a typical glass-half-full viewpoint shared by countless squads throughout the country at this point in the season. The buzz from the student body, from the city of Philadelphia, from the local and national media would remain undetectable. Villanova's students and alumni may have been vaguely aware that the football team would open against I-A Rutgers on September 10, but until the program started competing on the gridiron against other Big East rivals like Syracuse and Pittsburgh, few outsiders would be going crazy assessing football's spring development or recounting the sad tale of the past year and a half.

Had any member of the program been driven by outside expectations, they would have found their motivation at a low ebb. For the most part, the members of the football team would be playing for themselves and their teammates. In that sense, they were akin to participants in most of the other sports, and even extracurricular activities, on campus—all hard work, little glory. The only difference as far as football was concerned was that the price tag for this activity would exceed $3 million during 2005, which made the sport the most expensive for the university to field.

Many in the academic community had long compared the costs with the exposure and return on investment and wondered why. Some grimaced as they recalled that the school had been invited to join the Big East in football back in the mid-1990s, at the same time Connecticut had opted to ramp up its program. UConn now had a spanking new stadium that was filled every Saturday, was sharing in the mother lode of BCS dollars as a football-playing member of the Big East, and was fresh off its first-ever bowl appearance.

Others pondered why Villanova, if it wasn't interested in the big time, didn't scale back its football affiliation and join the lower-cost Patriot League. Nearby Patriot schools like Lehigh and Lafayette had been good enough to qualify for the I-AA playoffs despite a non-scholarship, need-based financial aid model for players that was similar to the Ivy League structure. Academically and otherwise, Villanova looked a great deal more like Lehigh and Lafayette than it did current league foes like New Hampshire or UMass, so why not tone things down and save a couple bucks?

Stuck in the middle of this debate was a group of fifty-eight players and ten coaches trying their best to concern themselves more with the real pigskin than with the political football being kicked about campus. Talley and his troops could only try to do things the right way, as out of style as that approach had become in the business of Division I football, in the hopes that enough of the school's powerbrokers would be satisfied with the results and allow them to exist as they were.

At Villanova, like at most I-AA programs, it wasn't enough for a player to block, tackle, punt, pass, or kick. It wasn't enough to get good grades, work earnestly toward a degree, or be a pillar of the campus community. With football sapping millions from the bottom line of dozens of university budgets from coast to coast, and the virtue and necessity of football constantly at issue, justifying your existence on campus was an unspoken part of every player's daily routine. Even on a perfect early-spring day, a football player at Villanova could easily find his outlook clouded.

2

THE COACH

For an outsider attending an ordinary practice for the first time, the identification of Villanova's head football coach could take roughly a dozen guesses. There was no Bear Bryant–like figure shouting instructions from a megaphone while perched like a deity atop a two-story coaching tower. There was no Vince Lombardi–like voice penetrating the spring air and making all who heard it stand up and take notice.

Andy Talley was in charge of the Wildcat program, but few would have described him as larger than life. At 5 feet 6 inches with graying hair and round spectacles, the sixty-two-year-old Talley wouldn't have looked out of place alongside the professors in the accounting or mathematics departments. That appraisal was just fine with Talley, who didn't fit the stereotype of football coach, nor did he desire to.

Talley didn't wake up at 4 a.m. every day dreaming about new offensive wrinkles or impenetrable defensive schemes. He hadn't had direct involvement with either side of the ball in over ten years, bowing out of the day-to-day operation of the offense when the various demands on his time as head coach became a disruption to game preparations. Talley now allowed his coordinators to concern themselves with the main details of actual football.

Sam Venuto had been a member of Talley's staff for ten years, six as the offensive coordinator, and had presided over one of the most potent aerial attacks in I-AA. The forty-six-year-old Venuto was reserved but rock-solid and had a full measure of respect from both the players and coaching staff.

As 2005 began, a new defensive coordinator, Mark Reardon, would be reporting to Talley. Reardon had been on the Villanova staff for four years, coaching defensive backs and special teams, and had been promoted when former coordinator Joe Trainer took the head coaching job at Division II Millersville University during the winter. Reardon was seen as an extension of the ultra-intense Trainer, a hard-nosed workaholic who demanded much of his charges and himself.

The third member of Talley's main triumvirate of advisors was assistant head coach and offensive line coach Mark Ferrante, the longest-tenured assistant on the current staff at nineteen years and the unspoken heir apparent to Talley in the head chair. Ferrante had been the quarterback on one of Talley's first teams at Division III St. Lawrence College in the early eighties, had joined the head coach's staff at Villanova in February 1987 and had never left. Ferrante oversaw many of the program's most vital administrative duties, including serving as recruiting coordinator, and there were those around the football office who argued that the day he left Villanova would be the day the program fell apart. Far from being a simple pencil-pusher, Ferrante's voice was the one heard most prominently at a typical Wildcat practice. He was a screamer, emotional and vocal, and seemed at times to relish a reputation as the "bad cop" on the staff.

For his part, Talley played the role of the good cop. Any involvement he had with players during practice was invariably to offer praise. Any extended discussion with players either on or off the field generally involved grades. Talley may not have known the intricacies of various coverage schemes or blitz packages, but he seemed to have an encyclopedic knowledge of the course of each player's study, his academic progress, and his social development on campus. Though nearly every coach has publicly heralded the importance of academics, not all have been devoted, or in Talley's case thoroughly obsessed, with graduating the players they brought onto campus.

It was little wonder then that Talley's main goal at the beginning of his career was to coach high school football and teach English.

"I played at Haverford High School and was a running back, went to Southern Connecticut and wasn't good enough to be a running back, or fast enough, and labored on the scout team for a couple of years. I played a lot my junior and senior year and started my senior year, but I was a very average player. And being a blue-collar person—my father drove a trash truck for Haverford Township, my mother was a cleaning lady—and the first one to really go to college in my family, there weren't a lot of options for me. I wanted to be a teacher and a coach, that's what I wanted to do. Money wasn't important to me. It was the early sixties, and football gave me an opportunity to literally get out of my environment and sort of make a name for myself. Coaching was something that I just knew that I wanted to do."

Talley's start on the sideline came at Simsbury High School in suburban Hartford, where his ambition soon outweighed his circumstances. After two seasons as an assistant, Talley realized that he would long be stuck serving a head coach who had no intention of leaving his post or the small community.

"I thought after two years I should have been the head coach," said Talley. "Like every young coach, I thought I really knew a lot. So I went to Springfield College, I GA'ed [served as a graduate assistant] there for one year, finished my master's degree and then I latched onto a guy who was on the move."

John Anderson, formerly the defensive coordinator at Boston College and a one-time assistant at Dartmouth, had taken the head job at tiny Middlebury College in Vermont, and began assembling a staff. With a wealth of youthful enthusiasm, no delusions of top-tier salary or family of which to speak, and possessing the people skills that are vital in recruiting, Talley was a perfect fit at Middlebury. Within a year, Talley had placed himself in Anderson's good graces by landing his first difference-making recruit, quarterback Bill Kuharich. Kuharich, from Malvern Prep in the Philadelphia area, was the son of then-Eagles head coach Joe Kuharich. The younger Kuharich would star for Middlebury and go on to serve as general manager of the New Orleans Saints and director of pro personnel for the Kansas City Chiefs.

"That was really the beginning for me of learning what college football was all about, and learning how to recruit," said Talley. "I spent three years there, in the tiny hamlet of Middlebury, Vermont, and worked with a Division I coach who really knew how to recruit and had a real good offensive system."

After three seasons of unprecedented success at Middlebury, Anderson was receiving plenty of notice from bigger programs. Brown University, which had familiarity with Anderson from his Dartmouth days, offered the head job, and Anderson accepted. Talley, who by this time had become the head coach's right-hand man, was offered Anderson's old position at Middlebury.

"I think I was twenty-nine," remembered Talley. "I knew that if I took the head job there, that I would never, ever go anywhere else, that I would stay in that little town for the rest of my life. I was enamored of the big time, I wanted to go to the big time, and in those days the Ivy League was really good football. So I turned the job down and went to Brown. Mickey Heineken, who was Tubby's [Raymond's] No. 1 assistant coach at Delaware, took the [Middlebury] job and stayed for thirty years."

At Brown, Talley was committed to perfecting his craft, despite Anderson's seeming allergy toward encouragement for any of his staff members. "I was determined to be the hardest worker on the staff, and I knew, since he was bringing me, that I'd have to be," said Talley. "And he was a taskmaster, he was a tough guy to work for. He was a tough, tough guy and a very demanding guy. He was very organized, very bright, but he was not a guy that would 'love you up' in any way, shape, or form."

Talley immediately built a reputation as Brown's top recruiter. The program's improvement was apparent, and he began fielding offers to become a head coach. Not far removed from his thirtieth birthday, Talley had received offers to coach at his alma mater, Southern Connecticut, and at King's Point in New York, but he spurned those positions in a quest to help lead Brown to an Ivy title. In Anderson and Talley's fourth season in Providence, the Bears won their first Ivy League crown in modern history, and by that time, Talley was ready to parlay the success into a head job. As luck would have it, there were no suitors at this time. As he labored on the staff for another two seasons, Talley's patience was dwindling.

"I really wanted to win an Ivy championship, because Brown had never won one, and we won it in '76. After that I felt like I had completed the assignment and started looking. And at that point I couldn't land one. I was in on a couple of little jobs but didn't get them.

"[Brown] was a happy time for me, but the last two years a lot of my friends started to leave the staff and I wasn't as comfortable there. And I probably was with the head coach too long. We were together nine years. John was an old-time coach from the old era and I was one of the new breed that was coming up and probably needed more strokes from time to time. Every young coach is insecure, and he wasn't the kind of guy that would pat you on the back and make you feel secure. He always liked to keep you in the corner, to keep you working, and not let you know that you were doing a good job."

Following the 1978 season, by now married to Arlene, a former gymnast at Southern Connecticut, and with a three-year-old son, Josh, Talley would have traveled to the ends of the earth to become a head coach. And that's exactly where he would have to go to realize that dream. At St. Lawrence College, a Division III school in the remote reaches of upstate New York, twenty-three miles from the Canadian border, the thirty-five-year-old Talley would finally receive his shot. At the hockey-mad school, to which the closest big city was Ottawa, Ontario, the young new leader would have to change the culture in order to succeed.

"People there were a little uncomfortable with me because I was a hard-charger, I wanted to do things in a first-class fashion, and I wanted coaches to work. Those guys [the former staff], once the football season was over, wanted to coach their other sports and just sort of live a low-profile life. I was constantly recruiting and constantly trying to upgrade the program. I was perceived negatively even by the players. I wanted an offseason program, and they had never done that. I wanted offseason lifting and they fought me on that. It was constantly pulling teeth to get everybody thinking about how to make football more important there, because it was a Division I hockey school. That was the sport and everything wrapped around the sport. So I used it to my advantage.

"If you brought fifteen or twenty players in on a weekend and they were playing Cornell in hockey, there were three thousand people in a hockey rink that was on top of everybody and you would just transfer that into 'Hey, that's the way football here is in the fall.' It was a great venue to sell what we were doing. You just hoped you could get them past the fact that it was twenty below zero outside."

Football, of course, was nothing like hockey at St. Lawrence, but that never got in the way of the patented Talley sales pitch. "You'd get your thousand people, and admission was free," recalled Talley. "You had dogs barking at one end of the stadium, running across the field, the game would have to be stopped to take the dog off the field, little kids running under the ropes. It was what college football used to be."

Despite the impediments, Talley built a winner out of a program that had formerly experienced a largely mediocre history. By his fourth season, he had led the team to the Division III semifinals before an injured Mark Ferrante failed to get the program past Augustana. Once again, Talley expected to be a hot commodity among larger programs looking for a new leader, but interest in him was lukewarm at best. "I was involved in the Connecticut job, I was involved in the Cornell job, and I was involved in the Penn job. Those were the three jobs I had interviewed for and didn't get any of them. I was there for five years. When I didn't get any of those jobs coming off of [the playoff] year, I had resigned myself to learn how to hunt, fish, and ski. I was going to be a lifer there. Because I was forty years old, I didn't get any of those jobs, and I couldn't have been any hotter as a Division III coach with Ivy background."

Before establishing permanent residency at St. Lawrence, Talley had one more intriguing offer to consider, as an assistant coach in the fledgling United States Football League (USFL). What may have initially seemed like another stroke of bad luck ended up as the most fortuitous bounce of Talley's career.

"I had a chance to go to the San Antonio Gunslingers of the USFL, I was offered the offensive backfield job with them. My wife was pregnant with our second child, and it was just a bad time to go. So I turned it down, but I was seriously thinking about taking it, and I wanted to take it. If she wasn't pregnant, I probably would have taken it. Three weeks later the offensive coordinator that was going to hire me, Larry Kuharich [the brother of Talley's first major recruit at Middlebury], got fired. Three weeks after that, the Villanova job opened up."

Villanova had not been on Talley's radar screen, mostly because Villanova was out of the football business in 1984. The program, which had been scraping by at the I-A level for years, was unceremoniously and controversially dropped by the university following the 1980 season. After a huge outcry by students and alumni, the administration voted to bring it back three years later, but as a member of the seemingly lower-profile, lower-cost world of Division I-AA. For Talley, who grew up walking distance from the Villanova campus and had regularly attended games there as a boy, the prospect of returning home was an attractive one.

"One of the coaching axioms that I had followed was, 'Do a good job where you are, win where you are and people will find you.' Axiom number two was, 'Don't follow a legend.' The great thing about the Villanova job was I wasn't following anybody, because there was no football. I really liked the fact that I could build something from scratch, and most of the jobs I had been involved with were all rebuilding jobs. I was good around programs that needed to be rebuilt. I kind of knew what needed to be done, I understood the kind of people you needed to bring in, I thought I was a good recruiter, and I felt like I could go out and find twenty or twenty-five kids a year that wanted what Villanova had."

First, Talley had to convince the university that it should want what he had. The Division III success story was a complete unknown in Philadelphia circles, and media reports at the time the program was revived pronounced Larry Glueck, a 1963 Villanova graduate who had played professionally for the Chicago Bears and was at the time an assistant at Harvard, as the leading candidate for the vacancy.

Talley had no idea what to expect when he met with the Villanova brain trust of Board of Trustees vice chairman Art Kania, Philadelphia Eagles general manager Jim Murray, and athletic director Ted Aceto, but the fact that he was asked to pay his own way for the interview did not fill him with optimism. By the third interview, in which he was asked to make a presentation to the full Board of Trustees, headed at the time by Chase Manhattan president Tom Labrecque, Talley's hopes were on the rise. The coach compiled individual three-ring binders for each member of the board, highlighting his goals along with the qualities that he felt would lend to making Villanova a strong program, and launched into a spirited oral presentation stressing the school's academic qualities and advantages in location.

"I got done talking in about an hour and fifteen minutes. I finally said to Father [John] Driscoll, who was the president at the time, 'Father, I'm out of breath.' And Tom Labrecque said, 'That's the best presentation that I've ever heard.' I felt coming from the chairman of the board at Chase Manhattan, that was pretty impressive. The guy's seen some presentations. But there's nothing like a football coach who's fired up, talking about something that he knows and believes in and is pretty excited about. And to these people it was like, 'God, this guy can actually speak English. He's organized.' I think they had a bad image of what football coaches were."

A blown-away board would cancel its interviews scheduled that evening with the remaining candidates, a group that included Glueck and Southern Connecticut coach Kevin Gilbride, who would go on to become head coach of the NFL San Diego Chargers. Aceto tracked Talley down at his mother's house at 1:30 a.m., summoning him back to campus.

Remembered Talley, "I said 'Jeez, it's 1:30 in the morning,' and he said 'No, just throw something on, we're all casual here.' So I went up and it was me, Ted and the president in the president's office. It was $45,000 to start, which was about $10,000 more than I was making at St. Lawrence. I didn't even read the contract, I just signed it, went home the next day and told my family, 'We're moving to Philly.'"

After arriving at Villanova, Talley set to tackling challenges. The school had no football offices, so he lured a few of the builders attending to the new on-campus basketball facility to assemble some makeshift offices beneath the bleachers of Villanova Stadium. Charged with hiring a staff on a paper-thin budget, Talley found young coaches who were more interested in greater responsibility than the pittance they would receive in their paychecks. Five former graduate assistants—Paul Ferraro (Syracuse), Brian Jones (RPI), Greg Olejack (Tulane), Dan MacNeill (Ithaca), and Craig Johnson (St. Lawrence)—made up the bulk of the staff. Dave White, an old friend of Talley's and the former head coach at RPI, and Lou Ferry, who had been the intramural director at VU since the football program was dropped in 1981, completed the first staff of the new era.

With a group of coaches in place, it was time to find some players. Villanova couldn't make promises of championships or eventual NFL stardom to its recruits, but it could guarantee its first batch of seventeen- and eighteen-year-old student-athletes something that most craved even more: immediate playing time. The program would initially consist of only freshmen and walk-on players who were already students at the university, along with three players who had signed letters of intent in 1981, just before the school dropped football. Defensive tackle Todd Piatnik, linebacker Roger Turner, and linebacker Pete Giombetti had been permitted to keep their scholarships and attend Villanova, and Talley convinced the trio to stick around for a fifth academic year, use their final season of eligibility, and do what they had initially come to Villanova to do—play football.

In 1985 and 1986, playing a limited schedule comprised mainly of Division III programs, the Wildcats went 5-0 and 8-1, respectively. In 1987, the roster of games was upgraded to consist of a number of I-AA opponents (the team was 6-4), and in 1988, Villanova entered the football-only Yankee Conference (later to be absorbed by the Atlantic 10). Playing an 11-game schedule for the first time since 1980, the young program went a respectable 5-5-1, including 4-4 in league play. The next season, the team arrived in earnest, finishing 8-4, winning the Yankee title, and making its first-ever trip to the I-AA playoffs. The Cats would lose, 52–36, to eventual national champion Georgia Southern in the first round, but clearly, the program had been placed back on the map. Villanova would go back to the postseason in 1991 and 1992, falling to Youngstown State both seasons, and some, including Talley, began to think bigger.

"I had hoped all along that as we continued to prosper, we would eventually move to Division I[-A]. Three out of four years we were a playoff team, and I was hoping that juice would propel us to the next level, but the philosophy of the university was more and more pulling away from I-A football and more settling in as a I-AA school because it was comfortable for them. They were really happy with the success the program had, we were graduating players, we didn't have problems on campus, the persona was good. Plus we had missed the curve of Division I-A, when the stadiums got bigger, bubbles were built, practice facilities, and Villanova financially at that time was still struggling to build their endowment. It was bad timing economically.

While Villanova had been out of the football business in the early eighties, another Catholic school that had once been an on-field rival and remained an academic rival, Boston College, had been undergoing a renaissance. Behind a talented young quarterback named Doug Flutie, BC was winning games against established powers from the south, appearing regularly on national television, and going to bowl games. By the time VU brought football back, Boston College, with alumni donations and money from television and ticket sales pouring in, had long since passed Villanova by. BC's football stadium, which once closely resembled Villanova's, had been renovated and expanded. Competing with a school like Boston College on the football field would take a major financial commitment, the kind that the school had attempted to eschew when it dropped the sport in 1981.

Any buzz about Villanova dipping its toe back into the big-time pool slowly died out, and the performance of the team had much to do with it. The Wildcats finished 3-8, 5-6, and 3-8 in 1993, '94, and '95, and won just five of 24 games in a newly expanded and deeper Yankee Conference over that stretch. Talley's concerns were no longer about his program reaching the next level. They were about keeping his job.

Aceto, the athletic director who had hired Talley, left Villanova in 1992 and was replaced by Gene DeFilippo, former associate AD at Kentucky. Father John Driscoll had departed four years prior, and the president's chair was now filled by Father Edmund J. Dobbin, who generally took a "hands-off" approach to football. Talley's fate would rest almost solely in the hands of DeFilippo, whose one-time status as the football coach's ally was beginning to fade.

"I coached Gene DeFilippo at Springfield College," said Talley. "Gene DeFilippo and I were friends. I was elated, I was ecstatic when Gene got the job, because we were finally hiring a football guy and somebody I knew, and somebody that had been at Kentucky, in the big time, and could really jettison our football program. Our relationship wasn't frosty, at first. Unfortunately, we went 3-8, 5-6, 3-8, and he reduced my contract."

Another element helping to strain the interaction between head coach and athletic director was the matter of DeFilippo's son, John, who was starring at nearby Radnor High School in the mid-nineties and was being pursued by a number of I-AA programs. Talley and his staff were interested in the younger DeFilippo but were also recruiting another local quarterback, Chris Gicking. Both had standing scholarship offers, but when Gicking beat DeFilippo to the punch by committing early, the athletic director was less than pleased. The younger DeFilippo eventually opted to attend James Madison (Gicking eventually transferred from Villanova to Shippensburg). And though Talley was simply looking out for the health of his program by recruiting two good players, his boss was believed to have taken the matter personally.

"I had a three-year revolving contract, and he came in after the 1995 season and said they were reducing my contract. So I now had two left on my contract. I felt that if we had a bad year in 1996, he would have fired me. They would have come up with a little settlement, I wasn't making enough for them to worry about it, and he could have gotten that done easily. The only thing I asked him to do was to tell me how many games we had to win. And he wouldn't. That's when I knew I was in big trouble.

"I didn't like the way he handled it, because he was involved in some other jobs at the time. And I said, 'Look, don't leave me here as a lame duck because if I get a new AD and I have a two-year contract, I'm in trouble.' I felt like my longevity here would have given me a little bit of an opportunity [to negotiate an extension]. But from his standpoint, we had three straight losing seasons. He didn't know the program as well as I did, and he didn't see how close we were."

Talley would force DeFilippo's hand after the 1996 season. Villanova reemerged that year, finishing 8-4 and returning to the playoffs, where they lost to East Tennessee State in the first round. New offensive coordinator Dave Clawson, a twenty-nine-year-old prodigy hired from the staff at Lehigh, had the team scoring points at will again. Talley was rewarded with a new contract, DeFilippo left to become AD at Boston College three games into the 1997 season, and suddenly, a major weight had been lifted off both the program and its leader.

The Wildcats rolled their way through 1997, finishing the regular season at 11-0 and spending six weeks at No. 1 behind future NFL players in wide receiver Brian Finneran and running back Brian Westbrook. Finneran would win the Walter Payton Award, the I-AA equivalent of the Heisman Trophy. Talley would take home countless coaching awards, including the Eddie Robinson Award as I-AA Coach of the Year. Though the season would end in a bittersweet fashion, as Villanova lost a 37–34 heartbreaker at home to Jim Tressel's Youngstown State team in the national quarterfinals, Talley was now in a position to remain at Villanova for the remainder of his career.

Villanova continued to achieve modest success, but it would take another five years for the program to return to the playoffs. The Wildcats were done in during 1999 by a late regular season loss to Youngstown

State, the last time Talley would face Tressel before the native Buckeye took over at Ohio State. In 2001, VU was 8-3 and won a piece of the conference title, but a strange midseason loss to Division II New Haven allowed the selection committee to keep the Wildcats out. Adding injury to insult, Talley would suffer a minor heart attack three weeks after the season was completed.

In 2002, with expectations low following Westbrook's graduation, the Wildcats jelled again. The season began with a 37–19 dismantling of Big East member Rutgers, and 5-foot-10 quarterback Brett Gordon placed the team on his narrow shoulders thereafter. The Cats found their way into the postseason, finishing 8-3 following a thrilling 38–34 win at Delaware in the regular season finale. Gordon guided Villanova to wins over Furman and Fordham in the first two playoff rounds, and Villanova was in the I-AA semifinals for the first time in its history. In the semis against top-seeded McNeese State, Villanova took a 21–7 lead into halftime before a series of highly questionable calls by the Big Sky Conference officiating crew turned the tide in favor of MSU. An apparent fumble return for a Wildcat touchdown was overturned when it was ruled that the McNeese ball carrier's forward progress had been stopped. There had been no whistle. Then, late in the game, with VU driving for the go-ahead score, a 30-yard completion was negated by an offensive pass interference call labeled as a bad one even by ESPN's objective announcing team. The Wildcats would leave Lake Charles, Louisiana, as 39–28 losers, but not before Talley said his piece.

In comments printed by the *Philadelphia Inquirer*, Talley complained, "I wish the officials would have let the players decide it. That last call really upset me. We were running crossing routes all day. Linebackers were bumping into receivers all day. They [the officiating crew] come from a conference that throws the ball all the time . . . surely we were going to take it in and win. We had run that play twenty times prior to that. Unbelievable. They stepped in and took away our opportunity to win on a play that's, at best, controversial. Why wait until that time to call it?"

Public complaints about officiating were rare in the NCAA playoffs, and charges that referees had determined the outcome of the game even rarer. Talley's comments drew an official written reprimand from the NCAA, as well as some venomous correspondence between Talley and Big Sky commissioner Doug Fullerton.

The McNeese tirade didn't come as a total surprise to those who knew Talley or had followed his career closely. The coach was good for a few freak-outs a season against the officials, could drive members of his own staff to distraction by not being engaged enough in X's and O's, and was not necessarily beloved by all of his fellow head coaches in the league. When assessing other teams or players to the media, Talley was known as something of a master of the backhanded compliment, and some questioned whether his outwardly friendly demeanor toward other coaches was always genuine.

Talley incited the private wrath of other coaches and schools in the league with an elitist mentality that placed Villanova on its own highbrow pedestal. He was quick to point out that the members of the league that had won national titles—UMass, Delaware, and James Madison—had all done so by welcoming in I-A or junior college transfers. The NCAA permitted players to transfer from a I-A to a I-AA program without sitting out a season, an allowance of which a good number of I-AA schools took advantage. But because of generally higher academic standards, Villanova was rarely able to take on a transfer, and Talley annually watched some of the "hired guns" that might have helped his team to a title matriculate elsewhere and thrive. His bitterness and outspokenness about the imbalance, and not-so-subtle suggestions that his contemporaries in the Atlantic 10 had it easier, even contributed to one of his former players and employees turning on him.

Mark Whipple, who had played quarterback at Brown when Talley was an assistant there and had coached on the same staff at St. Lawrence, had returned to Brown as the head coach before taking the reins at UMass in 1998. Whipple immediately took the Minutemen to the top of the ladder, turning around a program that had been 2-9 the year before and leading it to an unlikely national championship in his first year. Two keys to the title were a junior college transfer quarterback,

Todd Bankhead, and a I-A transfer wide receiver, Jimmy Moore. When Talley made public insinuations that UMass had an unfair advantage, Whipple was said to have privately seethed. Perhaps in reaction, Whipple in 1999 allowed game film on Villanova to be sent to Air Force, against which the Wildcats would be opening that season. Equipping nonconference opponents with game film of a fellow conference member was a no-no, and Talley phoned Whipple to vent his dissatisfaction with the act. (Whipple denied the charge when confronted, but Talley contends today that there is no doubt that UMass was the source of the film).

Though all remained well between the coaches on the surface, the simmering bad blood boiled over into a confrontation during the 2000 season.

With the Minutemen holding a comfortable 38–17 lead late in the fourth quarter against Villanova in Amherst, the Wildcats attempted to end an otherwise poor outing on a positive note by putting another touchdown on the board. As VU moved the ball nearer to the UMass goal line, and with most fans filing out of the stadium, Talley could hear shouts on the opposing side of the field. It was Whipple, who had walked all the way to the near-side hash mark between plays.

"Andy, what the fuck are you doing? It's over! We kicked your ass!"

Talley, not fond of humiliating losses or being called out by a former protégé before his own players, was incensed.

"When the game was over, it was a TV game as I recall, I basically had some options," remembered Talley. "I was so furious, that one of them was to walk off the field and just not shake hands with him. The second option would have been to take a swing at him, which I would never do. The third option is the one that I chose."

When the two coaches met at midfield, Talley gave his one-time pupil a caustic tongue-lashing. For his part, Whipple acted like the screaming fit of a few moments before had never taken place. The relationship between the two would never be fully mended, and Whipple left UMass to become quarterbacks coach for the NFL Pittsburgh Steelers in 2004.

Whipple wasn't the only former Talley assistant to draw his ex-boss's ire. By 2002, Dave Clawson had resurrected the long-moribund Fordham program to a point where it was participating in the I-AA playoffs. Clawson, who had helped save Talley's job in 1996 by ushering in his inspired offensive formula, happened to be pitted against Villanova in the quarterfinal round that season, the first time he would face VU as a head coach. At a team dinner on the eve of their matchup, someone at Fordham had fashioned table cards with a picture of the face of Villanova quarterback Brett Gordon and a pair of hands semi-imposed, a way of motivating the team and keeping it focused on the task at hand.

When Talley caught wind of the ploy, he was irate that the former Villanova assistant would seemingly condone what he saw to be the malicious targeting of a player that Clawson had once mentored as a Villanova assistant. Villanova would win the game the next day, but when the thumb on Gordon's throwing hand was broken late in the contest on a Fordham hit, Talley held Clawson responsible. When the season ended, and after weeks of lamenting Clawson's recruitment of "thugs" to get his program off the ground, Talley let Clawson have it in the form of a letter.

"I took at is if they had a personal vendetta to take Brett out of the game. There was a late hit on him early, and Fordham was a very rough-and-tumble football team. I didn't have a problem with that, but I just felt like they were really after Brett, and taking some cheap shots at him. After the game I wrote Dave a long letter basically telling him how much I respected him, and how much I liked him, but that I was disappointed with the picture on the table, I was disappointed in the fact that Brett got hit late, and I kind of saw it as a headhunting kind of a thing. . . . It was a positive letter. I said that [Clawson] was a first-class individual and a bright young head coach and that I didn't think that he should stoop to those kind of things. He didn't need to do that.

"He called me back, we talked about it, and he said that they did that for every game. They always put the star player on the table of the team that they had to stop. It was a mental sort of thing. So I accepted that. And that was the end of it."

Though he buried the hatchet with Clawson, who became the head coach at the University of Richmond in 2004, Talley was not always a diplomat, was not always great at maintaining friendships with peers, and like the large majority of college head coaches, was certainly not devoid of ego. He was acutely aware that he would always play second banana to the men's basketball coach at the school, and he was known to rebel against any second-class treatment he received from the university. At times, those traits had alienated him from his contemporaries and coworkers, but that same intensity had helped him survive an oft-demanding situation at Villanova. The coach's teams almost always took on his own "us against the world" mentality, often with positive consequences. You didn't always have to like Talley, but when taking a full view at what he had accomplished in twenty-one years at the university, even his most ardent detractor was forced to respect him.

"Here's what Villanova wants," said Talley. "They want all these kids to graduate. They want them to be squeaky clean. They want them to get good grades and win games. That's pretty hard to do, and for the most part, I think we're doing that."

3

GEARING UP

The heat. Football is not a sport generally associated with heat, instead married to images like the fabled "Ice Bowl," a 1967 game between the Dallas Cowboys and Green Bay Packers in which wind chills dipped to forty-eight below zero. But even those two teams had started that season by laboring through a training camp held in the stifling heat, as does basically every squad in the country, from the high school level right up through the NFL.

Villanova, which was officially back at it the first week of August, was no different in that regard. The Cats would be splitting time for the next month between the Villanova Stadium turf and the practice fields located directly across Lancaster Avenue from their home field. If a look at the lush, green, fake grass of the stadium failed to provide sufficient evidence that that the dog days of summer were nigh, then the sight of the practice fields could certainly snap an observer right back into reality. No matter how much watering the Nova facilities people did, and most involved with the program felt that it wasn't nearly enough, after a few practices the team was running through its drills on what amounted to a brown dirt lot. Even the yard lines that were painted prior to the team's arrival were more or less faded and gone by the end of the first week.

Andy Talley, who spent much of summer two-a-days motoring around the practice fields in his golf cart in an effort to efficiently monitor the team's personnel, was not pleased with the setup. As he watched his players, coaches, and trainers toiling in the heat, Talley was again feeling like one of the university's second-class citizens, railing about the number of camps that the university had put on the surface during the summer.

For the seventy-odd student-athletes, there would be little in their lives past, present, or future that they would remember with less fondness than August two-a-days. It was impossible for a bystander not to feel sympathy for a player who went out in temperatures of one hundred degrees, restricted the cooling of their bodies by strapping on a helmet and shoulder pads, then ran around in the heat for a pair of two-hour sessions.

It was hot enough that when a ruptured gas line on campus meant there was only cold water in the locker room shower for a couple of days, none of the players complained. Perhaps none noticed.

Amazingly, the players were not the most irritable people on the field at an August practice. That distinction belonged to the trainers and medical staff, particularly head athletic trainer Jeff Pierce and his subordinate, football athletic trainer Tiger Jarvis. Pierce would have been hard-pressed to crack a smile had he been lounging on a Caribbean beach with cocktail in hand, as he was that serious a person, but even the usually congenial Jarvis was every bit as stone-faced as his boss during the month of August.

It was Pierce and Jarvis who were primarily responsible for making sure that the players were hydrated and healthy and that they weren't being pushed too hard by the coaches. A rash of heat-related football deaths on campuses in recent years, and the subsequent lawsuits that had torn apart programs and athletic departments, had put the NCAA on edge, prompting all universities to cut back practice hours in the summer. But that mandate only made things slightly easier for Pierce and Jarvis, as practices were still brutal, and they were still responsible for watching everyone all the time.

Senior tri-captain and wide receiver John Dieser was sent to either the training room or the hospital for as many as five IVs a day. Dieser could break a sweat lacing up his cleats, and by the end of a two-hour practice his practice gear was drenched and his body was seemingly walking the fine line between solid and liquid. But Dieser was lean and athletic and in shape, which is more than could be said for many of the team's linemen.

If ever a body was not built to run the regiment of 40-yard "gassers" that the coaching staff forced every player to endure during August two-a-days, it was that of Casey Cosgrove. Cosgrove was a delightful kid with an easygoing manner that endeared him to nearly everyone on the team, but his 380-pound body simply did not scream "athlete." The trainers watched Cosgrove like a hawk.

Another nonspecimen was Alex Suder. Suder, who had missed the spring while on academic probation, had cleared up his problems in the classroom but was now facing battles in the lunchroom. A former starter who was being counted on to provide veteran leadership on a unit that was far greener than the practice field grass, Suder had shown up for August practice more than twenty-five pounds overweight. By the end of double-sessions, he was on the scout team, and the mention of his name in the vicinity of the coaches would make jaws clench in unison out of utter frustration.

The trainers were also keeping their eye on the group of true freshmen, who had not spent the summer in Villanova's regimented conditioning program and were likely to hit the wall earlier than the others. Talley and the coaching staff were equally interested in what their latest recruits had to offer, not only in terms of endurance but also toughness and ability.

From the outset, it was apparent that there were some big-time characters attempting to integrate themselves into the fabric of the team.

There was Mike Holland, a linebacker from Holy Spirit High School on the Jersey Shore, who on a generally buttoned-down and conservative Villanova campus was seen walking to his first day of classes as a collegian sans shirt. Holland seemed a little off his rocker, not unusual for a linebacker, but the coaches loved his aggressiveness and expected him and another first-year linebacker, Darrel Young, from Amityville, New York, to help the team right away.

On the other side of the polished versus raw spectrum from that pair was Antwon Young, a 6-foot-4, reed-thin quarterback from Fort Lauderdale. Young, an excellent golfer with a strong arm, was looking promising enough during drill work, but it quickly became apparent that he was not quite ready for the big time from a social standpoint. Young had little regard for locker room etiquette, and even less esteem for the leadership structure of the team. When a senior had forcefully reminded the signal-caller that there were no spikes allowed in the locker room, Young had replied, "I don't have to listen to you, motherfucker." On another occasion, he had challenged one of the team's other seniors to a fight.

When Talley met with his seniors privately after a practice in mid-August, he posed the question, "Are we going to have problems with any of the freshmen?" Almost in a chorus, the group had identified Antwon Young as the potential problem child, a situation that Talley had seen coming from a mile away.

Young had been raised by his maternal grandmother and had few strong male role models as a youth, so trust for any of the men that were suddenly barking orders in his direction was going to be hard-won at best. Talley had seen this defensiveness as a result of upbringing many times before, and his plan to get Young on track would be two-fold. First, he would have to handle the teenager with kid gloves. The phrase "love him up," one of Talley's favorites, would particularly apply here. Second, he would assign Marvin Burroughs, the team's starting quarterback and probably its most respected and well-liked member, to act as something of a big brother to Young. Between the head coach's gentleness and the starting quarterback's tutelage, Talley was sure he would be able to get Young in line.

Among the other freshman hopefuls was Mason Frakes, a California kid who was being counted on to solve the team's many problems in the area of long snapping. Frakes was given a half-scholarship, the very rare I-AA scholarship long-snapper who served no other function on the team. The Wildcats had endured many problems in 2004 with the taken-for-granted practice of long snapping, so many, quipped Talley, that specialist Adam James had been serving as the team's punter, place-kicker, and goalie. That's why Frakes was at Villanova, and everyone liked what they saw him from early.

But the story of the summer was Damian Kelley, and not for anything he did on the field. Kelley, a 3.5 GPA high school student from the Cincinnati area who had enrolled in the university's arduous civil engineering program, was being restricted from practicing by the NCAA. In what amounted to a paperwork snafu, his high school had failed to properly account for a grade change in an advanced placement course, which meant that he was technically short of the necessary credits to be deemed eligible by the NCAA clearinghouse. In today's world of NCAA bureaucracy, the error was not easily cleared up.

To ensure that student-athletes were not passing off false transcripts, the NCAA not only required a letter from the high school and the Villanova registrar to clear up the error, but also had to verify the teacher's grade book. Talley had the university's compliance people working overtime to iron out the oversight, but tracking down Cincinnati high school personnel at the beginning of August and demanding that they write letters and hand over grade books to the NCAA was not anywhere near as easy as inserting a new blocking scheme or ordering a new helmet. In this case, Talley was basically helpless, and was not afraid to mince words when it came to a certain legislative body and its red tape.

Some variation of "I hate the fucking NCAA" would spew forth from Talley's mouth multiple times for every day that Kelley was not cleared to practice. And Kelley, a promising defensive end, would stand for most of the month on the sideline in his practice jersey and no pads, staring at his new teammates as they worked and looking every day like he was about to burst into tears.

While awaiting clearance for Kelley, Talley and his staff were trying to gauge the competition at several key positions.

In the spring, the team had signed Joseph Marcoux, a highly touted kicker from Don Bosco Prep in north Jersey who had made good on a commitment to attend Villanova despite receiving late offers from the likes of LSU and Wisconsin. In an act of maturity and foresight not generally associated with seventeen-year-old athletes, Marcoux had chosen the better education that Villanova offered, realizing he was a snapped tendon away from being an anonymous teenager at a less-than-prestigious academic institution more than a thousand miles from home.

But Marcoux's decision had infuriated his coaches and most of his teammates at Don Bosco, who felt that his option not to play college football at the highest level reflected poorly on them and the powerhouse prep program. After committing to Villanova, Marcoux was surprised and hurt to find that his coaches and the team's I-A signees would scarcely speak to him. Marcoux was determined to prove to the folks back home that his decision had been the right one both from an academic and football standpoint, and his indisputable kicking talents made his battle with fifth-year senior Adam James one of the more interesting duels of August.

James had made his share of big kicks in his Villanova career, including a game-winner against Temple in overtime at the Linc in 2003, but his numbers had slipped every year since he arrived on campus. James had made a grand total of four field goals as a junior, and had missed four extra points after being perfect on points-after the season before, and the coaching staff's confidence in him had all but vanished. James had received his undergraduate degree from Villanova in spring 2005, and Talley had to decide whether to bring him back for a fourth year of eligibility or cut his losses and go with the untested Marcoux. Similar decisions were made about potential fifth-year players each season. Joe Casamento, the quarterback who had led the Cats to their 6-0 start in 2003 before losing his job to Marvin Burroughs, was one of the players not brought back for his fifth year in '05, and there was significant thought placed into letting James follow Casamento out the door.

But James would be luckier than Casamento, and he had no one but Talley to thank for his continued presence on the team. To a man, every

Villanova assistant coach had been in favor of excising James, as much for his aloof attitude as for his declining production as a kicker. Many of the assistants felt that James lacked a team mentality, and the staff had grown tired of his habit of pointing the finger at everyone but himself after a missed kick or botched punt. But Talley felt that trusting a true freshman to handle the kicking chores in a I-A stadium roughly a week after figuring out which buildings his classes were held in was too big a risk. Thus it was determined that field goal and punting duties would remain with James until further notice. Marcoux, who had a stronger leg, would kick off, but there was a general understanding among the coaching staff that if James continued to be inconsistent, the freshman would have a chance to take over placements as well.

James, who was genuinely perplexed at the staff's disaffection toward him, was okay with the setup, fully believing that if the snapper, holder, and offensive line did their jobs, he would never miss a kick and Marcoux would never be a factor.

While kicking may have been a concern, the quarterback position was not.

Marvin Burroughs was everything Talley and offensive coordinator Sam Venuto could have wanted in a signal-caller. Burroughs had a rocket arm that featured enough precision to run a Villanova offense built around a short passing game, was athletic enough to run the option and scramble if necessary, and even as a junior, had as much pocket presence as any quarterback Venuto had ever been around (a group that included former No. 1 NFL draft pick Jeff George, whom Venuto had helped tutor at Illinois). He had experience, having started all eleven games as a sophomore and played especially well late in the year. What's more, Burroughs had a magnetic personality that made him the team's most popular player, and he was beloved by every member of the coaching staff and athletics administration.

Burroughs was the Holy Grail of I-AA recruits, as the bigger programs never picked up his scent coming out of Atlantic City High School, which ran a wishbone offense that rarely allowed him to display his passing skills and had a coach that didn't do much to promote his players to colleges. Also, the athletic Burroughs was listed in the media guide at 6-foot-1, 215 pounds, meaning one of the football factories probably would have tried to switch him to safety or wide receiver. Sniffing out "'tweeners" like Burroughs was a major component of recruiting for I-AA programs, and Burroughs, for one, had proven to be well worth the search.

His development, as well as the presence of a couple of top-notch senior receivers like Dieser and the electrifying and flamboyant J. J. Outlaw, meant that the Wildcats would have every chance to be one of the top passing teams in I-AA in 2005.

Outlaw was Villanova's go-to guy, its present version of Brian Westbrook, a player with dazzling speed and enough versatility to be lined up not only at wide receiver but also at running back and kick returner. The Baltimore-area native also possessed an indisputable athletics pedigree, one that was undoubtedly a major reason for the cheerful embrace of his prominent role, as well as his affinity for the spotlight.

Outlaw's father, John, had played in the NFL with both the Patriots and Eagles, emerging as one of the league's most respected cornerbacks from 1969 through 1978. John Outlaw retired from the NFL before his only child was born, but he didn't stay away from pro sports very long, making a unique transition to the front office, and eventually the bench, in the NBA. The elder Outlaw followed his friend and longtime pro coach Bernie Bickerstaff from the Denver Nuggets to the Washington Wizards to the St. Louis Swarm of the short-lived International Basketball League and was now an assistant with the expansion Charlotte Bobcats. Meanwhile, J. J. Outlaw spent major chunks of his youth in NBA arenas, watching closely and intently the work of Bickerstaff, the boy's godfather, and modeling himself after the likes of players such as LaPhonso Ellis and Rod Strickland. That Outlaw, who eventually gravitated toward football, carried himself in a different, at times almost businesslike, manner was readily apparent to most outside observers. The Villanova coaching staff knew that Outlaw was comfortable in the spotlight and were counting on him to thrive in it during the 2005 season.

With Casamento gone, Burroughs' backup at the quarterback position would be sophomore Frank Jankowski, a player about whom Talley was particularly intrigued. Like Burroughs, Jankowski was seen as a strong athlete, one good enough to have served as a reliever on the Villanova baseball team in the spring. Jankowski also came from a first-rate program, Berwick High School in the coal region of eastern Pennsylvania near Allentown, an area known for its proud football heritage.

But Jankowski had missed part of spring practice due to his baseball commitments and wasn't looking very sharp during the summer sessions. The coaches hoped that part of the problem was that Jankowski was taking most of his reps with the second team. Since the first-team offensive line was something of question mark, it stood to reason that the second-stringers weren't going to protect any quarterback very well. Jankowski's second-team receivers were also inexperienced, perhaps helping to fuel his lackluster performances.

What the coaches liked was that Jankowski didn't seem to get down on himself when he made the wrong read or missed a receiver, instead showing enough confidence to march up to the line to take the next snap. When Talley gave Jankowski a gentle "get your ass in gear" speech after a poor showing in an August scrimmage, the quarterback insisted to Talley that he would be fine. And so Talley and his coaches took him at his word, and moved on to other, more pressing matters.

Another potential trouble spot weighing on the minds of Talley, Venuto, and the Wildcats' offensive coaches involved running back Moe Gibson. Gibson, a senior from the Washington, DC, area, would be taking over full-time starting duties from the graduated Terry Butler. Butler, who had posted a solid collegiate career after succeeding the incomparable Brian Westbrook in the backfield, was now in training camp with the NFL New York Jets, and the Villanova coaches were praying that they wouldn't miss him too much. The Wildcats had been known as a passing-oriented team for the past decade, but as Westbrook and Butler had shown, the presence of a multidimensional running back was key to the effectiveness of the scheme. The running back in the Villanova offense was asked to find tough running room in short-yardage situations and also to be a legitimate pass-catching threat and decent blocker.

The staff, which had struck out in an attempt to acquire admission for a I-A transfer running back during the offseason, were counting on Gibson to step up and fill the vacancy and were fairly certain that he had the ability to do so. But they also knew Gibson was a hypersensitive human being whose mood could deteriorate quickly when things weren't going well. Could Gibson carry the load, and moreover, could he handle the pressure? There was some reason to believe that he could not.

During the team's first formal scrimmage of the summer, Gibson and the Villanova offense failed on four touchdown tries from the 1-yard line, eliciting whoops and hollers of celebration from the defensive unit. As this scene unfolded, Gibson stomped to the sideline and dressed down his offensive line.

"What are they doing that we can't get 1 yard?" Gibson whined. "Seriously, man, what are they doing?" No one answered, and it was clear on this sweltering August day that the exhausted o-line wanted to pose the same question right back at Gibson.

As much as the efficiency of the offense was a major preseason topic at Villanova, there was plenty of concern over the play of the defense as well.

Everyone remembered how poorly the defense had played after Ray Ventrone was hurt in 2004, and Mark Reardon, the recently promoted coordinator, was looking long and hard for some leaders on his unit to ensure there wouldn't be a repeat of that scenario.

The best natural leader on the defense was end Darrell Adams, the amiable pro prospect who had sat out the spring following knee surgery. Adams had received a clean bill of health during the summer, but less than a week into two-a-days, his knee had swelled considerably, a situation that was nothing less than panic-inducing for all involved. If Adams wasn't healthy, he wouldn't be able to practice, and if he wasn't able to practice, he certainly wouldn't be able to play. Until he was right, the All-American didn't feel comfortable being vocal with his teammates, and so Reardon and the defensive coaches were left to play a waiting game, hoping that Adams would be of sound enough body and spirit to realize his potential as a senior and in turn give Villanova the boost it sorely needed.

Without Adams, there were no genuine leaders. Starting linebacker and tri-captain Brian Hulea (whose ailing mother was in treatment for her cancer and improving, thankfully) was a terrific football player and was well-respected on the team, but as the definition of the strong, silent type, his attempts at verbally motivating his teammates seemed at times to be more than a little forced. Fellow starting linebacker Bryan Adams fell into the same reserved boat.

The secondary had some burgeoning talents like free safety Allyn Bacchus and cornerback Rodney Badger, but both were young, and as members of a secondary that had led directly to the team's downfall in 2004, were in no position to serve as leaders, either.

And there was little doubt that there were players on defense that desperately needed to be guided, with sophomore end Russell McKittrick at the front of that line.

McKittrick was a 6-foot-3, 240-pound southern California native with a high motor and strong football instincts who had nonetheless been a major headache for Talley and the coaches since he first set foot on campus in 2003. The trouble started during his freshman year, when it was brought to the staff's attention that McKittrick had not been attending class regularly. Soon after it seemed that they had set him straight, McKittrick again went AWOL, upon which it was learned that he suffered from both attention deficit disorder (ADD) and attention deficit-hyperactivity disorder (ADHD), two similar-sounding afflictions with different symptoms of great concern. Talley and the trainers, in consultation with McKittrick's parents and a local physician, set to medicating him, but the treatment made McKittrick groggy and diminished the football intensity and drive that had turned him into a standout at San Marcos High School in the San Diego area. It was after McKittrick opted to cease taking the medication that Talley realized that he might have bigger problems than his attention span.

McKittrick once called Talley's cell phone to report that he had been hearing voices. Later, he casually told another member of the coaching staff that he was convinced that there was a secret society prepared to take over the world. Over the previous summer, McKittrick, who had remained on campus to attend summer school, was discovered by campus police perched atop the roof of one of the dormitory buildings without explanation. Every time McKittrick seemed to drift, the trainers and medical staff would change his medication to something that might help him without sapping him of the football ability that he was determined to maintain. Talley would monitor McKittrick closely, and every time the coach was convinced that he had finally turned the corner, McKittrick seemed to do something that would send up red flags.

As August prepared to turn into September, Talley found himself hoping against hope that McKittrick's newest medication would allow him to focus and develop into the standout player that he showed flashes of becoming. But in the back of their minds, Talley and his staff found themselves bracing for the worst.

Among those facing sleepless nights was Reardon—not that he would have slept even if he was tutoring some defense that was an amalgam of the 1975 Pittsburgh Steelers, 1985 Chicago Bears, and 2000 Baltimore Ravens. During the season, Reardon slept three hours a night at a maximum, with many of those "evening naps" taking place on an air mattress inflated on the floor of his tiny office beneath the stadium bleachers. The rest of Villanova's staff thought their friend and coworker was a little bit out of his mind in this respect, especially since he had two young children and a lovely wife sitting at home in south Jersey while he evaluated hours of film on the Main Line, but no one could ever question Reardon's level of dedication or preparation in performing his job.

Becoming acclimated to his new position was going to be more difficult for Reardon in light of the myriad staff changes that had taken place during the offseason. Along with former defensive coordinator Joe Trainer, popular D-line coach Clint Wiley had also departed from that side of the ball, and receivers coach Drew Maginnis as well as tight ends tutor Bill Lacey were gone from the offense.

Brendan Daly and Billy Crocker, two former Villanova assistants, had returned to campus to coach the defensive line and cornerbacks, respectively. Daly and Crocker were both well liked, hence the fact that Talley brought them back after respective absences of four and two years. But both had spent most of their young coaching careers on the offensive side of the football and were adjusting to their new positions at the same time that their direct supervisor, Reardon, was contending with his own enhanced level of responsibility.

Another new and especially loud voice on defense was that of Sean Spencer, who had coached the defensive line for four years under Talley's nemesis Mark Whipple at UMass and would be in charge of linebackers at Villanova.

The vocal and gregarious Spencer had arrived at Villanova in the spring with profoundly mixed emotions. After coaching for one year at Holy Cross in the Patriot League (he had lost his job at UMass when Whipple bolted to the Pittsburgh Steelers), Spencer was happy to be back in the scholarship world of the Atlantic 10, and after coaching the D-line for most of his career, he was also pleased at what was considered a promotion to the more demanding world of linebackers.

But shortly after having accepted his new and challenging assignment at Villanova, Spencer's wife of less than three years, Allyson, informed him that she would not be accompanying him to Philadelphia and would instead remain in New England and begin pursuing a divorce. Taking the Villanova job would not only mean walking away from any chance of reconciliation with his wife, but it would also keep Spencer apart from his infant daughter, Alysia. As an assistant football coach who worked long hours during the week and whose most important occupational tasks came on Saturdays, popping up to New England for the weekend to visit his only child was not going to be an option. So it was with the knowledge that the Villanova opportunity was a good one that might not pass this way again, and that the chance to better provide for his daughter in the long run would, however cruelly, force him to be away from her for long periods of time, that Spencer made his way to the Main Line.

Daly, Crocker, and Spencer weren't the only unfamiliar voices that the returning players would be hearing. On offense, another prodigal son, Brian Flinn, had returned to campus to coach wide receivers. Flinn, who had coached tight ends and assisted with the offensive line at Nova in 2000-01, was back following a four-year stint at Eastern Illinois University.

Two new graduate assistants, Mike Kraft and Justus Galac, would be helping out as well. Both Kraft and Galac had made sacrifices of varying degrees to pursue their love of football.

Kraft, a former punter and backup quarterback at Sacred Heart University in Fairfield, Connecticut, was a diehard New York Yankees fan who had given up a spot on a YES Network reality show called *Ultimate Road Trip*, in which he would have followed the Bronx Bombers for all 162 games plus the playoffs while a film crew tagged along, in order to work long hours for peanuts and live in a dorm at Villanova.

The proof of Galac's dedication to the game was of less recent vintage, but it was more impressive and significantly more mind-boggling than Kraft's sacrifice.

In the summer prior to his senior season as a nose tackle at Division III SUNY-Brockport near Rochester in 2001, Galac noticed a testicular lump and had the sinking feeling that the lump meant cancer. Knowing that such a diagnosis would mean a premature end to his collegiate football career, the recently named co-captain sought no medical treatment and told no one of his condition—not his parents, friends, or coaches—save a single teammate who was sworn to secrecy.

Though the lump continued to grow and his discomfort increased as the season wore on, Galac opted to wait until the end of the year to see a doctor. As it turned out, that season would be extended by a week when Brockport made the playoffs. Even after the team lost in the first round, Galac did not sprint directly to a hospital for treatment, as he was then afforded the opportunity to try out for the Rochester Brigade of Arena Football League 2. The Brigade gave Galac a physical but did not perform the traditional hernia test that would have undoubtedly revealed the condition.

He made the team.

Three months later, the Brigade released Galac, perhaps unknowingly saving the life of a young man to whom, with no risk of overstatement, football was more important than life itself.

Galac's potentially deadly gamble turned out just fine. After being released he underwent successful surgery and sought treatment for his illness, which was indeed diagnosed as cancer but had luckily not spread. Moreover, Galac would forever possess an airtight defense of his commitment to the game.

And though Galac's story would impress every Villanova football player who heard it, even he would not have as great a day-to-day impact on each individual team member as would new strength and conditioning coach Reggie Barton.

Talley, who was embroiled in an ongoing rift with the people currently in charge of the Villanova weight room, had fought for years for a full-time, football-only strength coach like most other I-AA scholarship schools employed. Villanova's players had long lacked much in the way of a supervised, regimented weight-training plan, and the inconsistency of the team's offensive and defensive lines were seen as a by-product of this setup. The Villanova athletic department finally relented in 2005 and allowed Talley to hire Barton, whose very presence would be sure to get the players' full attention.

Barton, a 6-foot-3, 280-pound former offensive lineman at Idaho State, was the type of frightening physical presence that even the toughest member of the team wouldn't think twice about messing with unless they also harbored a serious death wish. In addition to being a former player, Barton was also a professional power lifter who had won a "strongest man" competition in his home state of Idaho and looked like a man who spent his spare time bench-pressing Pontiac Bonnevilles. Barton knew exactly what it took to build strength, and he certainly wasn't afraid to voice his displeasure with any work habits that he viewed as less than acceptable. No player was going to mess with this guy, and even the most wizened members of the coaching staff would use the gentlest of tones in showing Barton the ropes.

Despite salaries that could only be viewed as average in comparison with Villanova's Atlantic 10 compatriots, a situation that helped ensure the type of turnover the program had experienced in the offseason, scoring a spot on Talley's staff was something of a prime assignment.

Talley wasn't viewed as being especially hard on his staff. On the contrary, he allowed his coaches to run their departments as they saw fit and rarely meddled without a very good reason to do so. This setup would allow a young coach to find his voice and polish his teaching tactics. In addition, Villanova's national recruiting approach, as opposed to the regional setup that most I-AA programs favored, meant that assistants were sent on the road to areas with prime high school football talent. The ability to develop contacts in prep hotbeds like Atlanta, Dallas/Fort Worth, Florida, and California looked terrific on a young up-and-comer's résumé.

Talley's somewhat detached approach to handling staff and players in a football-related capacity could have its drawbacks in certain situations, however. While all of the assistants appreciated being allowed to do their jobs, there were times when Talley might not have seen every nuance of every position battle or every team-related issue clearly. And after not having a great deal of personal involvement with players in practice, Talley's motivational speeches prior to games would inevitably ring hollow with some members of the team. Players would stare at the head coach quizzically at times during games, as he dressed someone down for committing a stupid penalty or dropping a pass after seemingly not showing much interest in the game plan during the previous week of preparations.

Talley knew that criticism of him, both internal and external, came with the territory, and he was well beyond worrying what anyone who didn't sign his paychecks or call him "dad" thought of him. In reality, if Talley had immersed himself knee-deep in film study or in the inner workings of the game plan, that involvement likely would have had an adverse effect on the things that had made Talley successful at Villanova for two-plus decades: the ability to closely monitor his players' grades and classwork, keep them out of trouble, and as soon as the offseason hit, find more student-athletes who would fit into both the university structure and the football program without giving anyone at the school headaches. In addition, no one, not the players, the assistants, and certainly not the fans or alumni, could appreciate the fact that it was Talley and Talley alone who was forced to consume himself with Villanova's on-campus politics, which had been stirred up yet again during the summer.

Father Edmund J. Dobbin, the Augustinian priest who had been the school president since 1988, announced on April 25 that he would be retiring at the end of the 2005–06 academic year. Dobbin was known to be a major college basketball fan, but his stance on football at Villanova had always cast him in the role of Switzerland—neutral, perhaps to a fault.

Dobbin was aware of the damage that dropping football had done to the university at the beginning of the 1980s, and no matter how much money the current edition of the program lost or how much certain sectors of the faculty or alumni base complained, he was not about to take Villanova in that direction again.

Although this was good for Talley and company, Dobbin was not going to be the man to ramp up the program's profile, either. The overriding feeling among some of those close to the situation was that Dobbin had been the most significant obstacle to the team moving to I-A and the Big East in the mid-nineties, and that he had commissioned a ruse of a I-A study during that time with the predetermined conclusion that a move up would be a bad idea. Dobbin, it was said, was terrified of the impact so-called major college football would have on the financial bottom line and academic reputation of the school, and he was worried that the ideals of a Catholic university and the pursuit of championships at the highest level of football would not easily mesh.

Because of his perceived ambivalence about football at Villanova, Dobbin's imminent departure raised some important issues as the sport was concerned. Would the next president share Dobbin's neutrality? Would he look at the financial bottom line and make a move toward the brighter lights and potentially bigger dollars of I-A? Or would he look at the financial bottom line, listen to the thoughts of some Augustinians and faculty, and say "enough is enough," downgrading the program to a nonscholarship entity, or worse, proposing to drop football altogether? No one knew as the sweltering days of August became a tired routine, but the point was worth considering, at least for Talley.

The Wildcat players and the rest of the coaching staff would not be giving much thought to these political machinations, which was a good thing, since the challenge of facing Rutgers on September 10 was more than enough to occupy their overworked minds and overheated bodies.

As balmy as August had been, everyone knew that once the calendar flipped to September, the heat would really be turned up.

4

THE BIG TIME

As the 2005 college football season began, the Villanova Wildcats watched and waited. The weekend of September 3, in which just about every team in college football played their opener, was designated as the bye week for the Cats, who would subsequently play the next eleven Saturdays, through the end of the regular season, without an open date. The players were eager to get started, but in a way, the extra week off was a blessing. Talley's staff would have an opportunity to slap another layer of polish onto its game plan, and his players would have another seven days to get game-ready from both a mental and physical standpoint.

Another potential benefit for the program was that it would have an opportunity to size up its first opponent of the 2005 campaign. Rutgers was opening its season on the afternoon of September 3 on national television at the University of Illinois, and all the Cats were anxious to see just how strong the Scarlet Knights were going to be.

For the past decade or so, Rutgers had been considered one of the weakest programs playing at the BCS level, if not in all of I-A. As 2005 began, the state of New Jersey's only I-A football program had gone twelve consecutive years without a winning season, had logged a composite record of 18-75-1 in the Big East since football was established as a conference sport in 1991, and hadn't made a trip to a bowl game since 1978.

But there had been positive signs seen in the program in recent years, as young head coach Greg Schiano finally began persuading some of New Jersey's rich crop of football talent to stay home and attend Rutgers.

At the end of the 2003 season, Rutgers had beaten perennial Big East stalwart Syracuse for just the second time in seventeen tries, and the team's confidence carried over to the following season when they began at 4-2 including what was considered a landmark win against Michigan State on national network TV. Of course, all of the good feeling faded when the Knights, true to form, lost their final five games and ended the year with a thud at 4-7. And though Schiano had the team competing in a way that it scarcely had before, Rutgers fans were expecting to see a winner in 2005, and anything less would turn those whispers about the head coach's job security into screams.

I-AA teams like Villanova didn't generally have realistic expectations of beating BCS-level behemoths, which had twenty-two more scholarships to make them stronger across all areas of the depth chart and possessed a higher national profile, sterling facilities, a weekly television presence that allowed them to recruit many more elite players, and beaucoup financial resources through their association with the BCS to help maintain the players' athletic talents and academic standing once they arrived on campus.

The main reason that most I-AAs even stepped up to play the major I-As was because of the paycheck. A school like Rutgers would give Villanova $200,000 just to drive up the New Jersey turnpike, a financial setup that went a long way toward balancing the athletic department budget and justifying the presence of football on campus. Elite-level I-As like Nebraska, Auburn, LSU, and Kansas State, all of which regularly hosted I-AAs, offered a financial guarantee closer to $500,000, and despite the physical and mental toll blowout losses at the hands of these giants would exact on the usually overmatched visitors, there was no way the cash-starved I-AAs (or, for that matter, the bottom-tier I-As in the Sun Belt or Mid-American Conference that were also forced to play these games) could turn the contests down.

Most I-AA coaches, including Talley, bemoaned the presence of guarantee games on their schedules, but they knew the games literally represented the cost of doing business. The glass-half-full types among this group would also speak highly of the experience and PR boost of playing the so-called big time programs and would use their presence on the schedule as a recruiting tool for potential players who might be attracted to the prospect of facing such elite competition.

Keeping any perceived slanted playing field in mind, there were few around the Villanova program who believed the Wildcats wouldn't have a realistic opportunity to beat Rutgers.

VU was one of the few I-AA programs that had proven itself adept enough to step up to the BCS level and win games, having taken down Big East members Rutgers and Temple in 2002 and 2003, respectively. The Wildcats hadn't lost a guarantee game since 2000, when a team that would eventually finish 5-6 fought gamely before losing at Rutgers (34–21). In Talley's 21 years at the university, Villanova had really been blown out only in one money game, when it traveled to the thin air of Colorado Springs and lost to Air Force 37–13 to open the 1999 season.

The Cats' last trip to Rutgers had ended in a 37–19 domination of the home team, as quarterback Brett Gordon picked apart Schiano's squad in a contest that some believed could have been a great deal more one-sided in favor of the I-AA school. Many of Villanova's top players in 2005 were freshmen that day in '02, and the ease of that victory remained fresh in their minds. Just about all members of the current edition of the Cats could recall that last season, one week after taking down Michigan State, Rutgers had embarrassingly fallen by double digits at the hands of none other than New Hampshire of the Atlantic 10.

But when the Villanova players and coaching staff tuned into ESPN2 at noon on September 3, they saw a much different Rutgers team than the hapless one with which they had previously been familiar.

Before a stunned crowd of more than 50,000 in Champaign, the Scarlet Knights spent most of the game's first 45 minutes running up and down the field against Illinois. Back in Philly, Mark Reardon winced as he watched Rutgers' 230-pound running back, Brian Leonard, overpower the Illini like a battering ram while his shifty backfield mate, Ray Rice, made tacklers miss. Illinois' offense could do nothing against the Rutgers defense for most of the first three quarters, managing more than 15 yards on just one of their first nine drives and turning the ball over three times. The score at the end of three quarters was only 27–10 in favor of the Scarlet Knights, but there was little dispute about which was the better team as the game moved into its final stage.

Then, the self-fulfilling prophecy stating that Rutgers would always find a way to blow it rushed to the fore yet again. After Knights kicker Jeremy Ito missed a field goal at the end of the third quarter, Illinois managed to put together its best drive since the first quarter, setting up a field goal to cut the lead to 27–13. Rutgers punted on its next drive, and four plays later, an Illinois touchdown pass cut the score to 27–20 and brought the formerly silent crowd right back to life. The Scarlet Knights nearly salted the game away on the ensuing drive, running 12 plays and nearly five minutes off the clock while moving deep into Illini territory, but an Ito field goal try that would have given Rutgers a comfortable 30–20 advantage was blocked. With the momentum squarely in its favor, Illinois drove right down the field again, and with just over a minute to play, a contest that had very recently looked to be in the books was tied at 27.

Predictably, Illinois answered a Rutgers field goal in the first overtime period with a short touchdown run, and the Scarlet Knights left town as 33–30 losers.

The men at Villanova watched all of this unfold with mixed emotions. There was little doubt that if Rutgers could play as well as it did on the road against a Big Ten team, than the smaller, thinner Cats would certainly face a daunting task. Talley and company also knew that in addition to being talented, the Scarlet Knights would be more than a little angry at the way their opener had ended, and would be seeking to take out their frustrations on VU. In addition, Rutgers didn't figure to be looking past a I-AA program as some I-As would, in light of the result the last time the teams had faced off back in '02 and the fresh reminder of the New Hampshire debacle in the Knights' past.

Still, the fact that Rutgers had spit the bit with the Illinois game on the line was cause for optimism. Villanova may have been facing something of a size and talent disadvantage in its opener, but the Wildcats had also won a lot more games than had Rutgers in recent years, and had a formula for success and a certain confidence that the Scarlet Knights hadn't displayed in a very long time.

Talley knew the opener would be a challenge, but he felt like his team could hang. "Right now, I would say they're about two touchdowns better than us," confided the coach as game week began. "But if we can get them into the fourth quarter, they're in trouble. I don't think they know how to win."

If there was a game on the schedule to which the bulk of Villanova's fans and alumni would pay attention, it was this one. The team's true-blue football fans would probably care at least equally as much about the season-ending installment of the University of Delaware rivalry, but the more sizeable base of Wildcat men's basketball fans that really followed the football team only when it was playing on a national stage (some within the Villanova athletic department would refer to this group as "the frauds") had a much easier time wrapping their minds around a game with a traditional Big East foe like Rutgers.

A considerable faction of fans and alumni felt it was teams like Rutgers, and not Northeastern or James Madison or William and Mary, that the Wildcats should have been playing on an annual basis in league play. Many within this contingent would speak with an air of regret and incredulity about a time when this move to the next level very nearly came to pass.

In 1994, three years after the formerly basketball-centered Big East Conference had added football to its roster of sports, a pair of universities that had previously been part of the league only for football, Rutgers and West Virginia, were invited to join the Big East for all sports. As a provision of the admission of those two schools (as well as Notre

Dame, which chose to participate in the league in everything but football), the conference's presidents determined that the league's remaining members that did not field I-A football—Connecticut, Georgetown, Providence, Seton Hall, St. John's, and Villanova—should also be given a chance to play the sport at the highest level, in turn reaping the full breadth of financial rewards (bowl payouts, TV contract dollars, etc.) that football would bring to the conference. Providence and Seton Hall, which did not field football programs and lacked the infrastructure or financial wherewithal to add the sport, chose not to seriously explore the idea of I-A football. Georgetown and St. John's, which at that time were playing at a pure nonscholarship level, gave the idea little consideration either. This left only Connecticut and Villanova, both of which had been playing scholarship football as part of the I-AA Yankee Conference, to take a maximum of three years to study the idea of ramping up their programs.

In order to enter the league as a football member, the Big East would require that Villanova meet the following seven requirements.

1. The stadium must meet the minimum NCAA I-AA seating capacity requirement (30,000).
2. Attendance at home contests must average 25,000 per game over a two-year period.
3. The conference receives first call on date and time for stadium availability on all Saturdays during the NCAA-approved season.
4. The stadium and institution must be able to move game times with twelve days' notice from afternoon to evening and vice versa to fulfill television obligations.
5. The institution must provide sufficient resources to enable the school to compete at the highest level.
6. The institution must provide the maximum number of grants-in-aid (scholarships) (85).
7. The institution must provide the maximum allowable coaching positions and sufficient administrative, conditioning, and sports information staff.

Considering the feasibility of meeting these seven tenets and also projecting the long-term potential for the success and viability of Villanova as a Big East football-playing member would be a committee comprised of university president Rev. Edmund J. Dobbin, director of athletics Gene DeFilippo, Villanova Board of Trustees members Tony Randazzo, Robert Birmingham, David Cook, Rosa Gatti, John Kolmer, and Mariellen Whelan, and Villanova alumnus and New Jersey Sports and Exposition Authority president Bob Mulcahy, later to become athletic director at Rutgers. Randazzo would chair the committee, and a pair of conference commissioners, Roy Kramer of the SEC and Mike Tranghese of the Big East, would assist in a consulting capacity.

In general, the committee's mission in studying the feasibility of Big East football at Villanova would boil down to one word: money. More specifically, how much money it would take to meet the criteria in order to make I-A football work, and where exactly the university was going to find this money.

The largest expense would undoubtedly be the stadium, and from the outset it was clear that Villanova football would require its own facility, preferably on campus. The valuable lesson here had been taught by Temple University, which had for years been playing off-campus at cavernous Veterans Stadium, a pro building almost always at least 75 percent empty. As Temple could attest to, the "first call" provision in the Big East requirements also made the prospect of sharing a facility with some other team problematic.

But Villanova's current on-campus venue was small (12,000 seats), aging (built in 1927), and located in the center of a campus within what was a thriving Main Line neighborhood, which meant that expansion or renovation of the facility would be a major hurdle. Radnor Township, in which the university was located, raised a major fuss whenever the school tried to erect even a new academic building. How enthusiastic would they be about the prospect of a 30,000-seat stadium, which would bring with it major traffic and parking concerns?

Money issue number two involved scholarships and the hiring of new personnel for the coaching staff and athletic department. While it may have seemed to some that moving from 63 to 85 scholarships wouldn't be a major impediment, what many outsiders didn't realize was that moving football to I-A would require the funding of 44 more scholarships, not just 22. Title IX regulations mandate that colleges and universities must fund the same number of athletic scholarships for both women and men. In this regard Villanova had a few options that were either expensive or would bring with them public relations difficulties: add a women's sport or two, furnish existing women's sports with more scholarships, drop a men's sport or two, or decrease the number of existing men's sports scholarships.

The third major obstacle would involve the Wildcats' mandatory four-year "transition period" to the big time. The NCAA stipulated that universities would not be considered full members of I-A until four years after the university had begun operating with a I-A commitment, and the Big East in turn would not be sharing the entire breadth of financial dividends with Villanova until the school became a full-fledged member of both the football conference and I-A. This meant that the university would spend the remainder of the millennium attempting to draw nearer to the other Big East football schools in terms of competitiveness on the gridiron, even as, unlike every other football-playing member of the league, it was forced to be at least somewhat self-sufficient in building its schedule, its fan base, and its recruiting strength.

With all this in mind, the prospects for I-A football at Villanova didn't look very promising as the special football advisory committee convened in 1996, roughly a year before the Big East deadline for a decision. Unlike most of the other schools playing football in the Big East (as well as UConn), Villanova was a small, private, academic-oriented institution that wasn't going to receive any state money to fund this enterprise.

And no matter what type of revisionist history some of the old alums were attempting to write, Villanova hadn't had much in the way of success or support for football when it had been playing at the highest level before dropping the program in 1980. The Wildcats made just two bowl appearances from 1950 until the program was dropped, and even when teams like Boston College, Cincinnati, and Temple were traveling to the Main Line, Villanova Stadium was not always filled to its modest capacity.

Had Villanovans supported football like their counterparts at Notre Dame or even BC, it seems unthinkable that the sport would have ever been dropped in the first place. What had changed in the last fifteen years that was going to boost the program's support level by half? Would Villanova eventually run into the same problems that had plagued Temple as it attempted to make a dent on the sports landscape of what was becoming more of a "pro town" with each passing year?

These concerns were legitimate, and yet, somewhat implausibly, Randazzo and his committee came extremely close to making all of the numbers line up. The stadium issue was among the first that the committee would address.

"An issue that we all knew was going to be a problem for us was the stadium," remembered Randazzo. "Radnor Township wasn't going to allow a football stadium to be either renovated, or a new one built on the premises. Trying to be objective, when you have 12,000 at a football game now, there's a bottleneck on the Main Line. If you were to increase that to 20 or 30,000, there's almost no way that the community could ever support that kind of a situation."

So DeFilippo, the athletic director, prospectively negotiated an attractive and financially reasonable short-term deal with Franklin Field, the former pro facility located eighteen miles away on Penn's campus. The notion of a brand new multipurpose athletics facility located closer to the Main Line was floated as the long-term solution.

"John Kolmer, who had come off of Wall Street working for First Boston, presented a model of how a stadium could be funded," said Randazzo. "But even that became secondary. We were convinced there was no way we were going to get a stadium built on the Main Line and approved by the township. At that time we did not envision the new stadium—Lincoln Financial Field—in Philadelphia. Ideally, it was thought land would be purchased—the Haverford Hospital property was one option—near the campus, to house an all-sports facility to include football, basketball, soccer, etc, thus freeing up valuable land for housing, classrooms, and an arts center."

The addition of both men's and women's scholarships, while costly, was a directive that the committee was able to spin positively as well.

"Part of the budget included the addition of twenty-two scholarships for football players, therefore twenty-two additional scholarships had to be added to the women's side to conform to Title IX gender equity requirements," remembered Randazzo. "During the process, we discovered there was already a shortfall of eight to ten women's scholarships that needed to added to be within compliance. These were also added to our budget. Our approach was to impress upon the Board that moving to Division I-A would obviously help increase the scholarships for women athletes. Conversely, dropping football would jeopardize the same sixty-three scholarships given to the women's sports."

But where would the money for the funding of these scholarships emanate from? Randazzo and the committee put a plan in place for a gradual escalation of the scholarship, administrative, and coaching needs, and though the Big East wouldn't be giving Villanova the full share of football revenues enjoyed by the current members of the league, Randazzo and others believed that the conference would help enough to offset many of the capital costs.

"The proposal we submitted was over a four-year period. We did not suggest going to twenty-two additional scholarships immediately. As we added 5 to 7 scholarships each year, there was a step-up in expenses to coincide with the increase in revenues. As such, we proposed an immediate participation in the revenue sharing from the Big East. At the time, Temple was receiving two million dollars a year through revenue sharing, and we were confident the same could be negotiated for Villanova. We were convinced that if the president was behind this, some of the onerous conditions being imposed upon us could be waived or negotiated. Rutgers and Temple were not meeting the attendance requirements, and Temple was not conforming to the stadium criteria. The budget over the four years was concise, structured, and well documented. The revenue sharing of the Big East was essential and without it, there would never be a reason to move up to Division I-A."

It was the perspective of Randazzo and other members of the committee that the dollar figures associated with being a part of the Big East for football would have ensured the program's financial stability beyond anything that the school's highest-profile program had experienced.

"The other point that was made very clear to us, and I'm not so sure that the Board recognized it until we presented it, was that the revenue sharing in football far exceeded anything that would be realized in basketball," said Randazzo. "When we started floating those numbers—TV contracts and sharing of the bowl revenues with the other football members—the numbers were extremely attractive. Football revenues, which were shared by eight schools, far exceeded the basketball revenues, which were shared by fourteen schools."

Those on the committee that crunched the numbers were also sure to point out to the I-A dissenters that the university could begin ramping up its program on a trial basis. If the arrangement didn't work during this period, the university would not have been wedded to any type of long-term, financially draining arrangement with I-A or the Big East.

Said Randazzo, "Our proposal to the Board suggested that we had this window of basically four years. We were going to be able to test the waters, and the Big East was going to test the waters too. Our proposal to the Board was, 'Let's try this for four years, if we can prove economically that we're not going to lose any more money than we're currently losing during this four-year period, let's go in and use Franklin Field, let's see if the alumni and the students are going to support the program, and what harm would it be? If we find that we have the support, then two or three years down the road, or four years down the road, we can decide what we want to do.'"

There was still much doubt about whether Villanovans would support the program, especially if it was playing home games off-campus, but committee members like Randazzo and Mulcahy felt that comparing the current state of the program to what could be achieved when playing more suitable rivals in the Big East was an argument of apples versus oranges. The university would simply be transferring already-existing rivalries in other sports, including men's basketball, to the gridiron, which would effectively alter the sentiments about the sport for the better. That would keep Villanova from suffering the erosion of interest that Temple had experienced, and the aggressive marketing plan included within the proposal would be another mark in favor of the move.

"Our program was very precise and sufficiently funded with a marketing program that was going to support that type of a program," remembered Randazzo. "Marketing the program was considered extremely important. We already had more season-ticket holders than Temple was averaging in attendance on a given day. Part of the proposal that we made to the committee was that before we would proceed, and before we would go into the fourth year, we had to have season tickets up to the fifteen thousand range, otherwise we weren't going to proceed. There was no way you could go into Division I-A and only have season ticket holders of two or three thousand."

As far as tradition was concerned, Board members such as Mulcahy thought I-A football at Villanova could work, and he used the success of another Catholic school as a reasonable proxy.

"Boston College had been in a similar situation," said Mulcahy. "Before Doug Flutie they were no better than we were. They had similar attendance problems, they had similar 'pro town' problems, and they were more of a commuter school than we were. You don't often get a Doug Flutie factor, but I felt that we had as much tradition, and certainly had been as successful in athletics as Boston College had in 1980 when we dropped football."

Mulcahy was one of those on the committee who was engaged in long-term thinking as it applied to the football program.

"My theory was that Villanova was one of the top three Catholic universities in the country, and the other two were Notre Dame and Boston College," argued Mulcahy. "And what going to Division I[-A] would do would achieve an elite status for the university and put it on the same level as those two schools. We had always had a history of being able to recruit good players, even when we had terrible facilities, and I felt that twenty years down the road this would be an important factor in recruiting students, forget players."

But even given the detailed proposal, the committee would meet its share of unforeseen obstacles, one of which was the lack of enthusiasm toward Villanova's I-A prospects by Big East commissioner Mike Tranghese, with whom Randazzo met to discuss the parameters of the potential move.

"I remember he made it clear that he was looking for higher-profile universities to add in football," said Randazzo. "He even mentioned to us that he was pursuing the academies. Army and Navy would be very attractive when negotiating the next TV contract. If he could have added either one or both of them, he would have preferred them to Villanova and Connecticut. He recognized that the invitation was extended, but he was not going to bend over backward to accommodate us in any way. It wasn't his decision to make, it would ultimately be in the hands of the Big East presidents, but he made it clear where he was coming from—Army and Navy as opposed to Villanova and Connecticut."

But Tranghese's lukewarm reception to Villanova's I-A feasibility study was nothing compared to what Randazzo and his pro-I-A associates on the committee were up against on their own campus. Immediately upon convening the committee, certain anti-football Board members began discussing the general value of the sport at the university on any level, a discussion that unsettled Randazzo and others.

"We had to balance very carefully that our mission did not become a referendum on football," recalled Randazzo. "The whole challenge for the committee was to evaluate the invitation to the Big East, but by some of the comments made it became clear to myself, John Kolmer, Dave Cook, and Rosa Gatti, who were members of the Board of Trustees, that some of these questions being asked were related to whether we should have football at all. Obviously that was not what we had intended, and was never supposed to be our charge. It was a balancing act that became really concerning to the board members that were on the committee."

Anti-football sentiment was by no means a new arrival at Villanova. In 1981, the university had eliminated the sport in a covert, dark-of-night exercise that had blindsided the entire team and coaching staff, not to mention the students, alumni, and several members of the Board of Trustees. Soon after the university released a meandering 573-word statement announcing football's elimination on April 15, 1981, it was discovered that the Board had voted to eliminate the sport despite the fact that the item had never been listed as an agenda item at the meeting, and that the measure was voted on in the absence of several key members of the Board. It was believed that several powerful Augustinians, along with anti-football trustees such as then-board-member Joseph Walters, had initiated the power play.

Bob Capone, a former player and assistant football coach at Villanova who was at that time working as the school's alumni director and was friendly with several members of the Board, remembered the shocking circumstances.

"The meeting of the Board was over, one of our guys was ready to light up his cigar, and they said, 'No, we've got one more thing, we're going to talk about dropping football.' There were two very influential members of the board who were not at the meeting, and one of the reasons that they picked that date was because Tom Labrecque, since deceased, the president of Chase Manhattan bank, wasn't at that meeting, nor was Tom Burke. Tom Burke is a third- or fourth-generation Villanovan who still works here now and was not at that meeting. And I think that the measure would have at least been put on hold had those two been there."

In a letter to Walters that was obtained by the school newspaper, The Villanovan, Labrecque wrote, "The peremptory process used to arrive at the decision was not one to be proud of," adding, "This is a low point in terms of our integrity in communicating with each other, and in the decision-making process."

"This was the best-kept secret since Pearl Harbor," said Capone. "I still just can't believe the methodology that was used. You would think that it was like a third-world problem and they were wiping it out. The entire thing was wrong. If they wanted to drop football, they should have put it out on the table and gotten the faculty, alumni, and students involved. But they did it really under the cloak of darkness."

The university press release cited the lack of conference affiliation for football as among the reasons for the move, also raising monetary concerns stemming from the cost of funding the program; heightened energy, social security and regulatory governmental costs; and educational budget cuts proposed by newly elected President Reagan. But those on the inside didn't believe that the bottom line was the biggest culprit in football's demise.

"I guess you could say money, but I don't believe that was the reason," said Capone. "I think there were those—some faculty, some Augustinians in high positions on campus—who just didn't think football belonged on campus. When the two alumni leaders went in there, Doug Murray, the president of the alumni said to [then-president] Father Driscoll, 'Father, give us 10 days, whatever money you need, we'll get it, we'll balance it. Why didn't you tell us, why didn't anybody say anything? Ring a bell [if] we've got some economic problems. We would have solved that.' But it was too late.

"In my heart I believe that it had very little to do with economics, it had to do with there were people who just don't like football. The unfortunate thing was that the people who didn't like football were all in positions of authority. And there were some people who like football at Villanova that never got into the quotient."

Roughly a year and a half later, following a giant outcry from students and alumni and a massive fundraising campaign set into motion by the Wildcat Club, a booster group, the wheels were set in motion to bring football back on campus. In late 1983, following a nearly two-year back-and-forth between the university's pro- and anti-football constituents that was referred to by the Daily News as the "War on the Main Line," the Board voted to restore football at the I-AA level. But now, more than a decade since the sport was reintroduced, the virtue of football was again in question. After all the heartbreak and ill feelings of the '80s, some Augustinians and certain members of both the Board of Trustees and I-A feasibility committee were questioning the value of the sport all over again.

"Some Augustinians have a cultural problem with football," said Randazzo. "They opposed football for reasons other than economics. They appreciate basketball and track but when it comes to football student-athletes their perception is not the same. They prefer not to have them on campus. We could deal with the facts and present a realistic budget but we were never going to overcome this bias. And yet, Andy Talley's program consistently has a very high graduation rate with very few problems. There is no reason to think the same could not be accomplished at a higher division."

Overcoming the perceptions that some on campus held about football players was easier said than done, however.

"Some voiced their opinion during these board meetings that we shouldn't be involved in football, that this type of element was not welcomed at the university," said Randazzo. "It was a prejudice that went back to the early 1980s, when we dropped football."

At one point during the study process, an Augustinian addressed the Board, claiming that he would chronicle how the graduation rates of college football players were well below the general population of students throughout the country, and how this element would effectively deteriorate Villanova's high academic standards. Board member Rosa Gatti attempted to dismiss that notion at the Board's following meeting, quoting statistics and providing research to prove that football players were in actuality performing better academically than much of the average student population, and also providing numbers comparing football players favorably to many of those participating in other sports. When it was the Augustinian's turn to document his side of the issue, sources revealed that he brought out the Boston Globe sports section, which included information about a past college basketball scandal as the sole basis for his argument against football. This nonsensical parallel bemused several members of the Board, who were left to lament the amount of illogical thinking that they might be up against during this process.

Dobbin, president at the time, was not going to shout down those irrational voices, though he dismissed the notion that all Augustinians had a cross to bear when it came to football on campus.

"This myth about the Augustinians being anti-football is simply not the case," said Dobbin. "If I were to look at people on the Board who were pro or con [on the issue of] going to I-A football, it would not fall according to Augustinian versus lay person at all. There wouldn't even be a correlation there."

The president's stated concern about the role of football on campus dealt with money, despite the fact that the meticulously labored-over financial aspects of the proposal seemed to be in order.

"The comment was made that he was not going to bankrupt the university over football," remembered Randazzo. "Somehow the perception of Villanova playing big-time Division I-A football just wasn't in the cards with him.

"We drew from experts in the field of football—[SEC commissioner] Roy Kramer, [Miami (FL) athletic director] Paul Dee, Bob Mulcahy—all of whom were favorably impressed with our approach and encouraged us to proceed. Our study included three scenarios. First was a worse case, that the program would not exceed the current deficit at the I-AA level. The second and third plans were at a break-even, and showing a profit, respectively. The scenarios each included revenue sharing from the Big East and increased attendance revenues. The risk was minimal during the four-year trial period, yet the national exposure and upside was very attractive."

But the notion of limited fiscal risk was not going to silence the very powerful voice of the President.

Remembered Mulcahy, "It came to a point where we asked Father Dobbin point-blank if he would support [the recommendation to the Board] if the committee decided to do it. He said no."

"Father Dobbin will be considered one of the most effective presidents in the history of Villanova University," said Randazzo. "His accomplishments are well documented and he deserves the credit he receives. No one was more dedicated to the university then he. [But] there was just no persuading him, and there was nothing we could do. So we went ahead and made the proposal on the basis that we still had the Board of Trustees. If we could convince them, it would be possible. But realistically, how are you going to have a football program if the chief administrator wasn't supporting it? We didn't really know what would happen if we were able to get the votes. How could you go ahead with a program knowing full well that the president of the university wasn't supporting it?

"We had no choice but to proceed with the study and make the presentation knowing we did not have the support of the president of the university. Our position was to convince enough Board members to decide the outcome on the merits of the report. Understandably some members voted no simply on the basis of the president's response."

Dobbin was likely astute enough to realize that several Board members, including a selection of those who held their positions at Villanova due to their association with the president, would align themselves with him irrespective of any facts that Randazzo and his committee might uncover supporting I-A football. Some would side with the president out of a sense of obedience or loyalty, and others were simply cognizant of the fact that the program would struggle to survive if Dobbin, who controlled the finances, as well as hiring and firing at the university, was not in support of it.

"I agree that there are people, at least in the presence of the president, who don't want to disagree," conceded Dobbin. "[But the I-A supporters] imply that that was really the dynamic behind this whole thing. I don't think our Board is that way. We have a great Board at the university, and have for many years now. They'll speak their minds, and they'll vote their minds, and they're not just going to do what I want them to do."

Flying in the face of that contention was the fact that one of the I-A committee's most influential voices, that of athletic director DeFilippo, bailed out in his support for the Big East measure at the eleventh hour.

"That was really disappointing for the rest of us on that committee," said Randazzo. "When we got to the point where we were going to vote, there were four trustees 'for' and three trustees 'opposed' to it. Gene DeFilippo and Bob Mulcahy were also allowed to vote as committee members. Bob was voting for it. Two or three days prior to us releasing the study in order for the committee to vote, Gene announced that he didn't think that it was proper for him to vote. And while he never said it, as an employee of the university, reporting to Father Dobbin, he was not going to vote for something that Father Dobbin opposed. He was really supportive throughout the year and a half. We could not have developed the results without his efforts. Behind the scenes he could see this working, and it hurt when he dropped out."

Though the requisite support existed on the I-A committee without DeFilippo's vote, a tactical error made early in the study process jeopardized the impact of the presentation that would be made to the full Board of Trustees.

"We had the votes in committee to make a favorable recommendation to the Board," recalled Randazzo. "However, during the early stages of the process of gathering information, the president made a request that the committee be unanimous in its decision whether to accept or reject the Big East invitation. Thinking we all had an open mind and would vote on the facts, we agreed to this stipulation. This was a mistake. We did not anticipate decisions would be made solely on emotions, not the facts. Strangely, as a committee, we were concerned those in favor of moving to Division I-A would try to influence us. On the contrary, the reverse was true. Those who opposed the invitation based their decision on something other than the facts in the report."

Despite this setback, and the president's tacit disapproval of the I-A measure, the pro–Big East findings of the committee made enough sense that the Board was nearly convinced to upgrade the football program, a circumstance that some felt made both Dobbin and the president's perceived loyalists such as Robert Birmingham extremely nervous.

"Finally, the presentation was made—'Here are the facts draw your own conclusions,' remembered Randazzo. "To their credit, most Board members read the detailed report and asked the proper questions. There was a sense that this was a viable option. We never could convince most of the Augustinians, though as questions were asked, the discussion became more interesting. A formal count was never recorded. Few people know that we came within a few raised hands of accepting the invitation."

Though Randazzo and his group defied the odds and came close, the I-A measure was still defeated, with what some believe to be a strategic power play by the university president proving too difficult to overcome. It was as the study concluded that some committee members suspected that Dobbin had known there would no I-A football at Villanova from the very beginning.

"In retrospect, the committee was given sufficient time to make a fair and complete evaluation," said Randazzo. "The university provided the resources for us to collect the data. The committee members spent an inordinate amount of their personal time to do a proper assessment. We were given the opportunity to present these findings to the Board. Unfortunately, we were used to legitimize a decision predetermined by the president. Without his support, a certain number of Board members were never going to vote in favor of the invitation. The process we worked so hard to protect had been contaminated. Money and the stadium issues were given as reasons for the rejection, though the committee proved the money issue was not valid, and the stadium issue had been addressed by the utilization of Franklin Field as a temporary site."

Multiple sources close to the situation later revealed that Father Dobbin passed out a statement, one written prior to the actual vote of the Board, outlining in press release form the fact that the university would not move to I-A in football, and the reasons for the decision. If there had ever been any doubt that the committee was being used to justify a predetermined response created by the president and other anti-I-A forces, this previously penned text eliminated it.

Dobbin denied that the release had been written prior to the Board's vote and also bristled at the notion that he had any type of agenda in respect to football.

"I certainly had nothing to do with it," Dobbin said of the release. "In fact, I doubt that I even saw it before the meeting. Nor did I write something else. I have no knowledge of a press release that I had prepared for this.

"Hardly am I anti-football or anti-I-A. I'm very pragmatic, and I'm not a manipulator. My whole approach to things is to let them play out, and I was the person who nominated every member for that committee, hoping that we'd get a real honest assessment that had credibility to it. And at the same time, I disagreed with the somewhat naïve optimism in the report at that time.

"I was open to it, but I had my doubts about the feasibility of it, which is precisely why I wanted a committee that would be able to assess it."

Dobbin disputed the possibility that Big East revenue sharing would have been an immediate option, claiming, "That wouldn't have happened, that was dreaming," and conceded that he could never see past the capital costs that would have been involved with the move to the big time.

"I saw that as the [challenge] that was most onerous for us to deal with," said Dobbin. "The other problems were basically when you have a smaller university, you're dealing with a different situation, having to compete at a very high level and compromise almost inevitably the quality of student that you were going to be taking if you were giving out eighty-five scholarships just for football, and plus more for all the other sports. This was a question that was raised, though it was not high on my agenda, I'll be very honest. My agenda was largely a financial one."

On October 15, 1997, the university released a statement indicating that it would remain at the full-scholarship Division I-AA level, citing financial concerns in opting not to move its football program to the Big East. The release contained no information regarding the possibility of the Big East's would-be financial contribution to the university during the transitional period, stating that, "During this transition period, new Big East teams do not share in the financial benefits of the conference." There was no mention of the bond and stadium scenarios that had been painstakingly outlined by John Kolmer, nor the Franklin

Field arrangement devised by Gene DeFilippo, with the only reference to the stadium coming in regard to the difficulty of expanding the current structure on the Main Line. Even the listing of the members of the committee was incorrect, but since the study was never made public, no outside observers could analyze the data that the committee had compiled.

And though money was the chief reason given for the decision to remain at I-AA, and Dobbin had seemingly avoided his stated nightmare of bankrupting the university, people like Randazzo felt that the president's stance had actually caused negative financial ramifications in the long-term.

"'I am not going to bankrupt this university,' it was stated more times than we liked to hear, and even in the face of data that proved otherwise," said Randazzo. "Everyone agreed I-AA football is a slow death. The two million deficit would increase each year. Expenses would increase as tuition increased, since the largest portion of the deficit is attributed to the tuition. Some universities exclude this cost as not being an out-of-pocket cash item. Our budget treated the tuition and room and board as a full cost. Revenue at the I-AA level is severely limited. Without television, there is very little revenue available. By going Division I-A, and the revenue-sharing within the Big East, there was a possibility if it was run properly that we could get to at least no worse than where we were, which was basically a two million dollar deficit. But the possibility of a break-even, or even making a small profit, at least existed."

Now, close to eight years later, Villanova football was successful at its own competitive level but was still losing millions. Temple, not Villanova, was the team sharing the Eagles' sparkling new facility in south Philadelphia. There was constant worry surrounding the basketball team's place in the Big East, as many believed that the league would eventually shift to a model built around its football membership, and would excise non-football-playing schools like Villanova at some point down the road. Invitations from BCS conferences to I-AA football teams were exceedingly rare, and in all likelihood, the Main Line school had seen its window of opportunity shut.

"I think it's a missed opportunity, there's no question about it," said Randazzo. "Lincoln Financial Field, that could have been Villanova and not Temple there. "We would not have had the crisis about whether our basketball team would survive as part of the Big East. It was Roy Kramer who said the leagues whose teams play all sports will survive and prosper, i.e., the SEC, ACC, Big Ten, etc. The only sport the Big East has in common is basketball. As football revenues continue to increase, the universities that are playing football as part of the conference will again look for alternatives. Whether there's still a chance [for Villanova to move to the Big East in football] or not, that's up for other people to make that decision. If this question is ever revisited again by the Board, my hope is that it is given a fair hearing."

As Andy Talley walked the Rutgers Stadium field two hours before kickoff, he knew every political reason why his team was there. He knew Villanova needed a guarantee game to help make ends meet, and he knew Rutgers was a logical option for an opponent in that regard. He knew the game was at least somewhat winnable, and he had long since considered that there was some benefit in having a chance to see Rutgers in Week 1, while Rutgers would be seeing the 2005 edition of the Wildcats for the first time.

But with the 3:30 game time drawing ever nearer, all that logic and positive thinking was out the window.

What Talley saw at the moment was a superior BCS-level opponent fresh off what should have been a victory in Big Ten country, a foe that had a chance to work out some of its kinks by playing sixty-plus minutes of live football, and a team that had a monumental advantage against his young, untested squad.

This rising tension was something of a normal routine for the head coach. Talley had no trouble putting up a happy front when he made pregame small-talk with the opposing head coach or with the officiating crew, but otherwise, "loose" wasn't quite the adjective an observer would assign to Talley at this juncture in the day.

The object of Talley's wrath, Villanova senior associate athletic director Bob Steitz, was not in close proximity as the head coach stood in the afternoon sun, but his presence could be clearly felt as far as Talley was concerned.

Steitz, who oversaw Villanova's football and men's basketball scheduling, was a veteran collegiate administrator whom Talley had known since Steitz had served as associate commissioner at the Atlantic 10 Conference in the 1990s. Steitz was the son of the late Ed Steitz, who was considered royalty in the world of college athletics administration for his instrumental role in the establishment of both the three-point line and shot clock in college basketball in the mid-1980s, and the younger Steitz had himself built a sterling reputation as an administrator in college sports for close to twenty-five years. There wasn't a nuance of the world of sports administration that Steitz didn't fully understand, and the success he had achieved in his field had been born of that understanding and an excruciating attention to detail.

But in the warmth department, Steitz was not exactly Mister Rogers, and though most who really knew him liked and respected him, Talley didn't get him at all. Steitz had convinced Talley to play just four games at home and seven on the road in 2005, as the Villanova athletic department opted to move what should have been a September 24 home game against Penn to the Quakers' home stadium, Franklin Field, in an effort to generate greater attendance at the larger facility. That alteration hadn't seemed especially significant at the time it was made, and it had been part of a tricky maneuver to get Penn onto the schedule for the next few years and another local team, Lehigh, back on the slate beginning in 2006. But as the "home" date with Penn drew closer, Talley was feeling less enthusiastic about the challenge.

And now, the fact that Villanova was playing its first of seven road games against a I-A team that already had a game under its belt was going to be dumped by the head coach primarily at the feet of the guy that oversaw the schedule.

As his players dressed in the humid Rutgers visitors' locker room, Talley could be heard ranting about Steitz and the competitive disadvantage that this schedule represented, how he and the other basketball-focused administrators with offices in Jake Nevin Field House were not sufficiently concerned about him, football, or the situation that the program had been placed in with this roster of games.

Talley's staff wasn't as outwardly irritable as 3:30 approached, but neither were they a barrel of laughs. The same coaches who had been cheerful and talkative just twenty-four hours earlier were now wound tight as a drum. This was serious business.

The players were looser than their coaches but seemed just as focused. The excitement of their first road trip of the year was giving way to acknowledgment of the task at hand. When the team's three buses, accompanied by a state police escort arranged by Rutgers, had made the short drive from the Piscataway Embassy Suites to the stadium, the bus was stone silent. This group wasn't just going to watch a college football game, it was on its way to try and win one.

In the locker room before kickoff, everyone seemed to have his own routine. Many of the players wore ear buds connected to iPods, trying to fire themselves up with a little hip-hop or driving metal.

J. J. Outlaw's music of choice was Phil Collins's "In the Air Tonight," and his selection of early eighties synth-pop as his warmup fare wasn't the only strange portion of Outlaw's pregame routine. Moments before the start of each game, Outlaw would dispense a team manager to head to the stadium concession area to get him two hot dogs, which he inhaled with the voracity of a contestant in the annual Nathan's hot dog eating contest.

Assistant head coach Mark Ferrante shook the hand of every player in the room, a practice that emanated from his time as a young staff member at Wagner College in the mid-eighties and was also a nod to late assistant Lou Ferry, who had partaken of the same ritual with his players.

Villanova offensive coordinator Sam Venuto would find a small corner of the locker room in which to meditate. On this day, in the cramped space assigned to Rutgers' visitors, Venuto sandwiched himself between a wall and a rolled-up tarp to try to find some peace and collect his thoughts.

With the intensity in the room at its most palpable point, Talley instructed his players to gather around and take a knee, at which time team chaplain and Augustinian priest Rev. Rob Hagan offered a blessing and led an "Our Father." Everyone associated with the program liked the forty-year-old Hagan, who was also an associate athletic director at the school and had left behind a thriving career as an attorney, including eight years as a criminal defense lawyer, in order to join the priesthood in 2003. On this day, Hagan's words would bring strength to many a player.

Once he was finished, it was Talley's turn to motivate. Knowing the players were champing at the bit to get going, he kept it brief.

"No matter what happens, the give, the sway, the back, the forth, you hang in the game," said Talley.

"Keep your head up. Doesn't matter what happens, get the next play, get back into the game, let's try to get these guys into the second half and then into the fourth quarter. If we can stay with them into the fourth quarter, we have a wonderful chance to win this game, okay, but you have to come out and play hard right off the bat. It's going to be a very, very fast pace. You gotta get up and running right off the bat . . . stick together, great opportunity, super day, let's go."

With Talley's final exhortation, the players let out a yell and began gathering near the entrance to the tunnel. All except Outlaw, who as another part of his unique routine, always insisted on saying a private prayer at his locker before being the last player out of the room. Some players, including Outlaw, would stop in front of Father Hagan to receive a quick private blessing.

Many teams emerge from the locker room voicing some kind of group chant as a means of self-motivation or intimidation of an opponent, and this would mark Villanova's debut performance of its new processional. Linebackers coach Sean Spencer had taught this one, which was chanted slowly and to the tune of the chorus of Steam's 1969 hit "Na Na Hey Hey (Kiss Him Good-bye)":

We ready
We ready
We ready
For y'awl

Many of the African American players, who seemed to relate most easily both with Spencer and the chant, expressed themselves loudly as they headed down the tunnel toward the field. The mostly East Coast–bred white players didn't seem quite so comfortable with the chant, sounding sort of like a chorus of Pat Boones butchering a Little Richard tune, but they respected Spencer too and gave it their best until, dripping with anticipation and adrenaline, they were finally allowed to storm out of the tunnel and take the Rutgers Stadium field on what had revealed itself to be a stunningly clear and pleasantly mild day in north Jersey.

Some of the players wore wide grins amid the boos and derisive chants emanating from the Rutgers student section, which was located behind and about 20 yards to the left of the Villanova bench. It had been more than nine months since the Wildcats had heard fan noise that had anything to do with them, and it also wasn't often that the Cats would get to play in front of this many spectators. The announced crowd of 32,412 (in reality closer to about 25,000) was roughly 20,000 folks larger than the Wildcats usually saw either at home or on the Atlantic 10 trail. Whether many of these fans were pulling for Villanova or not, this was the kind of football atmosphere these guys had dreamed about since they were handed their first sets of shoulder pads.

Rutgers won the coin toss and elected to receive, and it was finally time to get this thing going. As freshman Joe Marcoux teed the football up for the first kick of his collegiate career, Talley and his charges were more than ready to cash in on all the hard work that had begun on a similar-looking sunny day back in April. They were at last set to put the struggles of 2004 behind them—the death of their teammate, the season-ending injury to Ventrone, and the disappointing finish of a club that was supposed to make the playoffs. As Marcoux's pretty kickoff sailed end-over-end and reached its final descent inside the Rutgers 10-yard line, these guys were indeed "ready for y'awl."

Or so it seemed, for approximately 11 seconds.

Scarlet Knights return man Willie Foster fielded the kick cleanly, found a seam, made one cut, and dashed untouched for a 93-yard touchdown as Marcoux gave futile chase. The Rutgers crowd exploded. The Villanova sideline reacted with stony, disbelieving silence.

It was impossible to determine in real time what exactly had gone wrong, and it was probable that a number of players were at fault for the return, not to mention the fact that Foster was the fastest player on the field. What was immediately certain to defensive line coach Brendan Daly was that Wildcat freshman defensive end Dave Dalessandro had failed to take his position on the field goal block team, as Rutgers followed its touchdown by kicking a point-after against a defense that had just ten players on the field. Daly laced into Dalessandro on the sideline, and after a brief moment of shouting and chaos, Villanova was going to try to put the opening-play embarrassment behind them.

For a while, it looked as if the Cats would indeed let the touchdown roll right off their backs.

After the teams traded punts, Marvin Burroughs coolly led the offense on a nine-play, 80-yard drive that culminated in a pretty John Dieser 32-yard touchdown grab in the corner of the end zone. The momentum of the play was diminished somewhat by the ensuing Adam James extra point try, which was blocked to keep the score at 7–6. But with 7:21 to play in the first quarter, Villanova had proven that it could move the ball and score and could also stop the Rutgers offense. Things were looking up, but only for a little while.

The Scarlet Knights marched right back down the field with a 10-play, 71-yard drive that ended with a short Brian Leonard touchdown run to make the score 14–6. Burroughs moved the Cats right down inside the Rutgers 30 on the subsequent drive but lost a fumble on a third-down sack that was recovered by the Knights. Rutgers then put together another long drive, extended by a needless holding penalty by Wildcats safety Zach Mariacher and ending in a field goal. After

Villanova's ensuing three-and-out, the Knights went 88 yards in 11 plays to their third touchdown of the half, as Leonard and Rice carved up the Wildcat defense for 48 of those yards. Talley's team would get to the Rutgers 29 on their final drive of the second half but turned the ball over on downs and trotted to the locker room staring forlornly at a 24–6 scoreboard deficit.

Back inside the visitor's locker room, Talley was firm and encouraging, with just a hint of criticism.

"You're down two touchdowns and a field goal. That's all it is, that's going to happen in any game in the Atlantic 10. You're going to find out if you're able to come back. Let's get back offensively, you let some shit hang out there. We should be in great shape right now, we blew a whole score down there. Plus we have 'em stopped and we have a defensive holding call. We're making dumbass mistakes against a team that's pretty good. Guess what? You're going to see about eight of them in our league.

"Wake up. We're playing football now, the season has started. I'll tell you what, we are not that far away from these guys. You close the gap on them in the third quarter, and all of a sudden they'll start making mistakes. They're dumb-assed trying to throw the ball deep for touchdowns, wasting downs, if they were smart they could have buried us in the first half. But they're stupid, because they wanna look big in front of their crowd. Guess what, they left the door open for you, you decide if you want to walk through it."

Like Talley, most observers who had witnessed the first half would have likely argued that while Rutgers was the better team, Villanova possessed the ability to get back in it just like Illinois had a week ago. The Cats had moved the football and made some stops, but had done neither consistently. If, as Talley implored, the team could cut down on the mistakes and finish some drives, it seemed plausible that they would have a shot to make this a game.

And as Burroughs led the Cats' first drive of the second half, it appeared that those hopes were realistic. A pass interference call gave VU its initial first-down of the half, and a 16-yard pass play from Burroughs to tight end Matt Sherry on the next play already had the offense within sniffing distance of midfield.

Then, on first-and-ten from the Villanova 42, Burroughs started right on an option play, saw an opening, tucked the football, and ran. The quarterback had already gained 7 yards when Rutgers cornerback Joe Porter's helmet collided with Burroughs' left arm just above the elbow. At the exact same instant that the defensive back made his hit, another Knights' player delivered a blow to Burroughs' arm near the shoulder. The quarterback went to the ground, and as the pile of bodies was uncovered, Burroughs remained down. The hit hadn't looked all that menacing from a distance, and Burroughs appeared calm in his prone position. He wasn't rolling around or hollering in pain. Perhaps, thought his best friend and teammate Outlaw, Burroughs had simply had the wind knocked out of him.

Trainers Tiger Jarvis and Jeff Pierce hurried to midfield to take stock of the situation.

"What's up, Marv?" asked Jarvis.

With a whisper, Burroughs answered, "I got a Charlie horse, I took a helmet to my bicep. Just give me a couple of minutes and I'll be fine."

In evaluating the situation, Jarvis immediately began to suspect things were far more serious. Burroughs' left bicep was swelling at an alarming rate, leading the trainer to believe he might be dealing with a tear of the muscle. When Jarvis touched Burroughs' upper arm, however, he heard a crackling sound, which could mean only one thing: the quarterback's arm was broken.

Jarvis looked to the sideline, where Dr. Bill Emper, the team doctor as well as a renowned area orthopedic surgeon and former Harvard football player, stood watching. Emper generally steered clear of on-field injuries unless he was called upon, and he knew by looking into Jarvis's eyes that his services were about to be required.

Emper agreed with Jarvis's initial diagnosis, knew almost right away that Burroughs had snapped his humerus, and after doing his best to stabilize the quarterback, called for a cart to carry the team's best and most popular player from the Rutgers Stadium turf. Burroughs would immediately travel to the hospital, where an x-ray would confirm what Jarvis and Emper already knew, that the player expected to lead Villanova to a championship had a broken arm.

As Burroughs left the field, Talley quietly walked up to Jarvis.

"It's a fracture, right?" asked the coach, and Jarvis answered in the affirmative.

"What are we looking at? Six weeks? Eight weeks?"

Jarvis looked straight into Talley's eyes and broke the news as quickly and directly as he knew how.

"He's done for the year."

Talley, his staff, and any players who were of a mind to put two and two together were overcome with an almost immediate sense of nausea.

Both because they liked him and knew how important his presence and leadership were to the team's success, Burroughs undoubtedly would have ranked dead last on a list of Villanova players anyone would have wanted to see suffer an injury of this magnitude. Outlaw and running back Moe Gibson, who came in with Burroughs as freshmen and were his closest friends on the team, were suddenly forced to come to grips with the fact that they were unlikely to catch a pass or take a handoff from No. 17 ever again.

For Frank Jankowski, who had been the third-string quarterback for all of last season, the reality was beginning to sink in that he was going to be the No. 1 signal-caller for the next three months. For the moment, though, Jankowski would have to focus on Rutgers. He was either going to sink or swim in the first live action of his collegiate career, and as he had rarely appeared with the first-string in practice and the beginning of his road would come against a I-A team, an objective observer would not have been alone in sizing the sophomore up for a set of cast-iron ankle weights.

Jankowski completed his first two passes, but the drive Burroughs had begun stalled right around midfield, and a fake punt attempt on fourth-and-one was blown up by Rutgers. Three plays later, Scarlet Knights QB Ryan Hart threw a 15-yard touchdown pass to Clark Harris, and Villanova was in a 31–6 hole that even the most optimistic Wildcats diehard knew was just about insurmountable.

For the rest of the day, Villanova would throw on almost every down in an effort to move the ball quickly and score some points. And Jankowski did a decent job, completing 17 of 32 passes for 209 yards without an interception. But as they had in the first half, the Wildcats would consistently run out of gas in the red zone and would fail in every attempt to get their second touchdown of the day. For its part, Rutgers attempted to run the football and the clock, more or less calling off the dogs after the outcome was no longer in doubt.

Rutgers 38, Villanova 6. It could have gone a whole lot better. But as Talley pointed out in his postgame address to the team, it could have been a whole lot worse, too.

"Marv broke his arm, he's not going to play anymore this year," Talley began. "And I'm very sad and disappointed for Marvin and for our team. He's a great person. But it's what we've been talking about all along. The Lord giveth, the Lord taketh away. It can happen at any time if you don't relish what you have. But I can tell you right now that I saw a lot of things out there that we can be happy with. A lot of things.

"Frankie stepped in, did a hell of a job. We lost our stud QB, but we have a guy that we can win with. I think everyone here agrees that we can win with Frankie, he can take us a long way.

"I'm sorry we lost Marv. I'm sorry for you guys that we lost the game. But inside of me as a coach, there's a lot of hope. We can have a damn good football team, we really, really can. So what you need to do is put this one away."

Talley also couldn't resist taking his shot at Steitz and the schedule-makers.

"I want to apologize to you, because there's no way we should be playing a I-A team in the second game of their season. No way. That stinks from an administrative standpoint and I'll be talking to them on Monday. That's just a bad position to put a I-AA football team in. That team right there will prove to people that they're going to win six or seven games and be in a bowl game."

Talley's players weren't thinking much about the imbalance that playing a I-A in Week 2 had presented. Most felt that things could have gone a lot better if the breaks had gone their way, no pun intended, and though there was distress and more than a few tears over Burroughs' injury, the players, like Talley, knew there was plenty of cause for optimism.

When John Dieser, just minutes short of his next IV, gathered his offensive teammates for a few words, he knew it was Jankowski's team now, for better or for worse.

"We lost a hell of a player today, but Frankie showed us he can drive us like a leader," said Dieser. "We went up and down the field at will today when Frankie got in there. The bad thing is those four times in the red zone when we didn't get in."

As Dieser and the rest of the team began preparing to put the Rutgers loss behind them, Talley was meeting with a handful of assembled media outside the locker room. Again, he attempted to spin the loss of his starting quarterback in a positive fashion.

"We have a good second quarterback, Frank Jankowski, and I thought he played extremely well," said Talley. "[He] was a highly recruited quarterback out of Berwick, Pennsylvania, and we like him a lot. I felt we had two terrific quarterbacks, maybe two of the best in the league, 1-2, and I think Frank showed that today. We feel like we still have a shot to be a really good football team with him."

And after singing Jankowski's praises, Talley also took a public parting shot at the decision makers in the Villanova athletic department, laying the groundwork for a future meeting with Steitz and athletic director Vince Nicastro.

"I think it's really difficult for us to play a I-A team in their second game, in our first game. I don't ever want to do that again. It's bad enough we're playing a I-A team without having to play them in their second game."

After Talley had finished airing his feelings, Outlaw, with his eyes still damp and red over the fate of his roommate, suppressed his emotions long enough to say all the right things. Outlaw, whose father John had played in the NFL and was currently coaching in the NBA as an assistant with the Charlotte Bobcats, had seen and been a part of enough press conferences to know his duty in this situation was to pick up his teammates. When Terry Toohey of the *Delaware County Times* asked if Jankowski's strong play had surprised him, Outlaw, even through hurt, answered without hesitation.

"I would say no, because I knew he could do it. He didn't surprise me at all. He has an unbelievable arm. He's a 'front' guy, at times he likes to do his own thing. When things break down, he gets a little kooky out there. That's what we love about him, it's good to have a little variety in quarterbacks. Frank's a good teammate, all his teammates like him. We all believe in him."

As Talley, Venuto, and the offense rallied around Jankowski, much of Nova nation saw the score of the team's home football opener flash across any number of the Saturday TV scoreboard tickers.

The football fans of the bunch, who already knew the score and many of whom already knew about the Burroughs injury, were concerned but were aware that the real measure of their team's prospects would come in the Atlantic 10 home opener next Saturday, not against big-time Rutgers.

Meanwhile, the frauds would now be checking out in their attentiveness toward Villanova football in 2005. Some would yawn and await the release of the men's basketball schedule. Others would privately vocalize their disdain for the level of football at which their school participated, feeling for all the world that there was no way any Villanova team should be blown out by any Rutgers team.

For certain, not many in the latter group would be making their way to the Main Line in one week's time to watch a game against some Boston-area safety school called Northeastern.

5

LIGHTNING STRIKING AGAIN

DeQuese May sat down beside his locker, removed his arm and wrist bands, and with a silver marker the sophomore fullback wrote the number "17" in large block script along his inner forearm. It was two hours before kickoff, and May was paying tribute to his friend Marvin Burroughs, whose presence had been missed almost immediately in Villanova's offensive huddle.

Burroughs was still around as the team readied itself for its league and home opener against Northeastern, but the jovial Marv everyone had known was suddenly replaced by a heavily medicated, outwardly disappointed, arm-in-a-sling version of the former star quarterback. Burroughs had been excused from class during the week that followed his injury, meaning he had more time to reflect on his pain and a year of his football life that had been cruelly snuffed out before it had really begun. Talley and the NCAA compliance people at Villanova discussed applying for a medical redshirt on Burroughs' behalf, but since he had already redshirted during his freshman year, when Brett Gordon was firmly established as the QB, the odds were long that the signal-caller was going to play college football beyond 2006. The NCAA handed out a sixth year of eligibility only under extreme circumstances, and an injury to a quarterback was as routine as the falling of the autumn leaves.

As Burroughs sat dazed on the bench while watching his team practice without him, his teammates did their best to keep his spirits up. A saddened J. J. Outlaw, ever the professional, would run by his friend whenever he had an opportunity and chatter in his ear in an effort to make him feel a part of the team. The parents of reserve linebacker J. C. Cooper, in from their home in California for the Northeastern game, made Burroughs a tray of cookies. The team's coaches, medical staff, even the managers and equipment people did their best to keep Burroughs engaged. And the former starting quarterback would never shoo them away, instead politely answering all of their tired "How ya feel?" queries with a positive response and flashing that easy grin that belied an undeniable depression.

Andy Talley, meanwhile, had to walk a tightrope when it came to the quarterback situation. Talley knew it was his job to be a surrogate father to Burroughs, "love him up," tell him that everything was going to be okay and that he had the love and support of the entire Villanova family.

But he also knew that he couldn't let his team's season shatter along with Burroughs' left arm, and if he projected anything resembling a grim demeanor toward the players, they were going to pick up on it, carrying around their head coach's sense of unease and pessimism.

Talley was particularly concerned about the mood of the team's black players, particularly Burroughs' friends on the offensive side of the ball. The Villanova campus was predominantly white—"Vanillanova," according to some—with mostly white students, faculty, administrators, and, apart from Sean Spencer and special teams and running backs coach Apollo Wright, white football coaches. Having an African American giving the orders in the huddle, Talley had surmised, was incredibly inspiring, even empowering, for players like May, Outlaw, running back Moe Gibson, and center Christian Gaddis. Talley was wondering just whether all of the black players, particularly those who held long-standing friendships with Burroughs, would show as much natural enthusiasm toward and support for Frank Jankowski.

For his part, Jankowski had neither the time nor the inclination to consider the shifting sands of racial harmony within the offense. All

Jankowski knew as he dove headlong into the playbook was that the guys he was counting on to assist him in his first collegiate start—white, black, or otherwise—would be represented by the letter "X," while the enemy would be identified only with an "O."

The challenge was not one that the 6-foot-1, 210-pound Jankowski took lightly, but that didn't mean that he didn't feel with every fiber of his being that he could get the job done. Despite the fact that Villanova had two scholarship quarterbacks with a combined seven remaining seasons of eligibility when Jankowski signed his letter of intent in early 2003, Jankowski always felt that he was good enough to win a starting job. After all, folks in the coal region had been pegging him for stardom ever since his sophomore year of high school.

Born May 10, 1984, in Bethlehem, Pennsylvania, to pharmacist parents, the eldest of Fran and Honora Jankowski's two children showed an early affinity toward both football and baseball, but was kept off the gridiron until the eighth grade by a football-loving father who worried about what bad habits his only son might develop in the Pop Warner leagues.

"The first year I played organized football was in eighth grade," remembered Jankowski. "I always used to practice with my dad, my dad's kind of like my personal coach. . . . He's real knowledgeable about sports and quarterbacking specifically, so ever since I was little we always used to go over mechanics and drills. It would kind of be like a workout session."

Despite his limited experience on the field, Jankowski was good enough as a freshman to win the starting varsity quarterback job at Montoursville High School, the school in the small town near Williamsport where the family had moved when Jankowski was ten. Montoursville was a great area for baseball, best known as the hometown of major league pitcher Mike Mussina, and the high school also had a strong football program. Had Jankowski, by now also a promising pitcher on Montoursville's baseball team, remained at the school, baseball likely would have developed as his most natural route to a college scholarship. But during Jankowski's sophomore year, the family had a chance to move about sixty miles southeast to Berwick, closer to Fran and Honora's family in the town of Frackville. And at Berwick High School, which had won three national championships in football between 1983 and 1995, Jankowski's landscape was abruptly altered.

A normal teenager could transfer from Montoursville to Berwick and remain relatively anonymous, but around Berwick, where many folks already knew Jankowski's name and were aware of the fact that he had been on Joe Paterno and Penn State's radar screen since his freshman year at Montoursville, the transfer was considered headline news.

"At the time I guess it was considered a big deal," said Jankowski. "High school football is just taken so seriously in general in that area of the state and Pennsylvania as a whole, where obviously things are going to be really heightened during the fall season. Football is Berwick."

Mark Ferrante, who recruited Berwick and the entire coal region when Jankowski was in high school, agreed with the quarterback's assessment of the area.

"The coal region in general is different than most areas I've recruited," said Ferrante. "I don't know if it's expectation about playing at the next level, I don't know if it's just they think their football is the greatest football on earth, but the coal region in general is a little different than the counties down here, it's even different than Pittsburgh. [The quality of play has] dropped off over the years, but in their minds it hasn't."

Jankowski was almost immediately ordained the starter at Berwick, and even in the face of escalating expectations, his burgeoning confidence helped him to thrive.

"There were pressures, but where a lot of people would say 'pressure,' I like to say 'excitement.' The atmosphere on a Friday night under the lights. . . . Everybody knows 'Friday Night Lights,' but that really was that type of atmosphere in Berwick. The whole town's behind you, you get ten thousand people at a game, and you get more if it's a big playoff game or something like that. It's a really fun atmosphere, as well as you can be prepared to play college sports. You're used to the atmosphere, and [opposing teams], especially if you're from a good program, they're going to get up for you every week."

Jankowski produced a brilliant junior season at Berwick, throwing for more than 2,000 yards, rushing for nearly 1,000, and leading the team into the semifinals of the state tournament. By now the spotlight on Jankowski, both around the state and on the national recruiting scene, was white-hot. Berwick had recently produced a four-year quarterbacking starter at Notre Dame named Ron Powlus, and it looked like the region's latest gem would follow Powlus down the road to college stardom.

Though Jankowski lacked prototypical height at 6-foot-1, his natural athletic ability was a huge plus to the big schools, and a 4.0 high school GPA was icing on the cake. In addition to Penn State, schools like Notre Dame, Wisconsin, Syracuse, Northwestern, and Indiana had begun actively recruiting Jankowski by the end of his junior season. But despite the status of football in Berwick, Jankowski's talent for and lingering affection toward baseball left him with some doubts about his direction. The right-handed pitcher was receiving interest from the likes of Stanford (Mussina's alma mater) and Miami (FL) on the diamond, but since concentrating on football would afford Jankowski more college choices, the quarterback and his family determined that he would narrow his prospective college choices based on his opportunity to play football. The Jankowskis sat down with Berwick coach George Curry, singling out some of the best schools that ran the spread-based type of offense that could best accentuate Jankowski's skills as both a runner and passer.

Said Jankowski, "We came up with some schools that were actively pursuing me, were giving me phone calls on a regular basis at the end of my junior year that really fit where I might have wanted to go. I ended up going to football camp at Wisconsin, Northwestern—I didn't go to camp there because they didn't have camp the same week all the other ones did, I only took a visit there—and then I went to Notre Dame and Indiana. Those schools were all the schools that were really hot on me and were actively pursuing me, and that I wanted to pursue as well. I went to a "junior day" at Syracuse, and I was at Penn State so many times growing up that I didn't need to go to camp there that year. So that was that, I went to camps and did very well.

"I ran 4.6 [in the 40-yard dash] at Wisconsin, they said that was the fastest time they ever had for a quarterback. Actually Brooks Bollinger was there at the time, and they said that was a little faster than what he was running. He's a great quarterback, he's playing for the Jets now. I sat down with [head coach Barry] Alvarez, I sat down with their offensive coordinator [Brian] White, but their problem was that they were loaded with quarterbacks. They had six quarterbacks. Most of the big schools, they have five scholarship quarterbacks, and six was really stretching it.

"And then we went to Northwestern, they showed me around, it was really nice. The following day I went to Notre Dame. It was the same summer that Brady Quinn got offered, and they were going to offer two quarterbacks. There was a kid that went to Oregon State that was there, there was a kid that went to Illinois that was there, I was going against a kid that went to Kentucky. Me and these guys are going head-to-head at camp. I actually ended up being the number one guy out of camp, so they were really happy with me. The guy that recruited me was very high on me, [then–Notre Dame offensive coordinator Bill] Diedrick was very high on me. The only problem was [then–head coach Tyrone] Willingham wasn't there that day, because he had a prior commitment. But Diedrick said, 'You'll be getting a call.'

"And then from there I went to Indiana. The guy who was recruiting me and was the coordinator was Al Borges, who is the Auburn offensive coordinator right now, he really liked me. I went to camp, and I actually ended up taking an official visit there in January. Those were the schools I was really actively pursuing and vice versa, they were actively recruiting me. Indiana, Notre Dame, and Northwestern to start the year were really recruiting me."

As his senior year at Berwick began, Jankowski was among the nation's most highly sought-after quarterback prospects, and also happened to be the on-field leader of a team that was ranked No. 1 in the nation to begin the 2002 season. It was while atop this lofty perch that things began to unravel for Jankowski.

In Week 2 of the season, Jankowski suffered a serious deep thigh contusion that prevented him from walking for more than a week. With the quarterback out of the lineup the following Friday night, Berwick lost by one point and forfeited its number one ranking in the process. Though not fully healed, Jankowski was determined to get back on the field and not let either his bright college prospects or his team's season slip away. Perhaps to his detriment, Jankowski forced his way back into the lineup.

"I went and got [the leg] checked out by doctors to make sure there was nothing clotting, or anything really serious where it could threaten my life. They were worried about that because it swelled up so much. It was my senior year, so I'm trying to give it everything I got. I ended up playing after that but it wasn't until the winter when I could actually run again. I couldn't run throughout the whole year. Looking back, maybe I could have taken time off, maybe I could have taken like a month, month-and-a-half off then come back for the last couple of games and been healthy, but there really wouldn't have been a different result. I was trying to maximize every game as much as I could. You don't want to sit out for a month and a half in high school football because that's five games or so. You lose two, you might not make the playoffs.

"Things kind of snowballed from there in the wrong direction. One of my best friends [Mike Viti], who's the starting fullback at Army right now, he tore his knee. At the high school level, when you don't have a ton of bodies, it really gets tough. We had a couple of bad breaks that year. Going into that season I had a lot of team goals and individual goals which didn't become realized. But that's how sports goes, especially football. Injury's part of it and I was just happy that it wasn't anything that was super serious. But it was serious enough that I couldn't play how I could."

Berwick, the preseason number one team in the nation, missed the state playoffs in 2002, and Jankowski's play dropped off significantly due to the injury. The scrambling element of the quarterback's game had been marginalized, and though the college recruiters hadn't totally gone away, no longer was Jankowski considered the can't-miss prospect. Notre Dame, among other schools, was still interested but was no longer desperate to acquire Jankowski's services.

Weeks after Jankowski had set up an official visit to Notre Dame, the visit upon which he was told he would be offered a scholarship, the starting quarterback of the Fighting Irish, Carlyle Holiday, was injured. Holiday was replaced in the lineup by a walk-on, Pat Dillingham, who led Notre Dame to a couple of victories and played generally well, prompting head coach Tyrone Willingham to award him a scholarship for the following season. The scholarship that had once been reserved for a fifth quarterback, in this case Jankowski, was now unavailable. Jankowski, who was uninterested in the school's offer of having him become a "preferred walk-on," would not be following Powlus to Notre Dame.

"Obviously I wasn't happy at that moment, but there's really nothing you can do, because things are out of your hands. Maybe if my senior year went a different way, maybe if I didn't get hurt, maybe if my buddy didn't get hurt, maybe if things just would have fell through a little bit better, like they had the year before, you never know what can happen. But I always like to think that things happen for a reason."

Jankowski's story was hardly a unique one. Most regular players at Villanova, indeed most starters throughout the Atlantic 10, had been recruited by the so-called "big-time" programs (or at least the marginal I-As from the MAC or WAC) at some point but had slipped into the hands of I-AA programs during various stages of the process. Many, like Jankowski, had seen their college stock drop because of an ill-timed high school injury or a disappointing senior season. Some were "if" guys who had been strung along by bigger programs in the event that the player or players they really coveted opted not to sign at the last minute. Others ended up in I-AA because they were asked to play a different college position than the one they preferred. And just about to a man, no matter which category the player fell into, all thought that they truly belonged at the I-A level.

Irrespective of the circumstances, as a I-AA program, Villanova had to keep an eye on such prospects, and Jankowski's situation led to him being recruited by a school that, while having never been in serious contact with the player, was attractive in that it was roughly two hours from his home. By January, the only major college football offer Jankowski was considering was something of a vague verbal one from Indiana, and despite his concentration on football, Pittsburgh was still interested in his services as a baseball pitcher. But Jankowski was now unsure about attending college so far from his close-knit family. It was Villanova's close proximity that had led Honora Jankowski to contact Mark Ferrante in the first place.

Ferrante was of course familiar with Berwick, but Talley had made something of a blanket policy not to take players from the school. Just after Talley took over the program in 1985, Villanova had been burned by a Berwick recruit who committed to the school, but at the eleventh hour reneged in order to attend West Virginia. Talley blamed Curry, the Berwick head coach, and had vowed not to recruit from the school in the future. But Jankowski's obvious interest in Villanova, coupled with his much-publicized talents, led Talley and his coaching staff to reconsider the long-standing policy.

"We weren't recruiting Frank that much, but the mom was e-mailing me religiously," said Ferrante. "I didn't really start recruiting Frank until January, when normally you're on guys before December. Berwick was a school that Coach [Talley] was not overly excited about from way past history even before I got here, and then when I recruited the area I went up there and mended the fence so to speak. And then Frank's mom was e-mailing me a ton, so I finally got the film, and I said, 'Okay, I know where it's from but I'm going to show it [to Talley and the staff] anyway,' because I thought it was good enough. Sam [Venuto] liked it, Coach liked it, and that's when we started recruiting him. We probably only recruited him for the month of January. Both his mom and dad are pharmacists, so I think they were relatively excited about the quality of education, and I think the distance from home was not a bad thing."

Jankowski was attracted to the situation at Villanova, feeling immediately that he could perform well as both a student and college football player on the Main Line.

"What it came down to was that I just really felt the most comfortable, with all things considered, at Villanova for football," said Jankowski.

"Because I had a full scholarship, the scholarship is worth just as much as any athletic scholarship in the country. It's close to home. When you're weighing all the options, that's definitely a factor for me, I don't know how much it is for other people. But also, at the time, Villanova just came off their best year of football. Brett Gordon was the quarterback, and I liked the way he played, his style. He threw a lot. The offense really seemed like it was running smoothly. They made the semifinals. Obviously academics as well, academics played a very large part in why I'm here. All things considered, Villanova was just the place that made the most sense and I thought would be the best place for me."

And although the former Top 100 prep recruit would have figured to have a chance to excel at a I-AA program, the actual situation was nowhere near that simple. Though Gordon had graduated, his heir apparent, Joe Casamento, was a sophomore the coaching staff held in high esteem. The other quarterback on the roster, Burroughs, had four years of eligibility remaining, and some, including offensive coordinator Venuto, thought he had the potential to eventually unseat Casamento and become the best quarterback in the history of the program. Venuto had filled Jankowski in about the current state of the quarterback picture before he signed.

"I went up to Berwick and sat down and talked with him," recalled Venuto. "I think we did a pretty good job of laying out the scenarios for him, and I think we were pretty up front in saying, 'Hey you have a couple of pretty good guys that are here in front of you, so don't expect that you're going to come to Villanova and walk on campus and be the big man on campus,' You want to be honest with those guys, because if you're not it comes back to haunt you."

Venuto left Jankowski with the words, "The only thing I can promise you is you'll get a chance to compete, and you'll probably have a chance to run the whole show one year, at least."

That Villanova was not necessarily seeking another quarterback to compete for a job in 2003 apparently did not send up red flags for Jankowski or his family. Jankowski knew he had out-performed every quarterback at Notre Dame's camp roughly six months prior, so how could he not rise up the depth chart against seemingly lesser competition in I-AA?

"There's five quarterbacks at most of the big schools," reasoned Jankowski. "So I figured, there's two quarterbacks at Villanova, and not really putting anybody down, but I always feel like all I ever want to do is just have a chance to compete. As long as I can compete for something, I don't care if there are twenty quarterbacks. I have confidence in myself, and if I'm given a chance head to head on a level playing ground, I'll be able to get it done, just like I did at Notre Dame football camp . . . I liked the fact that I knew the quarterback that started was graduating so I'm thinking, 'Hey, maybe I can get a foot in there and maybe get to compete against some of the guys that were there.'"

Taking the probable long-term presence of Casamento and Burroughs into account, Talley, Ferrante, and the coaching staff were indeed surprised that a quarterback of Jankowski's ability was interested in matriculating at the university.

"Coach's philosophy generally is to try to take one every year, that's Coach Talley's general rule of thumb," said Ferrante. "We didn't have a great sell, and we knew that, so that's why on our list, there probably weren't a lot of names jumping out at me. And [Jankowski] knew that coming in.

"[The fear was that] you're one injury away, and all of a sudden you're too thin. I think that was the same year where James Madison got down to their third, and their quarterback after that was a converted DB. You look at those scenarios and you're like, 'Okay, we're not going to let that happen to us.' Coach's philosophy is he'd like to have four in the program and take one each year."

On paper, Villanova should have been thrilled that its recently signed third-string quarterback had been one bad break away from wearing a Notre Dame uniform. On paper, Jankowski should have been pleased that he had fewer rungs to climb on the depth chart than would have existed in South Bend or at one of the other football factories. But in reality, both parties had made a vital miscalculation.

Jankowski had underestimated how much Talley and Venuto believed in Casamento and Burroughs, and though he insists that he always considered both to be good players, Jankowski probably also underestimated the talents of both incumbent quarterbacks. In addition, though Jankowski expected to compete for a job right away, no true freshman had ever played a meaningful role at the quarterback position since Talley had been on the job, and almost all, including Gordon, Casamento, and Burroughs, had redshirted as freshmen.

For its part, Villanova had not properly gauged what Jankowski's immediate expectations about his role would be. As a former top prospect out of Berwick, Jankowski wasn't truly going to be happy unless he was given a full shot at the starting job, which meant the staff would have to take some practice reps from the still-developing Casamento and Burroughs and hand them to the freshman. Talley and Venuto were unprepared to do that, and thus commenced a two-year back-and-forth between player and staff that had only reached any semblance of a resolution when Burroughs was carted off the field at Rutgers.

Jankowski, who reported to Villanova in the summer ahead of the rest of the freshman, had been unhappy with the situation on his new team almost from the beginning.

"I showed up early, and I even tried to stir up some discussion about trying to learn the offense early in the summer. And I was told to not really worry about that, that the other quarterbacks can just call my plays for me during summer seven-on-sevens, where there's no coaches around or anything.

"I realized that Brett Gordon was graduating, so obviously there's going to be a new starting quarterback. I was told I was probably going to redshirt, and I don't have a problem with that, redshirting's a good thing, but the thing was, I was never even in the equation of possibly playing that year. It wasn't a situation where I came in and I was just way out of my league and Joe and Marv were so far ahead of me. It was a situation where they had their minds made up that they were going to have those two guys compete for a starting job when they came in. I was the third guy and I was going to redshirt no matter what…If it's Joe versus Marv, that's simple. And plus, when coaches get guys, they slot them into positions. They have preconceived notions of what they want to do with this person with their time at Villanova. And it was a thing where they wanted Joe and Marv to compete, they didn't want Joe, Marv, and Frank to compete."

Whatever objections the introverted Jankowski had to the arrangement didn't fully register with Venuto, nor would they have swayed the coach who knew better than anyone the complexities of the Villanova offense.

"We've always put a timetable on our guys," insisted Venuto, "That we never felt that they really got a grasp of the system until the spring of their sophomore year. Frank was a hard read because he was always so quiet and kind of reserved and didn't say much even in meetings, you really couldn't tell one way or another. You couldn't tell one way or another of what the frustration [level] was."

And so for the first time in his career at any level, Jankowski was not only a backup, but the backup's backup.

"I accepted it because I was redshirting, but it was very tough, because I have a lot of confidence in myself and I felt like I could help the team," said Jankowski. "I had no problem redshirting, but I would have liked to have competed and then redshirted. I always want to compete. I figured I would redshirt and compete after that."

Jankowski's assumption that he would be able to vie for the starting job as a redshirt freshman turned out to be misguided, and at least a tad naïve. If either Casamento or Burroughs played well in 2003 and established himself as the starter, it was unrealistic to think that Talley and Venuto would then take the counterproductive measure of holding open auditions for the quarterback job in '04. As it turned out, Casamento won starting duties in 2003, and engineered the 6-0 start that included the landmark win over Temple at Lincoln Financial Field. A shoulder injury at midseason caused Casamento's play to drop off, but Burroughs replaced him against Richmond and threw a jaw-dropping five touchdowns in his first career start. The quarterback picture was no less clear as 2003 drew to a close with a disappointing 7-4 mark, but it had more to do with the glimpses of greatness that both starting QBs had displayed rather than the team's failure to make the playoffs. The play of Casamento and Burroughs meant that though Jankowski was making strides, the former Berwick star was going to be on the outside looking in once again.

"In the spring, they opened it up," said Jankowski. "Joe had started the year, but they opened it up in the spring again. We have two scrimmages in the spring at Villanova, one [after] two weeks and then the last week. The first scrimmage comes along, and I end up getting the second-most reps out of the three quarterbacks, and Marv got the third-most. And I end up scoring the only touchdown on a 2-yard run. That was the only touchdown scored that day.

"And then the next scrimmage comes along, and I get ten plays at the end of the scrimmage, and then all of a sudden in that last week, Marv's named the starting quarterback. And this is out of nowhere. I remember even Joe was taken aback, because he and Marv were competing, and then all of a sudden Marv was just taking the first-string reps. I think Marv's a good football player, but the point of the matter with me personally is I never got to compete against him one-on-one, I never got to compete against him or Joe. It was one of those things where at the end of the spring they tell me I had a good spring but they really feel that Marv and Joe have a good grasp for the offense and those two are going to compete in the summer, so then I'm like, 'It's the same thing as the year before.' It's almost like they're waiting for one of those guys to separate themselves and that I'm the odd man out, and I don't even get the chance to compete."

Venuto's contention was that the depth chart at quarterback had as much to do with the experience of Burroughs and Casamento as it did with Jankowski's shortcomings.

"We had two quarterbacks who were proven players on the field, that both had a certain amount of success, competing for a starting job," noted Venuto. "Believe me, as a coach, if we felt that Frank was head and shoulders above either one of them in the categories that you have to be a successful and quality quarterback, we would have taken that into consideration and given him ample opportunity. Frank is a very fine passer with a strong and accurate arm, and we recognized that, but he wasn't a superior athlete, with all those intangibles, and there weren't two slouches at quarterback ahead of him either.

"He was obviously not mentally as good at that stage, and it was too much of a risk. In that case, you would have to shelve one of the two basically to get the other guy the reps. But we still felt highly about Frank. It was probably more of a numbers game, and having two guys right there ahead of him at the time, there's just not enough reps to go around. Was that fair to Frank? Probably not, if he thought he was going to compete for the job. But at that point there were two proven players that had already won football games for us that when you looked at it, Frank didn't stand out head and shoulders above them."

Despite the setup, Jankowski was more determined than ever to force the coaches' hand.

"I hear what they say, but I really don't accept it. I get a tape made of our offense, all the plays from the previous year, and I sit down and I start learning the offense, even more than I already had. The way I took it was, 'Okay, you're telling me I'm not going to do something, I'm going to work even harder.' My whole thing was I was trying to force them to give me a shot to compete. I worked hard, I was here, I was thinking I'm going to show up and I'm going to do very well, and they're going to give me a shot then. But I came and did as well as I could have done and it was still the same thing."

Burroughs started all eleven games in 2004, and though Villanova's season again ended in disappointing 6–5 fashion, the quarterback came on strong late in the season and had the offense running close to optimal efficiency again. Remembered Venuto, "From the third game of the season on, he had played very, very well. He was a little shaky at first, but from the New Hampshire game on, he played as well as any quarterback we've had, including [former All-American Chris] Boden and Gordon."

With Burroughs heading into his junior year as the established starter, and with the undeniably talented Jankowski desperate for a larger role on the team, the coaching staff opted not to bring Casamento back for his fourth year of eligibility and create a potentially unhealthy and divisive situation at the position heading into 2005. Jankowski entered the spring of '05 entrenched at the No. 2 slot, and while that spelled progress, it didn't satisfy the competitor in him in the least.

"They told me that they had decided to not bring [Casamento] back. So obviously that's good for me because it means its less quarterbacks. But that works in two ways. It helps me because there were two older than me and now there's only one older than me. But it was bad because then it gave them the ability to just name [Burroughs] the starter.

"You would think that you would give somebody the opportunity to compete at least once for a starting job, especially at quarterback, in their time at a school. It has nothing to do with Marv personally or Joe personally, it has to do with the fact that you expect, and it should be expected, just for reasons of competition and to make sure that you definitely have the right guy on the field. How come I'm the only one that never gets to compete for the starting job? And it's not because I couldn't compete against them. If I can't compete against them, and I'm not as good as them, then why not prove it on the field?"

The state of the quarterback picture led Jankowski to reconsider an idea Venuto had floated in the summer of 2004, when Jankowski's frustration about being stuck behind Burroughs and Casamento was at its highest point. Knowing that Jankowski had been a baseball standout in high school, the offensive coordinator suggested playing both sports at Villanova in an effort to satisfy his competitive fire.

"He's like, 'I know that you thought about baseball prior to coming to college, have you ever thought about that?' Not in a way that's pushing me out the door, but in a way that will keep me happy. That's important to the point that that keeps me from competing and it also keeps me happy, to keep me here. That was really recommended to me to keep me happy because I was not going to compete.

"And then [in 2005] I realized what was going to happen, so I sat down with Coach Talley and talked to Venuto and I asked them if I could partake in baseball as well. Because I realized I was not going to get a shot, I wasn't going to get an opportunity to compete. I'm a competitor and I love baseball, and I knew I could do both."

Jankowski pitched for Villanova in the spring of 2005, coming out of the bullpen and faring pretty well for a player that hadn't been on a mound in three years. At the same time, Jankowski was able to attend most of the football team's early-morning spring practices and felt prepared to hold down the No. 2 job in the fall. When the summer session started, knowing that he had received little time with the first team and that he was now just a heartbeat away from the starting job, Jankowski expected to finally see some significant work with the starting unit. Instead, it was mostly second-string again for the quarterback.

Said Jankowski, "You're with number twos, and that's not taking anything away from the number twos, but it's just that not as much is emphasized with those guys, especially as far as timing. When you're a quarterback, everything's about timing, that's why it makes such a big difference when there's a different quarterback in the game. The snap count, the cadence, the way a quarterback throws, the relationship between the quarterback and the running back as far as where their land points are for handing the ball off. The way they feel with the receivers—that's why quarterbacks throw to receivers all summer, because they have to develop that relationship.

"As far as any other positions, if there's any guy dinged up a little bit, say J. J. or Moe or Dieser or anybody, say they have a sore leg that day, that takes the second-string receiver up to the number ones, so then you move somebody else up to the number twos who has no idea what's going on. It's just something where I did the best with the situation that was given to me."

Despite what Jankowski considered to be steady play, it was still Burroughs who was running with the first team nearly 100 percent of the time. Knowing full well the regularity of injuries to quarterbacks, Jankowski feared he would eventually be placed in a game situation with players he hadn't often worked with and with whom he was not totally comfortable. Privately, Jankowski was ready to erupt by the week of the Rutgers game. When Talley took him aside after a practice to question why Jankowski's offensive unit looked a little out of sync, the backup's face turned crimson with anger.

"I told him, 'Yeah I'm going to be out of sync, how many reps have I run with the first-string team?' What team do you think is going to be more in-sync-looking, the first-string or the second-string?' We've got guys that are young, we've got guys that are just filling out positions. The emphasis is placed on the first-string, the second-string is there to really just aid the first string. Obviously there's going to be some inconsistencies within that framework. And he accepted it, he did not disagree with me, he agreed with me. And at that time, he said to make sure I was always ready."

To the surprise of everyone and bewilderment of most, Talley's directive was put into practice in the third quarter of Villanova's 2005 season. As the cart removed Burroughs from the Rutgers Stadium turf, both the head coach and former backup knew this was no longer a drill.

"Mentally I was ready," remembered Jankowski. "Right when I saw him down, I started playing catch. Nobody told me to play catch, I just started to play catch because I know what I have to do. I'm prepared, I'm totally into this. I'm not just playing football to play it. I'm into it. It's a big part of my life. I go in the game and in less than a half I end up throwing like thirty times, which is pretty outrageous considering I never threw a pass in a collegiate game in my life. I mean, I handed the ball off like three times in my career before that.

"As far as Marv getting hurt and me becoming the starter, if I could choose if Marv gets hurt or not, I would choose him not to get hurt. I honestly do not want anybody to get hurt which gives me a position. I would have rather had Marv been healthy and have me compete against him. Because I know what I can do and I know what would have been the result of that. That's reality though. Anytime in sports in general, but especially football, injury is a part of the game. And I realized, 'Hey, it's my job now.' Even though it's not how I wanted it or wished it to happen, it happened.

"I was very happy with myself after the game, not the fact that we lost, but it was the first time I ever got to play. I was satisfied and happy with myself that I did the best I could do, and I was not overwhelmed with the situation. I threw for over 200-and-some yards in that game in less than a half. Until you actually go in, you can be very confident and stuff but you don't definitely know. It seemed like I just took that natural step from high school to college, it didn't feel like it was anything different for me."

Clearly, Jankowski's efforts against Rutgers had been encouraging to Talley, but the quarterback had to stifle a smirk when he heard the head coach telling reporters about how he had always felt the player that had never been a realistic part of the starting quarterback competition was one of the league's best signal-callers. One week later, however, as Northeastern took the field, Jankowski couldn't afford to live in the past any more than his new offensive mates could afford to lament Burroughs' status as a cheerleader.

"Obviously it's a traumatic time for Moe, J. J., [wide receiver] Chris Polite, those guys have been best friends and roommates," remarked Jankowski. "That's a tough thing, your friend just got hurt, and he's my friend too. But I don't have time and neither do they at the moment to really sit and mourn for Marv. Otherwise, they're not doing justice to the team or to Marv. They've got to keep playing for him."

The time had come for Jankowski to make his first career start, an event that the former prep star hadn't expected to occur in his twenty-fourth game in a Villanova uniform. As always, his parents, younger sister, grandparents, and girlfriend made the trip to the Main Line. Only this time, unlike the others, the family had ample reason to be excited.

To the Jankowskis, the atmosphere had to feel like Berwick all over again. It was Parent's Weekend at Villanova, and on a beautiful eighty-degree late-summer evening, that meant a gathering of more than ten thousand would be in the stands by kickoff, a great crowd by Villanova football standards. The game would be televised locally by the CN8 cable network, one of just a handful of Wildcat games that warranted that status, and some players sensed that the media- and image-savvy Talley felt extra motivation when the game was on TV. The excitement in the air was palpable. Jankowski and his teammates, eager to shake off the one-sided loss at Rutgers, were focused. As they stretched, some remembered what Mark Reardon had said when he addressed the team in a meeting the night before.

In a spirited speech, Reardon had told the players of the importance of working without reward, of possessing will as well as strength, and the necessity of never taking defeat lightly.

"I love winning," Reardon had told the assembled team members. "But I work as hard as I do because I fucking hate losing. That's why. I hate it. I pulled over on the way home from Rutgers and I fucking threw up. Winning's great. But you gotta hate losing, you gotta, if you're going to be successful."

Reardon also relayed a sentiment first expressed by Talley in practice days earlier. After trying in vain to discern the identity of his team, Talley had told Reardon, "You're not going to have personality until you have some success." The players and coaches believed the emergence of that personality was imminent.

Northeastern was not one of the Atlantic 10's elite programs, but recent history encouraged Villanova's personnel to treat the Huskies as if they were. The Boston school had narrowly defeated the Wildcats 34–30 the year before, and back in 2002, Brett Gordon's eventual national semifinal club had been drilled 38–13 by a Northeastern team that wouldn't even reach the playoffs. Northeastern had begun the 2006 season with two tough losses to traditional I-AA powers Georgia Southern and Youngstown State, and Talley felt that if VU could jump on the Huskies early, they would quit. Based on the tape they had seen of Northeastern, the staff felt the Cats had the more talented roster, and most of Villanova's players were perceptive enough to infer the very same. After the long day of waiting and buildup that a night game mandated, everyone at Villanova was ready to get the Atlantic 10 season underway.

Finally, with the humid locker room bursting at the seams, Talley addressed the team.

"It's very important today to understand the climate that we're in. It's about as good as I've seen it in twenty-two years at Villanova. The weather is perfect, you have a huge sellout crowd, you're on eight million viewers of television watching every move you make. You're playing at seven o'clock at night, when a lot of the big games are over, and a lot of people are going to be watching. Villanova football on display. What could be better than that? Our parents are here, we've been to church, we hade a nice pre-game meal.

"You guys were born and bred to play football, that's what you do. And you have the perfect stage to exhibit what we have. It's a league game, Northeastern, a team last year that broke our hearts with a tough loss up there. We've got a chance to come back tonight and make amends. The Atlantic 10 is a league where you have to play every single Saturday, every minute you're on the field. It's that kind of a league. You have to break these guys. You have to go out in the first half and break these guys. It may take us three quarters, but you have to break them. They are 0-2.

"We have been to the mountaintop, and you've played against as good a guy as you're ever going to play against. You're going to play against a tough nut tonight. And you have to be ready to play and exhibit the gifts that the good lord gave you. This is our night. This is the beginning of a great campaign."

Talley then turned his attention to the championship banners hanging on the locker room walls, which for effect he utilized as an object of derision. "Man I'm tired of looking at this stuff, I might get these damn things ripped down, okay? 1992, 1996, 1997, 2001, 2002 . . . it's our time now, I don't want to talk about those guys anymore. This is your time, you decide if YOU want to get up on the wall."

The first two drives of Frank Jankowski's career as a starter, which resulted in a total of nine plays, 27 yards, and two punts, probably didn't make Marvin Burroughs fear for his job to any great degree. With just over six minutes to play in the first quarter, the Wildcats found themselves trailing by a 3-0 score when they felt the relief of their first truly positive moment since the Burroughs injury.

Northeastern punter Jared White dropped back to punt near his own 30-yard line, when Darrel Young, the true freshman linebacker, broke through the line to block the kick. Young had a good chance to field the football cleanly, but muffed it as it was rolling forward, before picking it up, running a few yards, then dropping it again. With several players from both teams now on the scene, the football was ambling like a greased pig toward the west end zone, and it looked for a moment like it might be pushed out the back for a safety. That's when Young made one last desperate leap toward the ball, somehow corralling it and finishing the play he had started with his first career touchdown.

The thrill of the team's second TD of the year, much like its first, was diminished by another botched PAT try. But the continued struggles of Adam James and the kicking game were long forgotten moments later when Jankowski engineered the first touchdown drive of his career, punctuated by a 2-yard touchdown run for reserve running back Matt Dicken. James hammered home the ensuing extra point, and with 42 seconds left in the first quarter, Nova boasted a comfortable 13-3 advantage.

The terrific Parent's Weekend crowd of more than ten thousand was alive and into the fast-paced game. Anyone watching locally on CN8 might think about sticking with a contest that looked like it could have the makings of a shootout. Then, as Joe Marcoux placed the football on the tee following the Nova touchdown, referee Jeff Maconaghy and just about all of the Villanova Stadium patrons saw a brief flash brighten the evening sky.

Lightning.

The presence of lightning at a college football game engendered a reaction not dissimilar to the announcement of the word "fire" in a crowded theater. Within minutes, the players and coaches had taken cover in the locker room. The fans, not willing to sit idly on the metal bleachers, had retreated to their vehicles. Some would head home, others would deliberate over whether or not to wait out the storm.

The Villanova coaches lingered on the field for a while, shaking their heads at the cruel hand that mother nature had dealt. Talley, who had curiously seen two previous Villanova home openers shut down prematurely because of lightning, knew exactly what this latest delay meant. The momentum that the Wildcats had built was all but vanished, along with most of the crowd and the television audience. Those previous two weather-abbreviated games had been in the second half and comfortably in Villanova's hands, but this time, Talley knew that coming back would mean playing out the final three quarters before an empty house. So much for putting Wildcat football on display.

For an hour that seemed closer to a week, the Villanova players sat at their lockers and felt their collective edge dissipate. No one knew just how long they would be sitting there, bored to tears in full uniform and anxiously waiting to return to the field. Every couple of minutes, Brian Hulea or John Dieser would walk through the spacious room and implore the players to stay mentally ready, but in their hearts even Hulea and Dieser knew that directive was easier commanded than executed. The third captain, Darrell Adams, was shivering under a blanket in the training room, as he battled an arm infection that was causing flu-like symptoms.

The coaches eventually convened in the football office beneath the stadium, concerned about the effect of the delay on the players and passing the time by comparing whatever notes they had assembled over the game's first 14-plus minutes.

Just after 9 PM, a time of day when the seven o'clock game should have been nearing its final stages, Maconaghy and his crew called the teams out of their locker rooms to resume the first quarter. By the time the players had gone through a brief warm-up period, and Marcoux again readied himself to kick off, the clock read 9:15. The delay had lasted one hour and twenty-one minutes. The stands, as Talley had predicted, were just about empty, with only parents left in the crowd who were watching a son in uniform. During the delay, the hopelessly out-of-date scoreboard clock had been struck by lightning, and Villanova's facilities people couldn't get it working again. With no fans and no scoreboard, this might as well have been a little league game.

Not surprisingly, the rest of the contest was less than memorable for most who either witnessed it or took part. Northeastern came out of the visitor's locker room with a touchdown drive to draw within 13–10, but Villanova kept the Huskies at arm's length throughout the remainder of the night. The Cats took a 26–10 lead into the halftime break (Dicken and Hulea both scored, while James missed another point-after), and when the second half started, after 10:00, Northeastern struggled to answer the bell. The visitors had already made plans to bus back to Boston following the game, and they played the second half like a team with a preoccupied awareness that it wouldn't be arriving home until six in the morning.

When the final second mercifully (and allegedly, given the state of the scoreboard) ticked off of the clock, a 38–20 Villanova win was at last in the books. Jankowski's first start had gone well, as he completed 16-of-25 passes for 241 yards with one touchdown and an interception. The first TD pass of the sophomore's career came in the form of a pretty 27-yard heave to Anton Ridley, one of his former second-string compatriots, late in the third quarter.

James had also recovered, banging home a couple of short field goals in the second half to keep the coaches off his back and Marcoux at least temporarily off his trail.

Most important, the win made the Cats 1-1, 1-0 in the Atlantic 10. Talley hoped that his team's first real success of the season would bring out its personality.

"I think we have some grit," Talley told a couple of reporters who had assembled in the tunnel between the locker room and the football office. "I feel we have a bunch of hard-nosed kids that are going to continue to play hard. The big question for me tonight was whether Frank was going to be able to put the thing in high gear and get it done. J. J. made some great catches for us, Dieser made some great catches. We had a little bit of a run to keep the pressure off of him. I think we can be the 30- to 35-point offense that we usually are."

Standing in the same tunnel, Jankowski shook off the questions about his nervousness, toed the party line in stressing the importance of the Atlantic 10 win, and praised his offensive line and receivers. The feeling that raced through his body was something midway between a knowing satisfaction and outright vindication.

"It was just a good experience and it felt normal," Jankowski told the press. "I didn't feel out of my element at all. I felt comfortable. I feel more comfortable doing that than being on the sideline."

6

THE FOURTH ESTATE

As was his morning custom, Villanova assistant athletic director for communications Dean Kenefick drove his SUV to the convenience store near his home in the western Philadelphia suburb of Drexel Hill on this, the Monday prior to the Wildcats' Saturday date with Penn. As the athletic department's top media relations and PR man, it was part of Kenefick's job to keep tabs on what the local press was writing and saying about the university's teams, and he was also responsible, among other things, for disseminating information about those teams to the city's print and electronic media outlets.

Having worked in media relations at Villanova for over a decade, Kenefick knew exactly what to expect when he opened the *Philadelphia Inquirer* and the *Philadelphia Daily News* on Monday morning, scanning to find any mention of the Wildcat football team or the upcoming game against Penn, their Philly-area rival: little to nothing.

The tabloid-style *Daily News* was the city's primary print resource for sports news, boasting a larger writing staff and seemingly more comprehensive sports coverage than its sister paper, the *Inquirer*, which was owned by the same company, Knight-Ridder.

Sure enough, on the Monday in question, the *Daily News* went all out, devoting its final fifty-two pages to sports coverage. The major story, to no one's surprise, involved the Philadelphia Eagles, who had routed the San Francisco 49ers to even their record at 1-1 on Sunday afternoon.

Somewhat astoundingly, Eagles coverage comprised the first seventeen pages of the *Daily News* sports. In addition to the game story, six different staff members were commissioned by the paper to write pieces about Eagles and 49ers. There was a detailed page of final statistics from the game, as well as a report card analyzing each area of the team's personnel during the win. Last but not least was a short piece previewing the Eagles' next game, against the Oakland Raiders, still some six days away.

It wasn't until the eighteenth page of the Monday sports section that there was a mention of the Phillies, who were at that point just one and a half games out of the wild card berth in the National League. Past the Phillies coverage was a lengthy piece about the NHL Philadelphia Flyers, still more than two weeks from their first regular season game. The story dealt with a training session the team held on the Schuylkill River. Next up were the 76ers of the NBA, who with six weeks to go until the regular season garnered an article about forward Chris Webber and his organization of Hurricane Katrina relief efforts.

Those who had either the time or the inclination to search further into the voluminous *Daily News* sports section would have found, thirty-six pages deep, columnist Mike Kern's page-long wrap-up of Saturday's activity in the world of college football (the *Daily News* had no Sunday paper, so all of its weekend coverage was pushed to Mondays). Kern had a page to touch on both the national and local college football scenes, and by being economical with his words and not overly sanctimonious with his opinions, he did a great job of hitting the highs and lows. He took a few paragraphs to discuss Villanova's win over Northeastern and Penn's victory over Duquesne, as well as Temple's loss to Toledo and La Salle's defeat at the hands of Division III Ursinus.

Kern also briefly mentioned the Villanova–Penn matchup, writing, "This Saturday night, the Wildcats will bus to Franklin Field for a home game against Penn," and adding, sarcastically, "Which means they should be wearing their blue jerseys."

Kern's quip would mark the final time until Thursday that the only college football game played between two Philadelphia-area Division I universities would get any ink from either of the city's two daily papers. In terms of inter-city rivalries, this was not USC–UCLA, and it wouldn't even approach the buildup that a big-time city basketball game like St. Joe's–Temple would.

Kenefick, Andy Talley, and the stakeholders in the Villanova football program had long since accepted, however grudgingly, that they would be basically ignored within the city media landscape. Perception and stigma were two of the central elements keeping Villanova and Penn from getting much ink.

First was the perception that the Eagles, more so than any other team in the city, sold newspapers, and that perception helped push everyone down, or sometimes off, the hierarchy of the sports pages. As the 2005 season began, the franchise had been the NFL's winningest over the past five years, was coming off its first Super Bowl appearance in twenty-four years, and was widely expected to make a run at another trip to the game's ultimate stage. The success had bred a sort of Eagles-mania throughout the city, and the local media came armed with an endless stream of lighter fluid to help keep the fire ablaze. Every team transaction or injury, however minor, was analyzed with the kind of electron microscope normally reserved for DNA analysis.

Said Pat McLoone, assistant managing editor at the *Daily News*, "Our philosophy is what we call 'play it at the top,' which means that we try to play the things at the pro level as hard as we can. We really kind of have a feel for what we think sells, and what that means is the Eagles, the Eagles, the Eagles, the Eagles, and the Eagles, and then the other pro sports sell well here as well."

There were those in the area, including a vocal selection of readers, who felt that the asymmetrical amount of coverage afforded the NFL team was a bit over the top, but there weren't nearly enough of those dissenters to change the newspapers' approach to the red-hot Eagles.

"There's some discussion of, 'I think people could have got by with seven Eagles stories,'" said McLoone. "And I understand peoples' frustration with that, but that's a judgment that we make. It's really done simply by feel."

Although their coverage could be viewed as excessive in some quarters, the papers, which employed generally solid, veteran reporters, were dealing mainly in facts when it came to the Eagles. WIP, the city's all-sports radio station and another of the coverage agenda-makers in Philly, was bound by no such tenant.

Some of the more popular hosts on the notoriously negative station would ratchet up Philly's Eagles hysteria by offering polarizing opinions designed to cater to the least common denominator of area sports fans and in turn generate ratings. Criticism of head coach Andy Reid, quarterback Donovan McNabb, and wide receiver Terrell Owens, who had just presided over the most successful season in the team's Super Bowl era, was part of the daily buffet of chatter. A vast number of the station's callers would offer up generally ludicrous opinions of their own on all things Eagles, and neither the best-known of the hosts nor the callers tended to deal in anything resembling perspective or nuance when it came to a given issue.

What WIP dealt with to an even lesser degree than the city's newspapers, or certainly the local television outlets, was discussion about college sports of any kind. There was a time when Talley's weekly radio show had been broadcast on WIP, but most of the city's major media players had long ago waved the white flag in acknowledgement that Philadelphia was a "pro town," meaning colleges got the short shrift when it came to normal coverage. When one of the city's major local basketball teams like St. Joseph's, Temple, or Villanova began making a run at or in the NCAA Tournament, the level of coverage, from the papers at least, would increase beyond its usual spate of game stories and the occasional column.

But apart from Temple, the city's college football teams played either at or below the I-AA level, considered a minor league even in the minor subgroup of Philadelphia college sports. The powerbrokers at the papers didn't devote much space to Penn or Villanova football, meaning the normal reader wasn't going to have any readily accessible means to read or hear about I-AA teams. And if those fans didn't seem interested, why would the papers devote major space or attention to the programs? This was the vicious circle in which the Wildcats, Quakers, and the rest of the city's college football–playing teams found themselves at the center.

As it presently stood, no one at either of the two schools ready to do battle on Saturday needed to wonder whether much external importance would be placed on the game.

"If we got 1,000 letters asking us why Villanova–Penn [coverage] was thirty-six pages in, we might have to take a look at that," said Kern. "My guess is we didn't get one letter. The only people that care about Villanova and Penn are the Villanova and Penn people, and if there were more people that cared, then Villanova would be getting more than eight thousand people on a Saturday, and Penn would be getting more than eight thousand people on a Saturday, and that's just the bottom line."

The only thing was, despite its having received little to no buildup in the media, the expected presence of more than twenty thousand attendees at the Villanova–Penn game strongly suggested that there was indeed local interest, at least for this week. There would be roughly as many people in the stands at Franklin Field on Saturday night as attended a Flyers or Sixers game at the Wachovia Center in south Philly, and more than three times the number of people who attended a typical college basketball game in the city.

There was a natural rivalry between the schools, aided by their longtime status as members of the basketball "Big 5," along with La Salle, St. Joseph's, and Temple. Since Penn football was not able to participate in the postseason as a member of the Ivy League, its fans would show up for what would arguably be the best and toughest game on its schedule. A good number of Villanova supporters would make the sojourn to West Philadelphia as well, since they could relate to Penn as a rival much easier than a William and Mary or a Hofstra. Many also enjoyed the atmosphere of historic Franklin Field, an eighty-year-old building that was once home to the Eagles and still hosted the legendary Penn Relays each spring. Franklin Field felt much more like the big time to Villanova's students and alumni than their own aging on-campus stadium ever would. In addition to those factors, the kickoff was scheduled for seven o'clock, and night games generally drew larger crowds than the afternoon variety.

Despite the promise of a good crowd for this Saturday night, Kern, also a part-time host (and one of the best and most knowledgeable ones) on WIP, knew that college football was a tough sell in the City of Brotherly Love. That struggling Temple was the city's highest-profile program certainly didn't help matters.

"The only I-A program in town has been struggling for so long, both to try and win games and put people in the stands," said Kern. "I think especially over the past twenty years, it's become a pro football town. We think Eagles, we breathe Eagles, it's Eagles 24/7. They dwarf the Phillies, they dwarf the Flyers, they dwarf the Sixers, and they're naturally going to dwarf college football. Penn, which is a great I-AA program in its own right, can't draw flies. Villanova can't draw, Temple can't draw, and Villanova and Penn certainly have been winning programs. You also have Penn State sort of dwarfing it. Even though it's three and a half hours away, it is a big deal to a lot of people in this area. For all those reasons, I think college football is a really, really tough thing to draw people and get people interested in the Philadelphia area."

Kern did not agree with the theory that the amount of media coverage affected interest in the teams in any meaningful way.

"I don't think WIP's going to sell tickets. If they talked about Villanova football for an hour, I don't think that's going to sell tickets to a Villanova football game. I make this argument all the time, if I wrote four stories about Temple in the paper in a given week, would that sell forty more tickets to a Temple game on a Saturday? I don't think so. I think the people that are going to go are going to go. The people who know that Villanova's playing New Hampshire on Saturday and both teams are 8-1 and it's for first place in their conference, they know that regardless. And I don't think the casual fan is walking up to the window on Saturday buying tickets. If I go on *Daily News Live* [a Crossfire-style cable talk show featuring the paper's sportswriters] and talk about Villanova football for fifteen minutes, does that do anything to generate an interest level? It certainly can't hurt, but I don't think it would change things to the point where it would make a noticeable difference."

Kern's experience had suggested that it was winning, above all other factors, that stoked the fires of coverage.

"Generally what happens in Philadelphia is if you're winning, at some point you get the coverage. Usually what's happened with Villanova is when they get toward the end of the season, and there are games on the line that mean something, we will probably step up our coverage a little bit. But it's just one of those things where it's a pro town, it's definitely a pro town, and it's always going to be that way."

Even despite its well-chronicled struggles, it was Temple that would continue to receive the highest level of college football coverage from the local media in the city. The fact that Villanova had been more successful than the Owls, and had even defeated them the last time the two met on the field, was beside the point. That computer rankings such as the USA Today–featured Sagarin Ratings annually assessed programs like Villanova and most of its brethren in the top tier of I-AA to be stronger than many of those in the bottom tier of I-A, such as Temple, was not enough to alter the sentiment of the mainstream press. Kern was one of those in the media who did not need to look any further than the dividing line that had been set by the NCAA back in the seventies to determine who was better. The Wildcats were inferior, the veteran reporter and most of his contemporaries believed, and thus deserved to be afforded less attention.

"Who's the Division I-A team? That factors into it. When they're scrolling across the boards on ESPN giving scores, which score is coming first, Temple–Western Michigan or Villanova–Penn? Villanova–Penn might not even make the scroll because it's I-AA.

"On any given day, could Delaware or Villanova or one of the I-AAs beat a MAC team? Sure. But there is a reason why somebody plays Division I[-A], and somebody plays Division I-AA. The players are better, you have more scholarships. Is Villanova maybe a better program than some of the bad programs in the MAC? Yeah, maybe. But when I-AA teams upset I-A teams, that just means on that day that they were better. It doesn't mean they're a better program for a long haul.

"Usually when you're perceived to be something, there's a reason why, because usually it's true. There's a reason that you play at the level you play at. If you want to be one of the big boys, then you move up to I-A."

Talley had long ago given up on any prospect of Villanova's move to the highest level and had grown accustomed to the bias against I-AA, and toward college football in general, in his hometown. But that didn't mean he wouldn't fight the setup when given the chance, and Villanova–Penn week afforded him just such an opportunity. At Wednesday's weekly college football writer's luncheon, attended by a handful of local writers as well as the head coaches of all the area teams other than Temple, the head coach addressed the local media agenda.

"We'll never knock the Eagles off the back pages," said Talley, in comments that were printed in Thursday's *Daily News*, "Which is extremely disappointing, because a game like this is great for college football in our area. We'll probably struggle to get twenty-five thousand. There should be forty-five thousand. But you can't fight the fact that it's a pro football town."

Kern, who had covered Villanova for the *Daily News* since the program was revived in 1984 and had a good relationship with Talley, was not surprised to hear the Wildcat head coach's two cents in respect to the press, or his connection between coverage and game attendance. On more than one occasion over the years, Talley had expressed disappointment to Kern on the issue of the failure of the *Daily News* to cover a big game involving his team. (The lack of a Sunday paper was the reason the paper covered few Saturday events. The *Inquirer* had sent a reporter to most of the significant games of the Talley era, however.) Kern and colleagues like the *Inquirer*'s Mike Jensen had been around long enough to know that the head coach's feelings came as a result of his investment of years of hard work in building the program, and all media who had dealt with Talley liked and respected him enough not to take it personally.

"I think Andy sometimes gets a little too concerned with what the media's doing instead of worrying about what he should be worried about," said Kern. "But that's okay. I give Andy every pass in the book, he's always been good to me and he was only looking out for the good of his program."

Talley knew a big crowd would be on hand Saturday night, and he knew what a special experience the game would be for his staff and players. From a practical football standpoint, however, he wasn't wild about the arrangement. In order to get Penn on the schedule in 2005, Villanova had to agree to play the game at Franklin Field, since the Quakers were unwilling to play six road games versus just four at home. Talley's daughter, Gina, was a senior at the university, and he was good friends with Penn head coach Al Bagnoli, and he didn't want to say no to playing the Quakers simply because of the absence of home-field advantage. Just as when he said yes to the Rutgers game, Talley offered Bob Steitz, Vince Nicastro, and the athletic department his approval when they made up the schedule. And just as with the Rutgers game, Talley was regretting his decision more and more with each day that the game drew nearer.

First of all, Penn was good. Bagnoli and the Quakers were annually either at or near the top of the Ivy League standings, and the programs on occasion found themselves recruiting the same local players. Though Villanova had beaten Penn in the three matchups the teams had played over the past six years, Bagnoli's team had given the Cats all that they could handle last year, losing 16–13 in the game in which Ray Ventrone was injured. Talley figured it was just a matter of time before Penn would break through and win one of these battles, and he knew the Quakers would come out fired up in a quest to end their losing streak against Nova.

At the same time, the Wildcats would not be heading to Franklin Field at a hundred percent. The elbow injury that was thought to have impacted the infection weakening All-American defensive end Darrell Adams during the Northeastern game had been deemed serious enough to require surgery and would keep Adams on the shelf against Penn. The Cats had as little depth on the defensive line as in any area of the team, meaning that a platoon of young players would take Adams's place, including Damian Kelley, the true freshman who had developed quickly after facing problems with the NCAA clearinghouse in August, and another true freshman, Greg Miller. Also expected to be sidelined was starting safety Terrance Reeves, who had injured an ankle in the latter stages of the Northeastern contest. Mark Reardon did not have a lot of reliable options to fill that void either, leading to the tension that Talley and his staff were feeling during game week.

As Villanova and Penn fans began to take their seats on a warm evening at Franklin Field, that tension was apparent. Talley continued to loudly bemoan the fact that the game was not being played at home. Reardon conferred with his staff and with unit leaders like Brian Hulea to stress the importance of the game plan he had obsessed over during the late-night film study he had engaged in during the week. But the mood of the staff was perhaps best encapsulated by strength and conditioning coach Reggie Barton, the mountain of a man whose job on game day was to serve as the "get back" coach, making sure the players on the sideline remained in the appropriate area and clear of the officials. As he milled around before kickoff, Barton noticed backup kicker Derek Fiorenza, a freshman walk-on who would have been a front-runner for "strangest Wildcat" honors, seated on the bench, quietly reading a book. Fiorenza would have been better off had he been holding a Penn flag.

Within earshot of much of the team, in a tirade that was amusing to all who heard it apart from Barton and Fiorenza, the hulking coach laced into the tiny kicker, sending him immediately to the locker room to dispose of the offending literature. Barton was still shaking his head in befuddlement fifteen minutes later, amazed that any player would be concentrating on anything other than football at this stage in the day.

"Reggie hates kickers," laughed Adam James.

After Villanova retreated to the small, decaying visitor's locker room, Talley gathered his team for the customary pregame address. The head coach's tack on this night would be to appeal to their sense of superiority.

"We play in another stratosphere, men. We play at a different level. So get ready to get up on the level where we belong. Do not play down to any level. Play at our level. They will come out high, guaranteed. They will come out very, very high. You've got to meet that high right away, very important. Third game of the year, eliminate mistakes. If you make one, go back and make us a great play. Forget about it and move on."

Talley also addressed the presence of the sizeable crowd on hand, the television audience that would be tuning in on CN8, and the lack of respect the media had for the Villanova program. Every week, Talley consulted the computer-driven Sagarin ratings, which projected a winner of each game, and also subscribed to Kickoff Magazine, which did the same. In addition to those publications, the school newspaper, *The Villanovan* (which for some reason would not send a reporter to this or any other Wildcat football game during the season), had also picked the team to lose.

"You've got a great crowd, you're in a great stadium, you have a historical background in front of you. It's a chance for you to play at the highest level in front of eight million people on television. That's what it's all about. Enjoy what we have, the opportunity that was given us tonight is a great opportunity to play a perennial Ivy League champion. They're playing a perennial Top 25 football team, who's dying to get back in the Top 25. If you want to get back in the Top 25, then you better tell the experts, who are picking you to lose, that they're full of bullshit. Sagarin ratings, Kickoff Magazine, WIP, and I read tonight in our school newspaper, they picked us to lose. Bullshit! Let's go."

Like last season's defensive affair, this year's edition of the Villanova–Penn matchup looked to be one in which scoring would come at a premium. Neither the Wildcats nor the Quakers crossed the 50-yard line in their first three drives combined, and when Penn managed to take the ball inside the Villanova 5 late in the first quarter, the Cats tightened up and held them to a 22-yard field goal to keep the score at 3–0. Penn was without its top rusher, Naval Academy transfer Sam Mathews, due to a persistent ankle injury, and the Wildcats could sense that the Quaker offense wasn't running at its optimal efficiency.

But some signs of worry crept in for Villanova just before the first quarter ended. Frank Jankowski, who had taken a hit to his non-throwing shoulder after delivering a first-quarter pass, threw an ill-timed interception, which Penn promptly converted into a seven-play, 58-yard touchdown drive capped off by a scoring run for backup running back Kyle Ambrogi. With Nova down 10–0 and in desperate need of some points, Jankowski made a bad read and threw another pick. Four plays later, Penn quarterback Pat McDermott hit Matt Carre for a 53-yard touchdown pass, placing Villanova in a 17–0 hole, as the large contingent of Quaker fans cheered the "visitors."

More disturbing than the score was the fact that the Wildcats were starting to bear the look of an intimidated team. Including the latter stages of the '04 game following Ventrone's injury, the Quakers had scored the last 30 points in the series and were obviously bursting with confidence. Most Villanova players remembered that Penn, despite the Ivy League university's elite image, was the mouthiest team it had faced in 2004. Kenefick, the sports information director, remembered with a laugh that some Penn players had come onto the field in a previous edition of the rivalry issuing taunts about how these soft Main Liners couldn't hack it against a hard-bitten city school. As if the sons of privilege at Penn played its games in the penal league rather than the Ivy League. Whatever the demographic realities, the current score wasn't going to shut Bagnoli's team up to any great degree.

In desperation mode, Villanova struck back. Jankowski opened the next drive with a 33-yard pass to J. J. Outlaw, DeQuese May went 25 yards on a subsequent screen pass to get the Wildcats inside the Quaker 20, and the quarterback capped off the drive with a 7-yard scoring strike to tight end Matt Sherry with 6:34 to play in the half. And for the first time all season, Adam James made his initial point-after try of a game, making the score 17–7.

Penn answered with a long drive near the end of the half but missed a field goal wide left to keep the margin at 10 heading into the locker room. In the cramped space beneath Franklin Field, Talley sounded his by now familiar encouraging tone.

"We gotta feed off each other and stick together," said Talley. "This is a great test for all of us because in the Atlantic 10, 10 points is nothing. Absolutely nothing. You're going to be behind by more than that in some games. You're going to have to fight back if you want to be a good team, and we can do it. You've seen what they can do, their best running back is out, Matthews isn't even playing. Offensively, we need one play at a time, put a score in there, 17–14, now it's a different game. Defensively, hang in there, no big plays, they may move the ball a little bit, that's okay. They have not turned the ball over, let's get a turnover."

As was his wont, Talley also addressed the big picture, affording Penn a bit more respect than he had in the pregame.

"Fellas, these are growing games. If you don't grow with these games, you're going to get blown away in our league. This is a very good team, [what would be an] upper level A-10 team. If you want to beat New Hampshire, Delaware, JMU, and the rest of the animals, you've got to come back in this game. So settle down, we'll be okay."

The defensive captains then said their piece.

"Keep your heads up, men," warned Brian Hulea. "We're getting fucking back in this game. You better believe this defines as a team. One fucking play at a time. Do not roll over."

Darrell Adams, sporting his uniform jersey on top of street clothes, also spoke up, "Come out in the second half like you know we're going to win this fucking game. How bad do you want to win? They ain't going to give it to us, we've gotta take it."

As forceful as Hulea and Adams were, it wasn't until Mark Reardon spoke to his charges that the defense was at full attention. Even the offensive group, by this point on the other side of the locker room conferring with Sam Venuto, couldn't help but hear the defensive coordinator's rant. Reardon, who had been witnessing up close and personal the bickering, pushing, and shoving going on between Villanova and Penn in the first half, let loose in a tirade that helped peel a little more paint off of the already patchy walls.

"You know what I'm sick of?" asked Reardon hypothetically. "I'm fucking sick of hearing you talk, and nobody going out there and fucking playing, that's what I'm sick of. Stop your fucking talking, stop the jabbering, and go play! Cuz that's what matters, none of this shit matters. Not a God damn thing I can say to you right now matters. Nothing. What matters is we go out and play. Cuz you know what? Penn is playing their ass off. And I told you before the game started, 'You're going to walk on that field and play an upper-level A-10 team,' and they're kicking our ass right now . . . we're going to be as good as you want to be. START FUCKING PLAYING!"

Villanova emerged from the locker room with fire, a flame that quickly flickered but nearly died despite Reardon's best efforts at motivation.

Penn took the opening kickoff and immediately drove into Wildcat territory. The Cats looked close to getting the ball back with little damage done after a third-and-five pass fell incomplete, but a substitution infraction on Villanova handed Penn a first down at the Wildcat 34. On the very next play, another backup Quaker running back, Joe Sandberg, shook off an arm tackle and dashed 34 yards for a touchdown, and it was suddenly 24–7 in favor of Penn early in the third. Bagnoli's team had been dominating in all phases, and now had momentum on its side to boot. Clearly, it was last-gasp time for Talley's crew.

The Wildcat offense fared much better on its first drive of the second half than had the defense. Early in the drive, Jankowski found wideout Chris Polite for 27 big yards on a third-and-seven play. Two plays later, it was Jankowski to John Dieser for 25, and next up was a 10-yard TD grab for Sherry, his second of the game. Villanova did exactly what it had to do, scoring quickly on just six plays and in a little more than two minutes to cut the score to 24–14 and regain some much-needed confidence.

Now it would be up to the patchwork defense to buckle down and do its job. And for perhaps the first time all day, the Cats were up to the task. In fact, four of the next five Penn drives lasted four plays or less, with each of the four resulting in punts. The Quakers' best drive over that stretch lasted six plays and ended when Hulea recovered a fumble caused by defensive tackle Matt Costantino, a former walk-on who had worked his way into a starting role as a senior.

The problem now was that Penn's defense wasn't giving an inch either. Villanova's second drive of the half stalled inside the Quaker 25, as the Wildcats opted not to attempt what would have been a 43-yard James field goal try, instead going for it on fourth-and-five. A pass to Outlaw netted 4 yards, and Penn took possession. The next two times Jankowski and company got the ball, they went three-and-out.

As Jankowski trotted back onto the field at the 11:20 mark of the fourth quarter, everyone wearing the home blue uniforms knew the team's window for a comeback was about to be slammed shut. But in only his second collegiate start, Jankowski displayed the steely reserve of a veteran. Moments apart, the sophomore completed huge first-down passes on second-and-twenty, then third-and-ten. Running back Moe Gibson, mostly invisible during the team's first two games, added value with a 14-yard run to move the chains. Finally, J. J. Outlaw scored on a 13-yard swing pass, diving just inside the right pylon on the east end zone. The Wildcat sideline erupted. James kicked his third extra point in as many tries. With 8:16 to play, Villanova had cut the lead to 24–21, and suddenly, Penn's players were doing a lot less yapping between snaps.

After the defense again held, Jankowski and the offense went to work from their own 11-yard line with 5:20 to play, for what would be the team's biggest drive of the young season. Again, there was immediate reason to believe the rally would fall short. On the drive's first play, DeQuese May was driven back 5 yards to his own 6, but Jankowski came back on the next snap and hit Dieser, who made an acrobatic diving catch for 27 yards. After driving the Wildcats into Penn territory, Jankowski was then faced with a third-and-one from the Penn 28. With the clock nearing the three-minute mark, and with Talley unlikely to count on James for a field goal from this distance, this was a crucial play. Jankowski, despite his bum shoulder, bulled ahead for 2 yards to extend the drive. On the very next snap, Dieser got behind the Penn safety, Jankowski hit him in stride with a perfect toss, and the senior streaked to the end zone to complete the touchdown drive with 2:51 to go. A stunned Penn sideline watched as the Franklin Field scoreboard switched to 28–24, Villanova.

But the drama was far from over. Penn had all three timeouts left and, no matter how poorly its offense had played over the past quarter-and-a-half, it wasn't going to give this one up without a fight.

The Quakers took their time, deliberately inching toward midfield. A critical fourth-and-two play from their own 33 netted 5 yards. Five plays later, with just 48 seconds left on the clock, Penn still hadn't reached the 50-yard line and was facing fourth-and-five. McDermott dropped to pass, was flushed from the pocket, and began rolling to his right. It appeared that Damian Kelley had the QB wrapped up, but the athletic McDermott squirmed out of danger, in the midst of which his helmet was jarred loose. Unable to see, but still running, McDermott whipped off the helmet and tossed it to the turf. Helmetless, he fired downfield to receiver Matt Carre, who dropped the football. The Villanova sideline celebrated. Until, that is, they saw the yellow flag. The call: a 15-yard face mask on the defense.

The by-now-enthusiastic Nova cheering session roared their disapproval, and Talley charged in the direction of the referee, Herb Stayton, to get an explanation. It appeared to most who witnessed the play live that the initial hit to McDermott had simply jarred the helmet loose, and that no Villanova player had ever grabbed his face mask. Replays would show that Kelley had indeed grabbed the face mask, and that the incomplete pass had been inconsequential because the officials blew the play dead as soon as McDermott removed his helmet.

The officials conferred, but the call would stand, moving the Quakers into Villanova territory. Though demoralized by the call and gassed by what was now a fourteen-play drive, the Wildcat defense again put the team in position to win. McDermott threw incomplete on first down, was sacked by freshman Darrel Young on second, and threw incomplete again on third. With fourteen seconds to play and no timeouts, Penn was looking at fourth-and-thirteen on the 45-yard line. The Quakers were going to need a miracle to pull this one out.

They very nearly got it.

McDermott dropped back, evaded pressure, and heaved a lob toward the goal line, where a large huddle of both Penn and Villanova players had gathered. With nearly a dozen arms outstretched, the football came to rest in the hands of 6-foot-3 Quakers sophomore Dan McDonald, who had out-leaped the shorter assortment of players and fallen to the turf at the 3-yard line. The hearts of the Wildcats and their fans sunk.

McDermott and Penn's offense raced toward the line of scrimmage as the clock ticked toward the five-second mark. They would probably have time for one more snap, unless they chose to spike the ball in order to set up a final play.

But Talley was taking no chances. He wanted to make sure his defensive players were set, had time to catch their breath, and had their heads on straight for the game's final play. He called timeout before McDermott could get under center.

With the tension mounting, Reardon gathered Hulea and his defensive leaders to talk strategy. Reardon figured Penn would look to pass the ball, since the Quaker running game hadn't done much in the second half and a passing play would give McDermott more options if things broke down. The coordinator looked out on the field, saw true freshmen like Kelley and Darrel Young rather than veterans such as Darrell Adams, and groaned. He knew what he had to do. If it didn't work, his customary postloss vomiting spell would be followed by at least a week of mostly sleepless nights spent in the football office.

The crowd buzzed with anticipation. The nervous players and coaches watched silently from both sidelines. McDermott strode confidently to the line of scrimmage, barked his cadence, and called for the snap. He dropped his usual three steps, began to look to his right where McDonald was in one-on-one coverage with Rodney Badger in the end zone, and was met head-on by blitzing linebacker Bryan Adams. Adams, who had slipped untouched between Penn's center and left guard, wrapped McDermott up in an immobilizing bear hug and drove him to the ground. Game over.

The rest of the defense mobbed Adams, a quiet but amiable junior whose career at Villanova had been marked by inconsistency. Reardon, who had called for Adams to attack the passer rather than hang back in coverage, took a deep breath of relief and ripped off his headset. The rest of the Wildcats stormed to the center of Franklin Field in jubilation.

But the celebration of their 28–24 win would be short-lived, and would give rise to almost immediate confrontation.

J. J. Outlaw, who had a huge game with eight catches for 103 yards, took a few steps toward the Penn sideline in what he insisted later was an attempt at sportsmanship but what some already bitter Quaker players and coaches interpreted to be taunting. Pushing and shoving ensued between Outlaw and some members of Penn's team, and just as Talley was set to give his postgame television interview, both squads charged each other. The Villanova players at the heart of the melee had seen little or no action in the game, with backup receiver Jonathan Hughes at the forefront of the pushing and reserve fullback Tyree Hughey screaming epithets and daring any Quaker player to mess with him. As both coaching staffs and administrators from both schools attempted to control the situation, shoving matches would flare up like brushfires elsewhere on the field. VU tackle Izzy Bauta, a tough Brooklyn kid who was no stranger to such confrontations, looked ready to unload on a Penn player before being pulled away by D-line coach Brendan Daly.

From the stands and on television, it looked every bit like a Florida versus Florida State–style melee, only the schools involved in this royal rumble were far better known for their arduous academic standards than their passions on the football field.

Just a friendly little intracity rivalry.

The players were finally brought under control and to the visitor's locker room, and the tension once again gave way to widespread joy. Father Hagan led a vocal, spirited recitation of the "Our Father," after which the Villanova players loudly mocked the "Who's house? Our house?" chant that Penn had entered the field with in pregame. The victorious group then gathered to hear their head coach.

"I had a heart attack about three years ago," began Talley. "I take a pill to slow my heartbeat down, and I usually take a half, but this morning I said, 'I don't know, I think I'm going to take two.'" The players laughed at this story, which all figured to be apocryphal (it was).

"And I took two," Talley continued, "cuz I needed to today. Hey, congratulations on a win that is so necessary to compete in the Atlantic 10. You have to do that to get back and be a champion in our league. You have to be able to come back. I'm so proud of all of the young freshmen and first-year players. The young guys really deserve a lot of credit, that's a tough arena to step into."

Before Talley could continue, a brief moment of chaos and concern erupted in the locker room. As the coach was speaking, backup cornerback Adam Clements clutched his chest and violently keeled over. Players began calling for the trainers, who were having trouble getting to Clements in the overcrowded locker room and yelled to everyone to give them space, which sent players and staff members scurrying toward the door.

Clements had passed out, and within a few moments Pierce and Jarvis ascertained that he was simply overheated from the seventy-degree night coupled with the humidity and stagnant air of the locker room. Still, the incident had muted the celebration. Even in moving to 2-1 and beating a city rival in a game that had not looked winnable in the early stages of the second half, the Wildcats' celebration was abbreviated.

Following a restful night, as he did every Sunday morning, Talley opened the September 24 *Philadelphia Inquirer* to find a story about the thrilling contest that had so tested his emotions. He was not shocked to find there was no such story on the front page of the sports, though there was a piece there about Temple's 19–16 home loss to Western Michigan, a game that had drawn roughly one-third of the fans that the Villanova–Penn contest had but had the coverage advantage of having been played in the afternoon. On page ten, Mike Jensen's Wildcats–Quakers game story summed up the particulars, including the post-game fight, but in part because the paper had to make room for another piece on the Temple game and two stories about high school sports, the reporter scarcely had the space to capture the mood of what had been, by all accounts, an extraordinarily entertaining back-and-forth game.

In Monday's *Daily News*, past ten stories about the Eagles' narrow win over the Raiders on Sunday, Mike Kern wrapped up Villanova–Penn in seven short paragraphs. The area's best-attended college football game of the 2005 season had for the most part eluded the attention of the media, and therefore the city's collective consciousness.

The Wildcats hadn't captured Philadelphia's imagination, but more importantly, at least as far as the coaches and players were concerned, they had captured the victory.

7

RECOVERY

Russell McKittrick had been struggling. By his own admission, he had played poorly in the first half of the Penn game before rallying and making a few plays as the team came back in the second. The inconsistent performance was a very good proxy on the sophomore defensive end's career to date at Villanova.

But the physical mistakes weren't what concerned Andy Talley and the coaching staff. In addition to lining up in the wrong spot on the field and missing assignments, McKittrick's devotion to his studies was still in question. Talley had arranged for McKittrick to live with Darrell Adams, John Dieser, and Brian Hulea during the 2005–06 school year so that the defensive end might be able to glean a sense of responsibility from the trio of team leaders, but McKittrick's grades and class attendance had still been erratic. With Adams set to come back from his elbow injury against New Hampshire, and with young ends like Damian Kelley, Greg Miller, and Dave Dalessandro also blossoming, the California native's stock was way down in the eyes of the staff.

"McKittrick is somewhere in deep space between Pluto and Saturn," said Talley. "The only way to get through to him is on some galactic wavelength."

Mark Reardon, who had recruited McKittrick and had a particular stake in his success, was nearly ready to throw in the towel in regard to the 245-pound end, noting, "He's all over the board mentally."

The twenty-one-year-old McKittrick had in the past five years also been all over the map geographically and emotionally, perhaps exacerbating the lack of stability he carried in what was now his third year on campus.

Growing up in Redmond, Washington, the only child of Scott and Liz McKittrick showed an aggressive streak early in life.

"I got kicked out of soccer just for being too physical, so my parents put me into football," said McKittrick. "I was like six years old. I played defensive tackle, and I also played fullback."

McKittrick enjoyed the excitement and competition of football but didn't consider participating in the sport at the next level until he was a teenager. Scott McKittrick, a pilot for Alaska Airlines, moved his family to San Marcos, California, thirty-five miles north of San Diego, when McKittrick was sixteen, and football soon rose on the growing high-schooler's list of importance.

"We had a really good coach," McKittrick recalled of his high school experience, which helped shift football into a spot among his chief priorities. "He was tough on us, and we didn't really have a lot of athletes compared to the other teams we played, so we lost a lot of games. But we always practiced really hard and we were probably in the best shape out of every team that we played."

San Marcos High School was by no means a powerhouse, but the energy displayed by the Royals' skinny defensive end got the attention of recruiters.

"I got a lot of letters and I talked to several coaches," remembered McKittrick. "USC, Arizona. But on the West Coast, there's not a lot of I-AA teams, and you have to be pretty good to get a scholarship to like USC, UCLA, San Diego State, Stanford, Berkeley, Arizona, Arizona State. There's not really that many schools. I didn't get offers from any of them, but they wanted me to walk on a lot of places."

Also scouring California for prospects was an East Coast school with which McKittrick had little familiarity but seemed to be keen on his making the cross-country trip to play football for them. After talking with Reardon, McKittrick visited Villanova, and though he was not fully comfortable with his foreign surroundings, the highschooler had a suitably entertaining time with his weekend host, then-VU fullback Phil DiGiacomo, to sign up as a Wildcat.

"I don't think I ever really felt a connection to Villanova," said McKittrick. "It was kind of a choice between go to community college, get into construction, join the military, or go to Villanova. And I had a really good time on my recruiting trip, plus I wanted to go to school and play football."

McKittrick was on the small side for a collegiate defensive end, and with stars like Darrell Adams, Terrence Taylor, and Jamil Butler firmly entrenched in the rotation at that position, he didn't have much hope of cracking the depth chart in 2003. McKittrick did get an opportunity to travel with the team during the latter stages of the year, but that turned out to be a mixed blessing for the confused player.

"I did really well on scout team," recalled McKittrick. "I was getting 'scout team player of the week' and stuff a lot, it was fun. Then they moved me to third-string fullback, and I didn't know anything. I would get yelled at all the time because I didn't know anything. They'd put me in for like one play all practice, and [otherwise] I'd just be standing there. I'd travel, go to Maine, stand on the sideline, freeze my ass off, that kind of stuff. That was the second half of the season, that really sucked."

McKittrick also began struggling off the field, as he tried to maintain a relationship with a girlfriend living twenty-seven hundred miles away in California. Talley privately snickered when it came to the freshmen and their natural though usually unrealistic inclination to maintain ties to girlfriends back home. Most of those relationships would fall apart before the first semester ended, but McKittrick fought hard to cling to his past, at the expense of his academic achievement.

"It was hard," said McKittrick, "But I don't think the material was overpowering for me. I could handle the material. A big thing for me was I wasn't getting enough sleep ever. I don't think I ever really got any sleep, and it was totally screwing me up. A lot of it was because of my girl back home, I was having a lot of trouble with her, and being away was a huge thing for me. It was hard for me to focus during class. I couldn't sleep. I wouldn't get to sleep until like four or five in the morning, and we're doing all the football stuff, so I need sleep. And then I'd sleep through class."

After catching wind of McKittrick's academic failings, and being concerned over his lack of focus and inability to sleep, Talley attempted to set his young player straight. McKittrick was sent for psychological evaluation, where he was diagnosed with attention-deficit disorder (ADD). After placing him on medication, the coaching staff expected McKittrick to fall into line. But the meds were not having the desired effect, for player or team.

"They got me assessed, and got me on this medication," said McKittrick. "I started off with Ritalin, and then they thought maybe it was something else, so [doctors prescribed] me antidepressant-type stuff. I think it screwed me up more than anything. My body chemistry was screwed up. I was on drugs—not street drugs, pharmaceutical drugs—but there was kind of a similar effect. My sleeping problems didn't get any better, they probably got worse. I was always stressed out because of my girl, and then I was stressed out because now I can't sleep, I have an appetite problem, I have to eat, I'm trying to keep up my weight, we're working out all the time, and I'm tired all day but I can't sleep at night."

Villanova's medical staff, in concert with McKittrick's psychologist, had changed his medication several times in the two-plus years that the player, since moved from fullback back to his original position of defensive end, had been on campus. The group believed they finally had a breakthrough in 2005, when McKittrick posted an encouraging spring, both on and off the field, which carried over to a good effort in summer two-a-days. McKittrick, now being counted on to help make up for the graduation of Taylor and Butler on the defensive line, had won a starting job. But in game one, against Rutgers, it all began to come apart for the player once again.

"The only thing I remember is being really, really, really tired, and feeling like I couldn't move," said McKittrick of the Rutgers loss. "I don't know what that was attributed to. I remember playing really hard and being really frustrated because I can't move. I was so tired."

McKittrick had not made much of an impact in the team's first three contests, and Talley suspected that he was starting to slip again in regard to academics. Talley wasn't certain that McKittrick could be counted on to take his medication, and was fearful that he might be drinking, which could only make things worse. Privately, the head coach wondered whether he was going to have to give McKittrick the Dave Dalessandro treatment.

Like McKittrick, Dalessandro was a defensive end who had originally been attracted to the physical elements of football. At North Hills, a Pittsburgh-area high school with a storied program, Dalessandro had blossomed into something of a star, a player of high-enough quality to be recruited by most teams in the Atlantic 10. But Dalessandro, one year behind McKittrick, was also low on the depth chart as a true freshman and had major trouble adjusting to life as a spectator during his redshirt season.

"It was really tough," recalled Dalessandro. "I remember sitting on the sideline and talking to [VU defensive lineman] Pete Caroppolo and being like, 'I can't do this.' I just wanted to go to war with everybody. I felt like I was not contributing. I'd look at everybody else playing, and it really bummed me out because I had never not played in a football game since I started."

Not making a difference on the field, Dalessandro looked for a distraction, one that, as on most college campuses, was readily available at Villanova.

"I remember sitting on the sidelines, and just thinking about drinking after a game, wondering why I'm not playing, being just a stupid kid," said Dalessandro. "I drank a lot of beer, and Jack Daniels a lot. Probably had a bottle a night, or I drank a good bit of beer. It was just in excess. I'd black out a lot and I'd wake up in my room, on the ground, and stuff like that. And then I'd have to get up and go to practice, and still be pretty drunk."

Dalessandro hadn't been on campus long before he was brought into Talley's office for disciplinary reasons stemming from his drinking.

"The first time, I was just sitting in the parking lot, I stood up, and I tripped. The public safety guy came over and he said, 'What's going on, did you have a couple beers?' I said, 'Yeah, I had a couple of beers,' and then he said, 'Well, we have to make sure you're okay,' and they called the ambulance. The ambulance came, and then I was at the hospital waiting, and I left the hospital. So I got in trouble for that.

"Then I got in a couple of minor things with drinking in the room, and having beers. I got in trouble for that a couple of weeks later. Coach T, I always felt like he was putting his faith in me that I was going to straighten up, but then I'd always go back and get drunk and get in trouble again."

The situation with Dalessandro had yet to be brought under control, and it came to a head in the aftermath of Villanova's win over Richmond in mid-October. Dalessandro had managed to steer clear of major trouble since his hospital visit-turned-defection early in the year, but his off-the-field lifestyle finally caught up with him.

"One time I was passed out and they took me to the hospital, but there were plenty of other times where I think somebody with good judgment would have probably taken me to the hospital. The last time I passed out, they were trying to carry me in the dorm, and Jamil Butler said, 'Take him to the hospital.' I had drunk way too much booze."

After Dalessandro was revived, treated, and eventually released from the hospital, Talley summoned him on Sunday morning to the football office along with his parents, who had been in town for the Richmond game. The head coach's message to the family was clear: Dalessandro was to go home and get his life under control.

"I knew at that time I was done drinking," reflected Dalessandro. "Because I looked at my mom, I can't see my mom in that kind of pain. And my dad was just all sad. So I said, 'This is it.' Coach T said to go home. He was keeping my scholarship around, thank God. I was ready to stop dragging around, and get down to business and start doing what I was supposed to do, instead of doing what I wanted to do."

Dalessandro went home to Pittsburgh, and per his head coach's mandate, got himself some help.

"It was three days a week for the outpatient rehab, three days a week, three hours a day," said Dalessandro, "And then I had to go to three AA meetings a week, for an hour a day, other than that. It was group rehab, all kinds of drugs and alcohol, and just sitting in a circle talking. The first day I went in, a girl was telling this story. She was crying her eyes out about how her fiancée died of a crack overdose, or was on a crack binge and had a heart attack or something. I was like, 'Oh my Lord.' It was helpful. It's good to hear how bad things can get.

"The first competition to get better is within yourself, and that's what it was. It was just me, I had to beat myself first to get out of this whole problem."

The hiatus from football, and the embarrassment about his exile from Villanova, only strengthened Dalessandro's resolve to return to campus.

"I was 100 percent sure I was going back," said the defensive end. "I got a job, lifted weights, and stayed away from the booze. I worked at Toys"R"Us assembling bikes, and just helped my mom out around the house and stuff. Just kept on the straight and narrow."

Since being cleared to return to Villanova, Dalessandro had been a model citizen and had improved immensely as a player. Though he hated to see a teammate like McKittrick suffering, Dalessandro also stood to get some of the playing time that the Californian seemed destined to dispense with due to his recent difficulties. The time away had helped Dalessandro grow up and gain some perspective, perspective that Villanova's coaching staff hoped might rub off on McKittrick.

"Looking back I just can't believe I'm such an idiot," said Dalessandro. "You get a scholarship to play football, and then you go out and booze it up? No wonder you're not playing, no wonder you're not in physical shape to play. And I look back on it and it angers me that I'd be that stupid to almost throw away something that great, and almost lose the love of my life—football."

Although Talley made a veritable mission out of recruiting student-athletes who could thrive as people and keep their noses clean at Villanova, with the size of his squad, problems like the ones experienced by McKittrick and Dalessandro were going to be constant no matter what type of precautions were taken.

Talley pondered whether Jay Wright felt the same sense of helplessness when it came to keeping the members of his program in line. Wright was the school's extraordinarily popular men's basketball coach, and though Villanova's athletics hierarchy meant that he operated in Wright's shadow, Talley counted the hoops coach as a friend. Wright and his players attended Villanova football games, even using them as a recruiting tool against rival programs that had no gridiron presence on their campus, and Wright often left encouraging voicemail messages for Talley during the course of the season. But in his heart, Talley had a hunch whose job was tougher.

"Here's the contrast," said Talley. "You have 90 players, 10 coaches, and two secretaries, all part of a family that requires constant care. In basketball, you have 12 players. You don't have to deal with the wind, the rain, the sun, and you dress in an Armani suit and make a million dollars a year. Which one would you rather coach?"

For the only time of the 2005 regular season, Villanova's football team would be boarding an airplane. Going to play the University of New Hampshire made air travel a must, not that the relatively short trip could be considered convenient for anyone involved. Joan McGuckin, the team's loyal and trusted football secretary, was the point person in charge of getting the entire travel party loaded on busses to Philadelphia International Airport on this Friday morning, making sure everyone was checked in and had boarded the Southwest Airlines flight to Manchester, then made it to the bus headed to the team hotel in Portsmouth. Equipment manager Tom Dunphy also had more than his usual share of work, since his normal routine of loading and unloading the team's gear would include two additional steps. The practice of moving a college football team was not one that most fans considered, but it was time-consuming and arduous. Dunphy and the team managers had the personal bags of fifty-six players, uniforms for Saturday, practice clothes for Friday's walkthrough, trunks full of backup helmets and shoulder pads, three laundry bins, four misting fans and an exercise bike for the bench area, and all of the trainers' medical trunks of which to take care.

The day was something of a grind, but Talley had through an alumnus arranged a huge barbecue lunch for the team in downtown Portsmouth prior to the Friday afternoon walkthrough. It would be a chance for the players to have a good meal, stretch their legs out a bit in the quaint town, and see more than just the inside of a hotel and a football field. Talley liked his players to have something to do beyond the game when they traveled, though there were members of his staff who quietly grumbled about this small allowance of freedom. The schedule would push back Friday's team meetings and took away from the notion of this being a "business trip," as opposed to a leisurely weekend in New England. But Talley wasn't programmed to think like most football coaches. When he complained from time to time about assistant coaches, not just on his staff but most in the profession, having "tunnel vision," this is what he meant. He considered himself an educator, not just a football coach, and he thought that he owed it to his students to allow them to get the most out of their travel experience.

The assistants, who knew that Saturday's contest would be perhaps the toughest on the team's Atlantic 10 slate, might have argued that this was a time when more than the usual amount of focus on football would be a necessity. New Hampshire was ranked No. 1 in I-AA, but stepping onto their decrepit home field, Cowell Stadium, an unknowing observer might have surmised that the school was ranked somewhere closer to number 101. Their head coach, Sean McDonnell, had led his version of Wildcats up the Atlantic 10 and I-AA charts despite resources that were severely lacking when compared with the company the team was keeping in the Top 25.

The sixty-five-hundred-seat stadium was outdated by about twenty-five years, by far the worst facility in the Atlantic 10. To get to their coaching box located in the brick athletic building adjacent to the field,

New Hampshire's assistants had to ascend a series of rickety ladders and shimmy across a couple of catwalks. The makeshift outdoor press box, which itself was up a treacherous ladder, had room for fewer than ten reporters. The natural grass playing surface looked okay on this, the first weekend in October, but by November it would be torn to shreds by a combination of the weather and a lack of care.

This is where you could find I-AA's premiere program of the moment.

And no upgrades were forthcoming at a school where hockey was No. 1 and football would always battle with men's basketball for No. 2 status. New Hampshire was a budget-challenged New England state to begin with, and the state university's administration had been part of a recent fact-finding mission investigating whether the reduction of football scholarships would garner widespread support in I-AA (it didn't) and could relieve some of the sport's financial overruns.

The mouths of Villanova's players may not have been agape at the site of New Hampshire's facilities, but they did have respect for the team they were about to face. UNH had put 51 points on the board at Villanova Stadium last season, and had in its past two games totaled 111 points in wins over Towson and Dartmouth. The quarterback, sophomore Ricky Santos, and top wideout, 6-foot-3 specimen David Ball, were both preseason All-Americans who had set prolific statistical paces during the 2005 campaign's first month.

With the potential aerial display in mind, Mark Reardon had to be wishing that Ray Ventrone was still around. Ventrone, on a day off from the Patriots, would travel to Durham for the game, but would of course be unavailable to suit up. His former teammates were glad to see Ventrone, who was accompanied by a female friend several of the players agreed was perhaps the most attractive blonde to set foot in the Granite State that day. Life in the NFL was treating Ventrone well, it seemed.

When they refocused their energies toward the task at hand on Saturday, team members knew that this game represented an opportunity. Beating the No. 1 team in the nation would be a statement win for the program, would undoubtedly place them in the Top 25 for the first time all year, and would formally announce the Wildcats' postseason aspirations. The first three games of the year had been important for their own reasons, but this was undoubtedly the biggest tilt in the team's opening four-game stretch.

In his pregame words to the players, Talley played the underdog angle and the theme of opportunity to the hilt.

"Once again, we must be the Rodney Dangerfield of football," Talley began. "Every time I look in the paper, I don't see us in the Top 25. I see us getting a few votes. *Kickoff Magazine* comes on Wednesday, I get it, we're 10-point underdogs. I look at the Sagarin Ratings, we're 11-point underdogs. And then that rag that we have at Villanova, those guys are homers, they're supposed to at least pick us once in a while, they picked us to lose. So I think everybody in the stadium pretty much feels that we're going to get beat today.

"But I'm pretty confident with what I saw Saturday night. We have the folks in this room to do what needs to be done. This is an elite game in the Atlantic 10. You have an opportunity today to show yourselves off nationally. You've got eight million people on TV, a lot of those guys vote, and you're playing a team that's supposedly one of the top teams in the country. We've played them before, men. We've played them before. You need to play at a high level today. We've had three games, we've had some mistakes, put those mistakes away and play Villanova football. If you want to be special in the Atlantic 10, you've gotta win on the road. In 1997 we went undefeated. We came back five times in the second half, five times, this game will be no different."

Frank Jankowski interrupted Talley's history lesson, trying to stir up the team's emotions with some inspirational words of his own.

"Hey, forget all your jitters, all the fucking everything else that goes into this game," Jankowski said. "Go out and punch them in the mouth for sixty minutes. Alright? This is football. We're a little nervous, they're a little nervous, go out and punch 'em in the mouth for sixty minutes. Don't stop, alright? Don't stop, alright? Let's fucking go."

With the starting quarterback's feelings on the record, Talley would take it from there. He mentioned the popular Ventrone, who had given the head coach a message before Villanova had retreated into the visitor's locker room.

"And the message was, kick some ass and take names. What do you say?"

But the No. 1 team in the nation did not bring out the best in Villanova.

After receiving the opening kickoff, the Wildcats got one first down before their stalled drive resulted in a punt. Then, on New Hampshire's first offensive play, from its own 34, Santos threw a bubble screen pass to running back John McCoy, who took two steps toward the line of scrimmage before stopping dead in his tracks and flipping the ball right back to the quarterback, who in turn winged a pass deep downfield to the waiting, and wide open, David Ball. Ball could have walked to the end zone on his hands. The near-capacity Cowell Stadium crowd exploded. For the fourth time in its first four games, Villanova had allowed its opponent to draw first blood.

The bleeding never stopped.

After the ensuing Villanova drive fizzled out at the UNH 33, Santos easily marched his Wildcats into the end zone on a nine-play, 67-yard drive that had included just one third-down situation. When wideout Aaron Brown crossed the goal line on a 27-yard pass play, Villanova was down 14–0 for the second straight week.

VU kicker Adam James got his team on the board with a 35-yard field goal later in the first quarter, but before the fifteen-minute frame had ended, a blocked James punt had been converted in short order to Santos's third touchdown pass of the game's first twelve and a half minutes, this one going again to Ball. The Cats were down 21–3, and the coaches were in search of sandbags to halt the surging tide. Reardon's defense, particularly his tiring secondary, had no answer for Santos and the UNH passing attack. Jankowski was moving the Villanova offense, but wasn't making big plays once the Wildcats got in reach of the end zone.

In the second quarter, the Wildcats briefly showed signs of life.

Jankowski hit J. J. Outlaw for a 34-yard touchdown pass to draw Villanova within 21–10, and on New Hampshire's next drive, Brian Hulea plucked a Santos pass out of the air for an interception that set the Cats up at the New Hampshire 45. Another touchdown here would thrust Talley's team right back into the game, just as a couple of quick scores had done at Penn one week prior.

But it wasn't to be. Villanova netted minus 1 yard on its next three plays combined, James punted to the New Hampshire three, and Santos made the opposing Cats look weak as kittens on the ensuing nine-play, 97-yard drive that put the top-ranked Wildcats right back up by 18. When Villanova picked up ground on another TD pass from Jankowski to Outlaw, Santos answered right back, hooking up with Ball for their third touchdown of the half.

As Talley and his team and staff shuffled toward the locker room, the scoreboard read 35–17, and New Hampshire had the look of a team that was just warming up.

The head coach was encouraging as he entered the locker room, insisting, "We have plenty of time. Three scores is no big deal, we can put three scores on. We need a couple of breaks, we need a couple of things to happen our way. But we can work our way back in this game. Okay, so hang in there, just keep playing. Whatever you do, keep playing."

Talley's calm tone did not transfer to his assistants.

Reardon unleashed his fury on the defense for the second straight week, especially the secondary that had allowed Santos to throw four touchdown passes and the pass rush that was allowing him to sit back and pick them apart. As Reardon's voice bounced off the metal lockers of the visitor's dressing room, the normally cool Venuto raised his volume as well, imploring his offense to finish off drives, and yelling, "I'm not asking you to do it, I'm expecting you to do it!"

Forceful though they were, Reardon's and Venuto's speeches sounded a little like verses of Brahms' Lullaby when Mark Ferrante was through with the players. The staff's most visible assistant coach, Ferrante had just watched his offensive line eliminate any chance for a late Villanova score by allowing an 11-yard sack of Jankowski on the final play of the half. This snafu, and the general temperament of the team, was on Ferrante's mind when he unleashed a ferocious and frightening screaming rant that turned his face beet red and allowed his voice to perfectly complement the intense image suggested by his Hulk Hogan–style mustache.

"We came out flat and stayed flat!" Ferrante screamed. "On the sidelines, everybody, we're all emotionless! Now pick your heads up and go out there and play football the way you're capable of playing! They did not do one thing, on either side of the ball, that we did not expect! They're just more ready to play than we are, every fucking one of them, number one to number 99! We didn't get off the bus, we didn't come out of the locker room and we didn't perform to our expectations. And that's the bottom line!"

As if he needed more emphasis to get his point across, Ferrante slapped the chalkboard, marked up with X's and O's freshly penned by Venuto. Referring to the gameplan, Ferrante continued.

"It ain't this, it ain't the defense, it's emotion! You gotta play with heart, and you're not doing it right now, and we're still in the game, and we're going up and down the field, and we didn't play with any fucking heart! Somebody inside this locker room punch somebody in the teeth and get it done! If you need me to start grabbing face masks, I will! There isn't one thing that you didn't expect! Fucking hit their ass. They didn't do one thing you didn't expect. Put the ball in the end zone and win this thing. Let's go!"

Ferrante's passionate exhortation clearly got the attention of the entire locker room, and had Villanova exited onto the field when the assistant head coach finished, his team probably would have showed some of the emotion it badly needed to get back into the game. But in his desperation to get through to the players, Ferrante had made a mistake of timing. There were still ten minutes on the halftime clock, which meant Ferrante would not have the final word, and his impassioned plea would lose at least some of its steam before the Wildcats retook the field.

Talley attempted to keep the locker room intensity high, but since he had already been encouraging and preached patience in his opening address, he couldn't very well make an about-face and lay into the team. In an effort to play both sides of the fence, Talley rambled.

"Alright now, probably one of the worst halves in the history of Villanova football. Probably one of the worst I've ever seen. So what? I'm sure I'm going to see a half somewhere down the line that'll be just as shitty. Okay, you're playing against a good football team, and they took advantage of every dumbass mistake we've made. That's the name of the game. So don't worry about this guy not blocking or that guy not catching something or this guy not tackling, it's a uniformly shitty job by us in the first half. Okay? We've done that before and won games, and we can do that today. Here's the program right now. We must kick off and be stout, you can't give them a cheap one. Offense, this game is in your hands. Okay? Stop dicking around and put some points on the board to help the defense. Okay? They're out there race-horsing the football right down your throat, and you guys are making every mistake in the book. Okay, so if you want to get in this game, you've gotta put some points on the board. I told you, you gotta keep playing, didn't I? All week. Two words, keep playing, that's the name of the game. We need some breaks, no question. We need a fumble, we need an interception, we need a couple of penalties against them, we need something good to happen, maybe a couple big plays on our part, but whatever it is we need it. Good experience for us right now. You're in a good situation. You've got a great day to go back in the second half and get back in the game. We are not showing anybody on TV Villanova football. TV [viewers] right now, Villanova football, they're laughing at us, fellas, they're laughing at us. And you young guys, give me a break. Give me a break. Come on, let's go. You got a V on your helmet, that means something. Let's start playing that way. Now hey, what are you going to do? We're behind, we got to kick ass, we've got to get going, we need some breaks but it can happen. Right now we need three scores, that's all, and defense, we need to be stout. We're in the same situation we were last week, it's the same exact situation."

Hulea gathered the players before it was finally time to go out for the second half, and his first order of business was to contradict what Talley had been preaching all week.

"Fuck 'keep playing,' let's start playing, alright? Because that is not us, man. That is not us. Let's go out there and stop all this fucking talk and fucking hit somebody."

But despite their best collective efforts, Hulea, Ferrante, Talley, Venuto, and Reardon could not inspire the team to come out strong in the second half. New Hampshire was forced into a fourth-down situation on their first drive, but converted a fake punt attempt and kept driving toward yet another TD pass from Santos. Villanova's first five offensive drives of the second half, on the other hand, ended thusly: interception, punt, fumble, interception, punt. For the first time since he had taken over for Marvin Burroughs, Jankowski was making critical mistakes and looking unsure of himself.

With New Hampshire up by a comfortable 45–17 margin at the 5:54 mark of the fourth quarter, Talley and Venuto decided to give Jankowski the hook. That meant true freshman Antwon Young, the kid who no one had expected to see the field in 2005, would garner his first time as a collegian. And Young played surprisingly well, albeit against New Hampshire's second string, completing three of his six pass attempts and leading a drive that got VU all the way to the UNH 10-yard line. Like so many of Villanova's other drives this day, Young's first effort fizzled out inside the 10, but Young had given Talley and Venuto some hope for the future. Though when the game finally ended, silver linings were difficult to find.

Back in the locker room, after trying hard to ignore some loud New Hampshire hecklers who serenaded his team as it left the field, the head coach let loose.

"Today we stunk," began Talley. "I don't know if you heard some fans up there telling us how bad we were, but they were right. I wanted to turn around and say, 'You guys are right back there, cuz we stink.' We played like shit. And the thing that pisses me off more than anything is we were not physical, not physical."

Talley's voice raised to an angered pitch for the first time all day.

"Not physical! Not once were we physical as a football team! And that's a disgrace. And that's the only thing I'm embarrassed about today. The score I don't give a shit about. We caused our own demise, we made more mistakes, but you were not physical. You were not a Villanova football team. They outhit you, they were tougher than you. That's why we got beat. Now, stick it in your pipe and suck on it, because that's the truth.

"They have guys on their team we wouldn't even recruit. Ask our coaches. We wouldn't recruit any of their kids. New Hampshire wanted a ton of you guys.

"Now, we're going to go back to the drawing board tomorrow . . . We're going to find guys who want to hit people, and we're going to find guys who want to play. You are not tough as a football team, you just aren't. There are some exceptions on our team, starting with Brian Hulea. But as a football team, we're all part of a team, and we are not physical and we are not tough enough. It's as simple as that. And you just got your ass embarrassed on television. You can do two things. Next week we can play like shit and get beat again, because Clawson's had two weeks to get ready for us. Richmond had a week off. Or we can put it back together again and go out and play Villanova football. Because today there was not one shred of Villanova football. Not one."

If the players thought that Talley's dressing-down would bring an end to the collective character assassination, they were wrong. Hulea brought the team together in a huddle, and clearly, he had had enough.

"Bring it in right fucking now," Hulea cautioned, at a sufficient decibel level that his speech could be heard in nearby Maine. "Everyone shut the fuck up. I'm so sick and fucking tired, I hear people who don't fucking come out and hit anybody fucking talking at halftime. Before the game, fucking talking about 'Oh, we're not ready,' this that and the fucking other thing. It's fucking bullshit. Fucking come together right now. Decide what fucking kind of team you have. We got seven more fucking games to get this shit right. God damn it. Fucking decide. Seven more fucking games. We got fucking embarrassed. Freshmen, if you get fucking beat like that another time in your fucking four years here that's fucking awful. Never got our fucking ass kicked like that in five fucking years. Fucking awful. I don't know what the fuck to say but I have fucking seven more fucking games. That's it. That's fucking it. I'm not fucking going like that man, I'm not fucking going down like that. We [must] have a fucking better week in practice, we can't fucking come in there and fucking jog on Sunday. We gotta fucking decide right now what kind of team we want to have. 6–5, do all of you fucking guys want to go fucking 6–5 and fucking hang out around campus fucking be happy with 6–5, or are you going to be a fucking playoff team? Cuz we have the fucking people. Make the fucking commitment. Tonight. Not fucking tomorrow. Tonight. When we get on the fucking airplane. Let's go."

Ricky Santos may have thrown for 371 yards and five touchdowns. David Ball may have gone for 128 receiving yards and three scores. But neither could have dreamed of pulling off the feat just achieved by Hulea, who after recording 15 tackles and an interception against the No. 1 team in the country, proceeded to drop thirty-nine f-bombs in a speech that had lasted just under two minutes.

Villanova dressed quickly, boarded its buses, and headed to Manchester to board its charter flight back to Philadelphia International. But before they could get back home, they'd have to wait for Tom Dunphy, who had to load the equipment on the chartered plane (which was an hour and a half late, leading to the delay), before returning the team's rented equipment truck. Finally, after an interminable delay, the overworked Dunphy returned, and the jet screamed down the runway.

The sound was all too fitting, on a day that would be best remembered for all the screaming.

1. Though loyal to Villanova, head coach Andy Talley at times felt like one of the university's second-class citizens.

2. *(Left)* Brian Hulea, the definition of the strong, silent type.

3. (*Opposite top*) Villanova's 2005 opener came against Rutgers, a team with football resources that dwarfed those of the Wildcats.

4. (*Opposite bottom*) Marvin Burroughs didn't even make it through the third quarter of the first game, but his presence affected Villanova's entire season.

5. (*Above*) Villanova's All-American Darrell Adams saw injuries place his future NFL plans in doubt.

6. (*Above*) The accidental quarterback, Frank Jankowski.

7. (*Opposite bottom*) Villanova's sure-handed tri-captain, John Dieser, made some huge catches for the Cats.

8. (*Right*) J. J. Outlaw: The Professional.

9. (*Below*) Darrell Adams sets his sights on the quarterback.

10. (*Above*) Sensitive senior running back Moe Gibson was terrific at times and absent from the game plan at others.

11. When Matt Sherry was on the field, he was one of VU's best pass-catching threats.

8

BITTEN BY THE SPIDERS

Villanova's coaching staff needed its players to toughen up, and quickly. With a 2-2 record, a loss to Richmond on Saturday would send the Wildcats' margin of error for reaching the I-AA playoffs plummeting to zero, and with potentially difficult games against William and Mary, James Madison, and Delaware still on the horizon to boot. A win, on the other hand, could start the team on a mini-roll, since contests against seemingly lesser foes Bucknell and Rhode Island were immediately to follow the trip to the capital of the confederacy. A victory in Richmond could clear a realistic path to a 5-2 mark entering the home stretch.

Richmond entered the game in a more difficult predicament than did Villanova. The Spiders were 1-3, with the win coming at Maine, and had scored just 19 points combined in their three losses. The team had been using two freshman quarterbacks, Levi Brown and Will Healy, who had struggled enough for the coaching staff to move former starter and then-wide receiver, Stacy Tutt, back to the position. Tutt had opened behind center in the team's most recent loss, to SEC foe Vanderbilt, and had played well enough in the respectable 37–13 defeat to be considered the best option at the position.

Richmond, which had been picked to finish fifth in the Atlantic 10 South division and was fresh off a 3-8 season in 2004, was not expected to be a factor in the league race, and the Spiders' poor play in September suggested that their preseason status was warranted.

But Andy Talley and his coaching staff had several reasons not to take this game lightly, not the least of which was the fact that Villanova had been so lifeless in New Hampshire. Talley suspected that the Spiders would be desperate to win a game in order to keep their season from spiraling completely out of control and would want to avenge the 49–10 drubbing that the Wildcats had leveled against them in 2004. The head coach also knew that Richmond would be fresh and well-rested since it was enjoying a bye week as Villanova was toiling in New Hampshire. But perhaps most significantly, Talley was well aware of the abilities of the Spiders' head coach, one Dave Clawson.

Talley had employed many successful assistants during his time at Villanova, but none had been as inextricably linked with him—for better or for worse—than Clawson. Hired off of Lehigh's staff by Talley to become Villanova's offensive coordinator prior to the 1996 season, the then-28-year-old Clawson had taken a major career gamble in accepting a job that was unlikely to remain his if the Wildcats failed to significantly improve on three consecutive losing seasons.

"I had originally deferred interest in the job," remembered Clawson. "It was intriguing because it was scholarship football, but at that point they had had three losing seasons in a row, and the rumor mill was that if they didn't win the following season, there was a possibility Coach could be fired. I had just started working for Kevin [Higgins] at Lehigh, we just won a championship. I thought Kevin had a huge upside, I loved working for Kevin, and I didn't want to leave. I was [28] years old, I was an offensive coordinator, and we had just won a championship.

"Coach Talley convinced me to meet with him to talk about the position, and after my meeting with Coach Talley, I said I would only consider the job if I was given a two-year contract.

"At the time Coach was trying to convince me it was a good opportunity, he said, 'We don't give two-year contracts to assistants.' And then [athletic director] Gene [DeFilippo] was part of my interview, and Gene said, 'Listen, Andy's got two more years on his contract, and we're not going to fire him, but we need to win, and I feel good about the direction of the program and I think we're going to win.' And I said, 'Well, if that's the case, then you shouldn't have a problem giving me two years.' And he said, 'You got it, I'll tie your contract to Andy's.'"

Had Villanova suffered through another dismal season, both Talley and Clawson would have in all likelihood been bought out, and though Clawson would have definitely been paid and perhaps reassigned to another job on campus, the potential damage to his reputation and career might have been difficult to overcome. If he was going to try and turn the offense around, Clawson needed to first find out if he had any talent with which to work. Fortunately, he did.

"I watched the film and I saw Brian Finneran," recalled Clawson, referring to the receiver who would eventually become the national player of the year and an NFL starter when all was said and done.

"He had been hurt the year before, but even when he played, they were trying to pound the football, they were a run-oriented team. The reason I took the job is I thought their personnel was very suited to the things that we were doing at the time at Lehigh. I remember getting three or four Villanova tapes that Coach Talley sent me, and I evaluated the personnel with Andy Coen [now the head coach, then an assistant at Lehigh], and I said, 'What do you think?' and he said, 'Some of those wideouts look like they might be pretty good.' I mean, heck, if we throw those kids the ball a little bit more we could win a couple more games."

Clawson took the job, and Talley began singing his public praises before the new coordinator had even donned a headset for his new employer. Talley had Clawson accompany him to alumni and university events, introducing him as the boy wonder that was going to help Villanova turn the tide and get its program back on track. Those close to the situation at the time remember Clawson being less than comfortable with the pressure that Talley's probably well-meaning advertisements placed upon him, but that didn't mean Clawson wasn't confident that he could succeed.

Said Clawson, "I just remember about halfway through the spring, talking to Dan MacNeill, the defensive coordinator. I said, 'Dan, you guys are pretty good on defense, right?' He said, 'Yeah,' and I said, 'I think this receiver [Finneran] is pretty good. I think we can win some games next year.' I just remember leaving spring feeling like we had a chance to be pretty good. And the quarterback, Clint Park, was not a perfect fit for the system, but he was athletic, and he was smart. I remember just being very optimistic that we could really surprise people. I just thought that if we could get Brian healthy and get him more involved with the offense and try to feature him, that he was a kid that was probably better than the league. And I thought the complements around him were good enough that we would keep people honest."

Clawson's gut instincts turned out to be correct. The Wildcats went 8-3 in 1996, making their first playoff appearance since 1992. The offense that had averaged 18.6 points per game in the year before Clawson's arrival jumped to 31.5 a game in 1996, and Finneran recorded over 1,200 receiving yards en route to being named an All-American.

Villanova's '96 season ended in the first round of the playoffs at East Tennessee State, but with Finneran, a couple of other strong receivers including his twin brother Brad, and the school's first-ever 1,000-yard rusher in Curtis Sifford coming back in 1997, Clawson would be in charge of an attack that looked like it could carry the program toward a serious run at the I-AA national title. Also on that team would be an intriguing freshman named Brian Westbrook, a former star two-sport athlete at DeMatha Catholic in the Washington, DC, area who had been shunned by the big-time programs because of an untimely high school injury.

Clawson wasn't counting on a contribution from Westbrook, who had received just one other scholarship offer, from Richmond, but still had reason to believe his offense would continue to run up and down the field.

"At that time we didn't know Brian Westbrook was Brian Westbrook. He's a true freshman. He's not even the starter to begin the season. And the skilled group from '96 had returned. So the thing to me still centered around Brian [Finneran], and [receiver] Josh Dolbin emerged as a very good player, and we were going to throw the ball, and keep defenses off-balance enough by running the football when we got favorable numbers to do so."

The major question mark in 1997 was the quarterback position. Clint Park was an honor student who opted not to return to the team after graduating in the spring, but Clawson was high on a lanky sophomore from California named Chris Boden.

"You feel like you have a good nucleus of skilled kids, and then it's just a matter of the quarterback, and I had been a big Chris Boden fan from day one. When I got the job, Coach Talley sent me about fifteen films, and he asked, 'Who do you want?' and I picked Boden. And I really felt we could be successful with Chris Boden as a freshman, he was very close to competing with Clint Park for the job that year. And when Clint decided not to come back, I really felt we could be successful with Chris Boden."

Clawson's feelings about Boden, who threw for an astounding 3,707 yards and 42 touchdowns against just five interceptions as a sophomore, proved to be accurate. His emergence helped Brian Finneran catch 96 passes and win the Walter Payton Award, emblematic of the top player in I-AA, in a landslide. Westbrook, the true freshman, seized the starting running back job from Sifford by midseason and averaged 6.5 yards per carry. Clawson's offense was virtually unstoppable, a fact that quickly became apparent when the Wildcats scored 64 points in the first half of their opener against West Chester. For the season, Villanova would average more than 40 points per contest, and in storming through the campaign at 11-0, would defeat six of its eight Atlantic 10 opponents by double digits. Talley's team was No. 1 in the nation for the final six weeks of the year leading up to the playoffs, the first time the program had been ranked atop the I-AA charts, and as the obvious number one seed in the 16-team playoff field, it was the odds-on favorite to capture the national title. The program was now receiving more media attention around Philadelphia and nationally than it had since the program had been revived in 1984, and that positive press and the high-octane offense had improved attendance considerably on the Main Line.

For the first time, Villanova would host I-AA playoff games in the late fall of 1997, and the campus was abuzz. After routing Colgate in the first round, the Wildcats were stunned by Jim Tressel and Youngstown State, which erased a 21–0 deficit to win 37–34 on a windy early December day that wreaked havoc with the Villanova passing game.

Despite the heartbreaking defeat and the fact that he was just thirty years old, the record-setting pace of the Villanova offense led a head coaching opportunity directly to Clawson's doorstep following the 1997 season. Fordham, a Jesuit-run Catholic university in the heart of the Bronx, came calling, and the coordinator listened intently, but when it was made clear that the school wanted him to retain the previous coach's staff, Clawson took his name out of consideration.

Still, it was just a matter of time until Clawson would move into a head coach's chair at some institution, and everyone involved with the program who was of a mind to consider such matters understood that to be the situation. Talley saw the writing on the wall as 1998 began, and there were some close to the program who believed the head coach might not have been incredibly disappointed to see Clawson leave.

There were suspicions that Talley felt that Clawson was receiving too much of the credit for the program's resurgence, that he didn't like the way the coordinator related to certain players and coaches on the staff, and that he had been uncomfortable with what he perceived to be Clawson's politically motivated relationships with members of the athletics administration. People associated with the program at that time revealed that Clawson, whom Talley had introduced at functions as the man who would help save the program, was not seen accompanying the head coach to many of those same functions after the successes of 1996 and 1997.

Adding to the strain between head coach and coordinator was a disappointing 1998 season that saw the team go 6-5 and miss the postseason. Clawson's offense was still scoring over 30 points, but without the Finnerans and Josh Dolbin, it wasn't nearly as consistent.

When the season ended, the same head coaching job that Clawson had considered one year prior was once again open. Ken O'Keefe, who had taken the Fordham position in 1998, left after one season. Suddenly, the chance to move up seemed much more enticing to Clawson.

"The following year, I was going to be able to hire the coaches I wanted, and at that time too, my wife was pregnant with our first child," said Clawson. "I loved working at Villanova, but it was going to be hard to support a family off an assistant coach's salary, and so things changed in my life personally and the job was more attractive because of the staffing situation.

"I was excited about it, but it was hard to leave Villanova. It was a good place to work, great school, easy to recruit for, I was recruiting California at the time and enjoyed doing that. But I figured I had been an offensive coordinator at that level for five years and was excited about a new challenge."

Clawson left Villanova on good terms, and his relationship with Talley, despite any underlying tension that might have lingered, was as healthy as it had ever been. Talley even lent a valuable hand to Clawson during his transition.

"He was very good to me, he was very supportive, and I never felt that he had an agenda other than to help me," said Clawson of Talley. "He gave me good advice on how to evaluate whether it was a good job or not. And the bottom line was, 'Can you win?' And I think he prompted me to ask the right questions and get satisfactory answers that I don't know if I would have gotten without his help. He said, 'Hey, I don't want to lose you, but when you have a chance to become a head coach, it's hard to turn that down.'"

Talley's support of Clawson continued into 1999, when Fordham went 0-11 and folks around the New York City school were wondering where the hot young offensive mastermind they had heard about actually was.

"During the 0-11 season, he called me I would say every other week to say, 'Hey, you hanging in there, you doing okay, just thinking of you, you'll be fine.' When we were 0-11 he was tremendous to me. 'Hey, you'll be fine, it's a hard job, you knew it.' He said all the right things. And when you're going through an 0-11 season it feels good to hear that.

"If you go through an 0-11 season it is so humbling. I really left Villanova thinking that, 'Boy, I'm pretty good at what I do.' I take over a head job, I think I'm ready, and 0-11? It humbles you and it makes you appreciate, 'Jeez, at Villanova we did have great players,' and Coach recruited all of those kids. And its not about being a hotshot this or that, its about trying to build a really good solid program and having the players come out of it with a great experience."

Ironically, what turned out to be the nadir of Clawson's coaching career was probably in actuality the apex of the young head coach's relationship with his former boss. As Clawson changed the culture of the Fordham program, turning the Rams into a major player in the Patriot League by his third season there, Talley and Villanova were in the midst of a three-season stretch during which they started strong but missed the postseason each year. The offense had continued to run at a high level under new coordinator Sam Venuto, the former wide receivers coach, with the amazing Brian Westbrook at the forefront of the attack, but the fact was lost on few that the team had not returned to the playoffs since Clawson left.

It was only in the 2002 season that Villanova, led by senior quarterback Brett Gordon, emerged as a playoff team again, in the same season that Clawson guided Fordham to its first-ever postseason appearance. After Villanova upset Furman in the first round of the playoffs, and Fordham shocked Atlantic 10 champion Northeastern on the road on the same Saturday, Clawson was suddenly about to head back to the Main Line to face his one-time employer. With nearly four years having passed since his departure from Villanova, Clawson succeeded in his attempts not to dwell on his personal connection to his forthcoming opponent.

"I didn't think about it until it actually happened, because I don't think anybody expected us to beat Northeastern, and I don't think people expected Villanova to beat Furman.

"When it's the season, it's the season, and you're getting ready for the game and you're preparing your players. You're getting ready for the defense and the offense, and I'm just so preoccupied with what we're doing that, I'm not trying to minimize it, but it was really not that big of an issue. If anything, I was glad there was a familiarity of where we were playing and the stadium and the setup and the locker room.

"Villanova had had a good run, they had some good receivers, Brett Gordon was an excellent quarterback, and I was just getting ready for the game. You try never to make it personal."

And though an early-week conversation between the former coworkers went well, it was about to get more personal than either coach ever could have predicted. In the second half of a quarterfinal matchup that Villanova won with relative ease, 24–10, Gordon took a hit to the thumb on his throwing hand, a seemingly routine injury of which Clawson and the Fordham coaching staff had not even been aware.

"I think he was running to the sideline and got hit," said Clawson. "I didn't even know he hurt himself. You look at his numbers that game, how would you know? He was on the sideline and our kid made a clean hit on him and he got tackled, and he got up, and our kid got up. I think Brett hit every pass but one the rest of the game. In the press conference they asked me, 'Did you do anything different when he hurt himself?' I said, 'When did he get hurt?'"

It was revealed after the game that Gordon had broken his thumb, and privately, Talley was steamed about what he considered to be a dirty hit. The reason he suspected that Clawson had ordered Fordham's players to injure his quarterback wouldn't be disclosed for roughly six weeks, but in the meantime, Villanova had a semifinal game for which to prepare. Gordon managed to play well in the first half against McNeese State despite his damaged thumb, but when the injection that he had received just prior to the second half made his hand go numb, Gordon's play dropped off and McNeese rallied and won the contest, 39–28. Little did Clawson know as he watched the McNeese–Villanova game on national television that he, along with the game officials, would be made the scapegoat for the defeat by his former boss.

The night before the Fordham–Villanova game, at a standard NCAA prechampionship meeting held in this case at the visiting Rams' hotel in King of Prussia, Dave White, an associate athletic director at

Villanova and a former member of Talley's football staff, had walked through the dining room that had been set for Fordham's team meal. On each table White, who had Talley's ear and was thought by some within the athletic department and football office to be overly meddlesome in football-related affairs, noticed a photograph of Gordon with a pair of hands semi-imposed on each, and jumped to the extreme conclusion that the photographs represented a bounty placed by the Fordham coaches on the Villanova quarterback. White in turn reported his "findings" to Talley, and the head coach, already edgy due to the tension of the postseason run, took them at face value.

More than a month after the season had ended, Talley wrote Clawson a letter airing his feelings about Fordham's perceived dirty tactics, and Clawson was as infuriated by the accusation as by his former boss's method of information gathering. What White had seen, according to Clawson, was simply an innocent reminder from the coaching staff to Fordham's defensive players to get their hands in the face of the 5-foot-10 Gordon, a game plan directive that the staff had stressed all week in practice.

"It was out of left field, I had no idea," said Clawson. "I never even thought twice about [the table photos], because I knew what our coaches were telling the kids about getting hands in the face. I just thought, 'Man, that's a pretty neat way of communicating to have your hands in his face.' And at first I was upset because to be accused of that really bothered me. I worked for him for three years and we had a really great relationship at that point for six years. And for him to think that I would even do something like that bothered me. Number two, for him to sit on that as long as he had bothered me even more, that he didn't address it right away. Then I was upset.

"I said that it was news to me, and he just said that he was very upset, that he thought it was wrong and then," said Clawson with a laugh, "when I found out where he got the information from . . .

"My question to him was, 'Do you really think I would do that, because if you really think that I would do that, then we don't have a relationship, it's not even worth saving.' His answer was more or less,

'No, I didn't think you would do that, but then someone told me you did, and then I didn't know what to make of it.' And then on top of that, coincidentally, Brett gets hurt, so now he's thinking that not only did I put a hit, but the kids did it. I mean a hit, how do you put on a hit?"

The conflict was resolved amicably, but Talley's suspicion, coupled with Clawson's bitterness about the accusation, changed the relationship between the two forever. And now, Clawson was in his second year at Richmond, coaching in the same division in the same league as Talley, meaning things weren't going to get any less strained.

"I think we got over it, we've talked since then, but it's different," said Clawson. "And now I'm in a league where I'm competing against him. Our jobs in this league are very similar. We're both at private, academically demanding schools in a state school league. Certainly, one of the schools we need to beat is Villanova, and one of the schools he needs to beat is Richmond. Whenever you compete against somebody, you'd like to say things are normal, but it definitely puts a strain on things.

"At times that I've still talked to him we've been good and at other times before we play them in a game it's different. The only thing different about that is that here's a guy I worked for for three years and spent every day with, and you're recruiting with him for three or four days at a time, spending twenty-four hours with each other, and I think that those transitions make it hard. It's just part of coaching, it's part of life. Coach and I have always maintained a good relationship yet we have always had these little tensions in between."

Matt Sherry woke up on the Tuesday morning prior to the Richmond game with an itch on his left arm. The sophomore tight end's self-examination revealed a small, clear, bump that looked a lot like a mosquito bite, and Sherry thought little about it for the rest of the day.

By Wednesday, the red mark looked bigger, almost like a large pimple, and Sherry showed it to football trainer Dan Jarvis. Jarvis wasn't sure what it was, but scrubbed the protuberance, cleaned it, and sent Sherry on his way without much in the way of concern. On Thursday, Sherry noticed that the bump was a louder shade of red, had grown to an inch in diameter, and by the end of practice, was beginning to cause the player significant pain. Jarvis then failed in an attempt to pop the blistering edifice, and his efforts caused the mark to throb throughout the night. Sherry watched TV on Thursday night with his arm raised above his head to control the throbbing, and his discomfort allowed him to get only around two hours of sleep. By the time Friday morning arrived and it was time for the team to board its busses for the trip down to Richmond, Sherry felt miserable, and Talley and Jarvis were beginning to come to the conclusion that their starting tight end, a key to the team's offense and a player who looked just about ready to arrive as a star in the Atlantic 10, might not be able to play on Saturday. And though no one could figure out just what Sherry had, his injury history at Villanova was such that the coaches were hardly surprised. The 6–4, 255-pounder from Rhode Island had looked like he might develop into a pro prospect almost from the day he stepped onto campus, but bad luck had prevented him from delivering on that promise as of yet.

Sherry had missed some of spring ball prior to the 2004 season due to a hip pointer, and in summer camp that year, while blocking, Sherry stepped in a practice field divot and sprained the peroneal muscle in his foot, forcing him to wear a boot for 10 days and miss important practice time. Once he was back on the field, Sherry got all the way to game six before hyperextending his elbow against Northeastern, an injury that bothered him for the rest of the 2004 season. The tight end was healthy by the spring of '05, until he dove for an overthrown ball in a scrimmage, landed awkwardly, and separated his shoulder.

Unlike some other players on the team, Sherry wasn't suspected to be the type of player who would nurse an injury, he was simply a tough kid whose injuries gave the indication that he was made of glass.

Sherry wasn't the quarterback or No. 1 receiver, he was a tight end with fourteen catches on the year, but Villanova would still be in trouble without him. The young offensive line was already without big right tackle Mike Costanzo, who wasn't making the trip, and left tackle John Finneran was expected to play but was struggling with an ankle injury. If Sherry couldn't go, undersized redshirt freshman Mike Bradway, the son of New York Jets general manager Terry Bradway, was going to be thrown into the already-youthful mix.

As soon as the bus arrived in Richmond, Sherry, accompanied by Jarvis, went to the hospital. The attending doctor didn't know what Sherry's ailment was any more that Jarvis did, but gave him some antibiotics and told him to come back in the morning so that his colleague, who just happened to be Richmond's team doctor, could check it out. On Saturday morning, Sherry and Jarvis went back to the facility, where the problem that had been plaguing Sherry since Tuesday was finally diagnosed as a brown recluse spider bite.

On the day that Sherry's team was set to play the Richmond Spiders, the news was more than a little bizarre. The recommendation was made that Sherry not play, but after arriving in Richmond, Villanova team doctor Bill Emper argued that since the bite wasn't going to get any worse, it would be Sherry's decision. With his family flying down from Rhode Island for the game, there wasn't much doubt what the player would opt to do. Talley and the rest of the Villanova coaching staff weren't going to dissuade him either. This game was too important.

Sherry's situation was at least as concerning to the head coach as was the forecast. Talley often joked that he felt like a weatherman much of the time, as he attempted to discern which way a storm front would break and how it might impact his game plan. Saturday's forecast in Richmond called for rain in the morning, which since the Spiders' playing surface was natural grass, was bad news on two fronts. A damp and muddy field would slow down Villanova's offensive speed, and a wet football would also be a major problem in a system that made most of its bones on quick precision passing.

The rain came down in sheets as Villanova's busses pulled up outside UR Stadium, but just before noon, it began to subside. Talley walked the field and was satisfied that it would be dry enough not to slow the attack down considerably. The team had had a sharp week of practice following the New Hampshire debacle, and Sherry's attempts to play were yet another positive sign that things would break in the Wildcats' favor after all. As Talley addressed the team, his positivity was shining through.

"You've all been on the field, it's a good field, so we're really in good shape," started Talley. "You guys can run and play your game. You must hold onto the football, because the ball can come up wet just from the grass, which means getting a wet ball on a pass or a run. Two hands on the ball, be secure and feel confident of the way you handle yourself out there on the grass."

Remembering what had happened on New Hampshire's first offensive play one week prior, Talley implored his defense to stay alert.

"Defensive backs, defense, first play of the game, what we're always concerned about is a special play, so get ready for something crazy. Be ready for it. We're not interested in safeties and corners coming up and making tackles 2 yards behind the line of scrimmage on the first play of the game. Be smart and look at what's going on. Don't forget, they've had two weeks to prepare so he may have some other things in the vault for us today. We've got to see them early, and adjust to them.

"With our offense, I can only go on past experience, it is always just a matter of time. It is a matter of time before we figure out what we have to do, and expect that big plays are going to happen and points are going to happen. So it's a matter of time, stick with it, be patient, don't worry about anything.

"This is the fifth game of the year, it is a critical game at which point we determine what kind of football team we want to be. I don't want to be a football team that goes out on the field and worries about everything. I don't want to be a football team that goes out and jumps offsides and is itchy. We want a football team that goes out and plays Villanova football, which is consistently good football for four quarters of the game. Not super jacked-up, not flat, but at a point where you go out and hit the field and you play football on every single play. And that's what we're looking for today, so we can establish ourselves in this league and be who we should be.

"Now you young guys aren't young anymore. This is your fifth game, do not fear, nothing can happen to you that hasn't already happened. What else could happen that hasn't happened? Nothing. So let's just go play. You're in a great venue, we always play well in Richmond, we always win in Richmond. So here's the deal, we're going to hit the field quickly, let's get some scores on the board. Defensively, get after them. Here's what I want to see from the defense, one thing, what is it? Physical! That's what I'm looking for, let's get after them, and smack 'em, and let's play great Villanova football."

Talley's teams had been in many shootouts during his years at Villanova, and the first four minutes of the Richmond game appeared that it would reflect that trend.

On just the seventh play of the contest, Frank Jankowski dropped back and found J. J. Outlaw wide open over the middle for a 51-yard touchdown pass. For the first time all season, Villanova had scored first. This was the break in the clouds that Talley and his staff had been waiting for.

Richmond answered right back, as Tutt drove the Spiders quickly down the field before hitting running back David Freeman with a 32-yard TD pass. The ensuing point-after tied the score, but Villanova reclaimed the momentum in short order. On the next drive, Jankowski threw a deep ball to John Dieser, who was in one-on-one coverage on the right side of the field. Dieser caught the jump-ball lob, the Richmond cornerback fell down, and the senior tri-captain sprinted 57 yards to the end zone.

Adam James made the score 14–7 with 11:08 to play in the first quarter. The legions of fans who had decided to stay home due to the threat of inclement weather were missing a game that promised to be an exciting, back-and-forth, flag football-style affair. Talley was fine with that pace, which clearly favored Villanova.

But things would calm down considerably for both teams thereafter. It would be early in the second quarter before anyone scored again, as Richmond cut the lead to 14–10 on a field goal. The Spider defense had adjusted after giving up the two early touchdown passes, and Jankowski and the offense were now having trouble sustaining drives. Moe Gibson and the running game were nowhere to be found, as Richmond was winning the battle with the young VU offensive line, and Jankowski was feeling the heat behind this green unit as well. Matt Sherry had caught two passes on the same drive near the end of the first quarter, but didn't seem himself. Sherry, run down from lack of sleep and with a course of antibiotics running through his system, came to the sideline and threw up after a stalled Wildcat drive. The coaching staff, in consultation with Jarvis, would shut him down for the rest of the afternoon.

Amid these developments, the Wildcat defense was holding its own, keeping the team in the game during a more than twenty-minute stretch of the first half when the offense couldn't get anything going. The unit's first sign of wear on the hot and humid Virginia afternoon came near the end of the second quarter, when a Jankowski interception near midfield was followed by a 26-yard scramble for a touchdown by Tutt that gave the Spiders their first lead of the game.

Villanova threatened to tie the game or take the lead when it got the football at the Richmond 49-yard line with 49 seconds left, but Jankowski drove the team no further than the 30-yard line before another drive sputtered and the first-half clock expired.

The Wildcats hadn't scored a point in the final twenty-six-plus minutes of the half, and Richmond was winning the war in the trenches. Still, the score was a manageable 17–14, and Talley and the coaching staff had every expectation that they could rebound. After all, this was a team that had erased a 17-point deficit at Penn just two weeks prior.

"We'll make adjustments at halftime, get it done in the second half," said Talley. "You guys are playing great, you let a lot of things off the hook in the first half offensively, but we'll be alright. You're in an A-10 game, let's play.

"Settle down, settle down, settle down, we're fine. 17–14, it's not a big deal. Settle down, make plays in the second half. Defense, you're doing a great job. Offense, we're getting the ball, but we're making mistakes and turnovers. We have to stop that. Just relax. You're in good shape here. The weather's fine, we can win this game, make some big plays, enjoy it. Let's go. In this league, you never know. Right now New Hampshire's getting beat 28–10 by William and Mary. Three weeks ago, William and Mary gets killed by Rhode Island. You've got to keep playing. Who's going to make the big play? Just keep playing. Don't get down, keep your chin up, stay positive, no more bitching on the sideline, let's come together and support each other. That's what you do when you're on the road.

"Last year, the score was 14–10 at halftime, they were losing. We beat them 49–10. See what I'm saying? Now you're ready to win the second half, you are totally prepared to do this. Have they done anything defensively that you haven't seen? Have they done anything offensively that you haven't seen? Okay, so let's go out there now and take this game, everybody together, take control of the game."

Villanova had not been immediately energized by similar halftime speeches made by Talley against either Penn or New Hampshire, but this time, the head coach's exhortation seemed to have a positive effect.

Richmond fumbled the opening kickoff, which was recovered by alert Wildcat safety Allyn Bacchus at the Spider 37. Jankowski then promptly led an eight-play drive lasting more than four minutes, including a key conversion on a fourth-and-six play from the 33 to Bradway, Sherry's young replacement at tight end. Moments later, Jankowski hit Outlaw with a 15-yard strike to get Villanova inside the Richmond 10-yard line, and a 4-yard pass to Outlaw two plays after that got Villanova back in the end zone for the first time since the early stages of the game. James had the ensuing point-after blocked, which elicited groans from the sideline, but the game was back in control of the Wildcats, 20–17.

The remainder of the third quarter looked a great deal like most of the first half. The Villanova defense was again stiff, forcing Richmond's next two drives to end in punts. The Wildcat offense was also struggling, with its two third-quarter drives following the touchdown resulting in punts as well. By this point, Ferrante's offensive line was paper thin. In addition to Costanzo and Sherry, John Finneran had succumbed to his ankle injury and was shut down for the day. Also in the second half, center Christian Gaddis, the anchor of the unit, left with an ankle injury of his own. As the fourth quarter approached, the Villanova offensive line consisted of four redshirt freshman, including seldom-used walk-on center Mike Probasco, and true freshman Mike Sheridan at one of the tackles.

Villanova may have been winning the game as the final frame began, but Richmond could smell blood in the water. The defense was still carrying the Wildcats, and the Spiders' first drive of the fourth quarter, a 13-play, 87-yard march that used up nearly five minutes of clock time and ended with a 5-yard touchdown pass from Tutt to wideout Matt Hale, showed that Mark Reardon's troops were beginning to crumble under the weight of that burden.

With 10:36 to play and his defense winded, Talley needed his sophomore quarterback and the offense to answer in a decisive fashion. Little did the head coach know, however, that Jankowski was about to begin the worst quarter of his young collegiate career.

On the second play of the ensuing drive, Jankowski threw downfield into the waiting arms of Richmond free safety Andrew Harris. True to form, the Villanova defense held and got Jankowski the ball back, but on a second-down play on a crucial Wildcat drive just south of the 6:00 mark, the inexperienced o-line was blown up, Jankowski was hit 10 yards deep in his own backfield by defensive tackle Johnny Campbell, and he fumbled the football in the process. Campbell fell on the ball at the Villanova 20, the Richmond sideline celebrated, and a spent Villanova defense in just three plays allowed David Freeman to run the 20 yards to the end zone, punctuated by a 6-yard touchdown run with 4:25 to go.

The score was now 31–20. Any Villanovan who held out hope that their team would make a miracle comeback was cured of that thinking on the Wildcats' very next offensive play, as Jankowski's tipped pass was intercepted by Richmond linebacker Brian Burnette, who calmly returned it 31 yards for the Spiders' third touchdown in just over six minutes. Villanova wasn't coming back from this.

The Wildcat sideline watched in disbelief as the clock ran out on an 18-point loss that had so recently looked like it would go down as the team's third win of the year.

In reality, it wasn't a game that Villanova deserved to win, even though the defense had put up a gallant effort throughout. After scoring 14 points in the contest's first 3:52, the Wildcats had managed just

6 over the final 46:08, and that touchdown came on a short field that followed a fumble.

After committing four costly turnovers and sustaining four sacks, it would have been easy to lay the offensive struggles directly at Jankowski's feet, though doing so was somewhat unfair. The quarterback was a sophomore making only his fourth collegiate start, and his inexperience, coupled with the disastrous state of the offensive line and the invisibility of the running game, had melded into a situation that simmered for the game's first fifty minutes before boiling over in the final ten.

When they shook hands at midfield, Dave Clawson told Talley that Richmond was lucky to win the game, and while the former Villanova coordinator may have felt that way, a long look at the circumstances proved that Richmond was just plain better. In giving their head coach his first win in eight tries against a former employer (Clawson had gone 0-5 against Lehigh while at Fordham, and was 0-2 against Villanova entering the 2005 matchup), the Spiders had proven that they were onto something big and might have a chance to build toward a winning season or better.

Villanova, meanwhile, could only search for answers. Talley's frustration with the loss, and the direction the season was moving, was apparent when the head coach addressed his team in the locker room beneath UR Stadium.

"The point is this: In the Atlantic 10, if you don't take advantage of opportunities when you have them, you're a dead man. We should have been up 21–7 without a problem. We need to have some auditions on the offense, I'll tell you that right now, because that is not the type of exhibition that we can have here. We're a losing football team right now because we do losing things during the course of a football game. Turnovers, offensively like that, are you kidding me? [Richmond is] a mediocre team, and on the scoreboard it looks like we got our ass kicked. Turn the ball over in this league, you're dead, you will bleed to death in a heartbeat."

For the first time all season, Talley called out his starting quarterback in the postgame, but was also sure to hoist part of the blame for the offense's struggles onto the shoulders of other members of the unit as well.

"Frank, you better continue to grow up," Talley began. "Offensive line, you better continue to grow up and give him some time. And we need a running game, because we're going nowhere throwing the ball as much as we have to throw it. Simple as that.

"They did not beat us, we beat ourselves. That's the tragedy, we beat Villanova. You can do two things, you can put your head in the sand and go south on us, or you can keep your head up and keep playing. I've been with Villanova teams before at this point that picked their head up and kept playing, I've been with a couple that put their head down and got their ass kicked. Decide what you want to do."

9

ACADEMICALLY SPEAKING

On Saturday, October 8, Kyle Ambrogi, a twenty-one-year-old senior running back at Penn, scored two touchdowns as the Quakers routed Bucknell 53–7 to help his team move to 3-1 on the season.

Two days later, on a normal Monday afternoon, the honor student from the university's prestigious Wharton business school drove to Philadelphia's South Street area, purchased a gun, went to the basement of his mother's home in the city's western suburb of Havertown, placed the gun to his head, and pulled the trigger, ending his young life.

Ambrogi, who had scored Penn's first touchdown in the Villanova game just a few weeks before, had reportedly been battling depression, and though the Quaker coaching staff had been keeping a close eye on the former local prep star as had his family (including brother Greg, a sophomore on the Penn football team), Ambrogi had succumbed to forces that even his closest friends and family struggled to comprehend.

The news, which put Penn football in the papers and on television in a way the program never would have wished for, made Andy Talley numb and more than a little nauseous. He knew that his friend Al Bagnoli had done everything in his power to help Ambrogi, and he knew that as a head coach watching over ninety-plus players, the situation was ultimately well beyond Bagnoli's control.

More than even most college head football coaches, Talley interacted with his players on a personal level. He monitored their academic standing and social development on campus, had a good feel for their family situations, and made sure to keep his antenna up for any warning signs that suggested potentially troubling off-the-field problems. But there was no way in the world he would be able to reach them all, and the troubled and sensitive ones, guys like Kyle Ambrogi, weren't often going to come knocking on his door if they had a problem.

Talley's thoughts drifted immediately to Russell McKittrick. McKittrick wasn't suicidal as far as Talley or anybody else knew, but it was hard enough to figure out what made the kid tick that Talley was sufficiently petrified. McKittrick was barely playing as the team readied itself for the Bucknell game, having been stripped of his starting duties following the New Hampshire loss after continuing to miss assignments and lining up out of position on multiple occasions. Mark Reardon had more faith in a couple of true freshmen defensive ends, Damian Kelley and Greg Miller, than he had in McKittrick at this stage, and thus McKittrick was relegated to duties with the kickoff team.

It was the right thing to do from a football standpoint, but Talley had no idea how losing his starting job would affect McKittrick off the field. Would he feel any incentive to go to class, take his medication, and keep his drinking under control if he wasn't playing meaningful minutes on Saturdays? Talley hoped that McKittrick would focus his energies in a positive way if only in an effort to reclaim his starting job, but he had his doubts.

After two consecutive dispiriting losses, the Bucknell game couldn't come soon enough for Talley, McKittrick, or any of the stakeholders in the Villanova football program. The last of the Wildcats' three out-of-conference opponents, Bucknell was 1-4, and judging by the score of the Penn game, it was a shell of the team that had finished 7-4 and played Villanova within six points in 2004. The Bison were using a converted defensive back, Dante Ross, as the quarterback in their option-based offensive scheme, due mainly to the fact that he was the only player on the team explosive enough to keep opposing defenses somewhat honest.

Villanova was in a position to concede nothing at this stage, especially in another road game, but when the Wildcat coaching staff watched the opponent's film, they were fairly certain that even on their worst day, their team was head and shoulders ahead of Bucknell in terms of talent.

That should have always been the case when an Atlantic 10 team took on a Patriot League foe, though the better Patriot clubs did step up and beat A-10 opponents on a fairly regular basis. Members of the Patriot League, like those in the Ivy League, did not technically allow athletic scholarships, but neither were they a pure Division III-style nonscholarship model. The disparity between the Patriot-Ivy model and the Division III model, or for that matter the Patriot-Ivy model and the full-scholarship Atlantic 10 model, was not fully understood by many people not directly involved with one of the programs, but there had been a quiet throng of Villanova supporters who felt that the university was better suited to be a member of the Patriot League in football.

Folks in that camp reasoned that as a private school with strong academics, Villanova would fit easily into a league with Bucknell, Colgate, Fordham, Georgetown, Holy Cross, Lafayette, and Lehigh. Bucknell, Lafayette, and Lehigh were all located in eastern Pennsylvania like Villanova, which meant natural rivalries would almost certainly develop. Fordham, Georgetown, and Holy Cross were all Catholic schools like Villanova, and Georgetown was even a core member of the Big East like Villanova.

The argument for the Patriot League was also an argument against the Atlantic 10. The football end of the conference was, as Dave Clawson pointed out, largely a "state school" league. There were five "Universities of": Delaware, Maine, Massachusetts, New Hampshire, and Rhode Island; two state schools with by all accounts modest academic standards: James Madison and Towson; and two private schools that fit the same "come one, come all" demographic: Hofstra and Northeastern. Within the Atlantic 10, Villanova had the most in common, both academically and demographically, with Richmond and William and Mary.

Bob Mulcahy, the current Rutgers AD and Villanova alumnus who had been a proponent of the football program's move to I-A, was among those who felt that if the Big East was not a workable option, than the seemingly less competitive Patriot League was the better gridiron home for his alma mater.

"We have no long-term rivalry with Richmond and William and Mary," argued Mulcahy. "We'd be better off playing Lehigh and Lafayette than Richmond and William and Mary. Frankly, playing Maine and Northeastern and a lot of those schools doesn't mean anything. Delaware's worthwhile, but if you're not going to play I-A, then go play Lehigh and Lafayette and the schools that are going to have some local rivalry."

The financial component also played into the stance held by Mulcahy and many of his fellow alumni, not to mention some campus administrators and faculty.

"The problem with playing at the [current] level is that you don't have any real support," said Mulcahy.

And while keeping up as a member of the Atlantic 10 meant funding at least sixty football scholarships, that commitment didn't necessarily guarantee any more strength or success than did being in the Patriot League. Colgate had reached the I-AA national title game in 2003 (where it was promptly trounced by Delaware) despite its "nonscholarship" status, while Villanova had never advanced that far in the postseason. Lehigh had been a Top 25 team for years and had defeated two Atlantic 10 champions in the playoffs in the previous decade. Fordham, with the fewest football resources and most recruiting challenges in the conference, had been to the national quarterfinals in 2002.

There was every bit as much logic to suggest that Villanova could thrive competitively in the Patriot League, perhaps even more so, than to suggest that Villanova could thrive in the Big East and I-A.

But whenever public whispers were made linking Villanova to the Patriot League, Talley would quash them, and the main reason was that such rumors could impact recruiting in a profoundly negative way. The university would have to honor any scholarship promises that were made to recruits and current players if such a decision were ever made, but many top recruits would be far less inclined to attend or even consider a school that was kicking around the notion of moving to a conference where the overall quality of play was unquestionably inferior.

It was believable that Talley may have also turned his nose up at the Patriot League talk because of his own ego, and if that was in fact the case, it would have been difficult to blame him. He had built the Villanova program from scratch in the mid-eighties, had built it so well and so quickly that talk of moving to the BCS level warranted serious discussion in the mid-nineties. He had also been a faithful soldier in standing by the school when it opted to remain at the I-AA scholarship level, even when that decision meant his own career would be perhaps perpetually stuck in neutral. Ratcheting the program down would have been a slap in the face in light of all that Talley had accomplished at Villanova and would have represented a veritable demotion for a coach who strongly suspected that he could have been successful at the game's highest level.

Most Villanovans felt the same way Talley did: that if anything, the university's approach should be to invest more in the program, not less. But even some of those supporters figured that if a move to I-A would never happen, what was the point of hanging around in the Atlantic 10 with the Maines and New Hampshires of the world, when Villanova's fan base was completely uninspired by the competition in the league as it was? To some, the university was needlessly hedging its bets. If the answer was always going to be I-AA, and the prospect of winning a national title was only marginally more difficult in the Patriot League, then why not look into the more cost-effective, more academically suitable model?

As part of the mid-nineties I-A feasibility study that had effectively become a referendum on the issue of football at Villanova, Tony Randazzo and his committee were forced to answer many of those very questions.

"We addressed that as part of our committee, because it did come up from some of the other trustees," remembered Randazzo. "We had one or two trustees in particular who said our peer group was the Lehighs and Lafayettes and Bucknells, and they said, 'Why not play football there?'

"We said if the university or the trustees are hell-bent on joining the Patriot League, then we should do it for all sports. And we knew that was never going to fly with basketball, so any discussion about the Patriot League was put aside."

And while having all of the university's teams in one league was indeed the ideal, Villanova was already a football-only member of the Atlantic 10, so what would be the major challenge in being a football-only member of the Patriot League?

The prospect of Villanova football's membership in the nonscholarship conference seemed plausible, though many of those who considered the Patriot League option attractive failed to realize that a move there would change the recruiting landscape in a way that could quickly render the football program at the school uncompetitive.

Talley's recruiting strategy, above all else, was the reason that Villanova had been able to remain competitive in the Atlantic 10. Had Villanova attempted to regularly go head-to-head with a school like Delaware for local players, the larger school, almost solely by virtue of its stadium that was filled to its weekly capacity of twenty-two thousand, would have left Talley's program in the dust. Similarly, if Villanova went after many of UMass's or Maine's recruits, the Wildcats would have oftentimes been on the losing end of battles with its own admissions office.

So Talley's approach was to expand his recruiting into places like California, where if a highschooler wasn't among the elite players sought by the Pac-10 schools, his options were limited. Prospects with above-average academics or better weren't always enamored of low-level I-A schools like Fresno State, San Jose State, or Utah State, or the remote locations of many of the better football-playing universities in the I-AA Big Sky Conference, and were thus willing to give the strong academic institution located just outside of Philadelphia a long look. It was this approach that had landed Villanova Californians like Brian and Brad Finneran, Chris Boden, and other major components of the team's success over the years.

As a member of the Patriot League, Villanova would have a much tougher sell to these players. The quality of play in the I-AA Atlantic 10 and I-A Western Athletic Conference may have been comparable, but there was a significantly wider gap between the Patriot League and the WAC. The existing Patriot League schools already recruited nationally as it was, and universities like Lehigh and Lafayette would have beaten out Villanova for the same player at least seven times out of ten because of their generally stronger academic reputations.

That thinking reflected the logic of the situation, though there were some associated with Villanova that didn't necessarily buy it.

Said Mulcahy, "You have a network from Catholic high schools that you would be able to draw from. A lot of these kids are I-AA players. Plus, they might wind up playing Princeton and Harvard and some of the other schools, and frankly, there would be as much interest if not more than they have now, just from alumni."

What Mulcahy did not address was the issue of money, perhaps the most misunderstood element of the entire Patriot–Ivy League discussion. Many of those who supported Villanova exploring the notion of "nonscholarship" football were under the misapprehension that excising sixty-plus scholarships would ease the most significant financial chunk of the university's commitment to football, that is, wiping out 60 scholarships at an annual cost of $37,000 each would mean an immediate savings of $2.2 million upon the program's relocation to the Patriot League.

Many outsiders believed that a school like Lehigh or Penn was competing effectively with Villanova and Delaware on the gridiron in spite of the fact that the members of their starting lineups were paying full tuition to attend school. The notion that the Patriot and Ivy schools could find just as many players, who were almost as good as their counterparts in the I-AA scholarship leagues, to attend their school despite the lack of a financial incentive was highly illogical, but some coaches, academics, and administrators in Patriot and Ivy circles heralded their "nonscholarship" conference's "last amateurs" model of football with a straight face on a regular basis anyway.

The reality of Patriot and Ivy League recruiting was this. Schools like Lehigh and Penn cast wide national nets, in search of the best low I-A or high I-AA players around the country who were within reach of the university's academic standards. A handful of the most highly sought-after players in this group were those whose families could afford to send them to school and would be thrilled to pony up the bucks if their son was admitted. But more often that not, the best players in the Ivy League and Patriot League were those who, due to financial hardship, qualified for full or substantial "grant-to-need" packages, which were not officially considered scholarships but functioned as such. Players were not required to pay back any portion of the grant like a normal student who was awarded financial aid, meaning that at Lehigh, just as at a scholarship institution like Villanova, the university bore the brunt of the financial burden.

Clawson, who coached for eight years in the Patriot League, five as a head coach, estimated that one-third to forty percent of his final team at Fordham were receiving full grants, and that roughly seventy percent were receiving at least partial grant money. Patriot League schools, like all I-AA institutions, were permitted to fund the equivalent of no more than sixty-three grants-in-aid but were allowed to have up to 98 players on their rosters, as opposed to ninety in the rest of I-AA. If Clawson's Fordham squad was at its maximum of ninety-eight, by his estimate, up to forty players were receiving a full ride, and close to seventy were receiving some amount of nonreturnable grant money. That setup didn't quite level the playing field with the scholarship I-AAs and their sixty-plus full grants-in-aid, but it certainly helped them remain competitive.

Educating players within the Patriot League model was by no means cheap, nor was the process of locating them. Sniffing out "need" students who were good football players and not serious academic risks to fit into the fabric of elite institutions was extremely difficult, which was why a school like Fordham or Lehigh also spent major recruiting dollars to find such student-athletes. In many cases, a Patriot League school was forced to outspend a contemporary in the Atlantic 10 in its quest for contributors.

"In a lot of ways, they've got to be bigger," said Clawson of the Patriot League recruiting budgets, "because number one, you're bringing in bigger classes; number two, you're not redshirting kids, so you're on a four-year cycle as opposed to a five-year cycle; number three, you're allowed to have ninety-eight guys on your team as opposed to ninety, so you have a bigger team; number four, you've got to field a JV program; number five, because you're not giving kids full scholarships, there's a lot more attrition."

Pete Lembo, who served as head coach at Lehigh for five seasons before taking over at Elon University in 2006, agreed with Clawson's perspective on the increased emphasis on recruiting budgets.

"Typically they are going to be bigger, because you need to go further to find your pool," said Lembo. "And it's not just sending a coach to that area that's more costly, it's then flying that recruit in, and going back in the spring to locate more juniors, and so on. You really have to be able to recruit large numbers. There are more steps to the process, you have to be more thorough, and you have to be more organized."

And while in theory, the Patriot League model was supposed to yield a higher-quality student than in the scholarship world, that was not necessarily the case in practice. All the football programs in the Patriot were supposed to operate within the framework of an academic index, a formula factoring in SAT score, GPA, and class rank whereby recruits had to be within two standard deviations of the average for the entire student body of the university. But the notion of the academic index was a policy to be enacted on an institution-by-institution basis, as opposed to a hard-standing, enforceable rule, and a few of the better Patriot League schools had been known to look the other way here and there on recruits that might not have fallen within the two-standard-deviation line.

A major problem lending itself to this abuse of the policy was that the best of the academically oriented players on the radar screens of Patriot League schools were probably also being recruited by the Ivy League, and with all things being equal, few were going to pass up the perceived better education in the Ivy to attend a Patriot university. If a player was not quite Ivy material academically but was a targeted Patriot League prospect for football-related reasons, the Atlantic 10 or another full-scholarship league would likely snap him up with their more enticing financial offer and the prospect of playing in a better conference. The net effect of the arrangement, as far as the Patriot League was concerned, was that the academic profile of the football team was potentially not as good as it would have been if the school awarded actual scholarships.

"You lose the better students," explained Clawson. "If those kids can get into an Ivy League school, they're not going to pick the Patriot over the Ivy, because the financial package is going to be similar. Whereas at Richmond or at Villanova, occasionally we would beat the Ivy League on players because number one, it was a full scholarship so the financial difference could be substantial enough, and number two, the kid perceived it as a much better level of football. You have a chance to play for a national championship, which you can't do in the Ivy. In the Patriot, you're never beating the A-10 [for players] and you're rarely ever beating an Ivy, unless there's a special situation. Most kids, if they have a scholarship offer, aren't even going to fill out those financial aid forms."

Like Clawson, Lembo had met with both sides of the double-edged Patriot League sword while coaching at Lehigh. "If I went down to south Jersey and recruited a kid from Shawnee High School and Penn wanted him, nine times out of ten we were going to lose him to Penn," said Lembo. "Because the way that family would look at it is, 'I'm going to pay the same amount to go to Lehigh or Penn, I might as well get that degree with the three letters next to it.'

"And at the same time, I was in a household where we lost a kid to a very, very average academic institution who could have gotten a good summer job and probably paid the amount he needed to pay to come to our place, simply because it was not a full scholarship. That was the mindset of that family, and that was more valuable than the Lehigh degree."

Essentially, the schools in the Patriot League were attempting to find players who fit in the small window between Ivy League academics and Atlantic 10 talent, a major challenge that didn't always satisfy either the academic mission of the school or the football program's quest for a championship.

"It's hard recruiting in that league," said Clawson. "You're trying to find kids that you can get in, but can't get into an Ivy. The Ivy League, those programs are very well-run, they're very well-coached and they're very thorough in recruiting. You're not going to find a kid that's a great student that nobody in the Ivy has found, and so you're working a very fine line of guys that aren't quite Ivy, but they can still get into your schools.

"It's very hard, that's why we had to recruit nationally, to find a guy, one that can get in, two that can help you win, that is also a high-need kid. There were a lot of great kids that were great fits for Fordham that we couldn't make it affordable for because the parents were middle-class."

Clawson was among those who believed that the Patriot League football system, while well-meaning in its quest to promote academics above athletics, was inherently flawed at its core.

"I think the sell is, 'Hey, we're like all the other students,' but they're not," said Clawson. "They're still getting preferential packages. And I think to a certain degree the [schools in the Patriot League have] admitted it doesn't work, because they give scholarships in basketball now. If it's such a great model, why do they give scholarships in basketball?"

As Lembo saw it, the scholarship football model currently employed at Villanova for football was the preferable option to the Patriot League way of doing business, and the state of basketball in his former league was a case study for that argument.

"Going scholarship in basketball has allowed the Patriot League schools to recruit a better-quality student, because the kid who might otherwise go to an Ivy and pay twenty or thirty thousand dollars, now [Patriot universities] have a legitimate chance to beat [the Ivies] head-to-head on," said Lembo. "And that same kid, now knowing he can go to Lehigh for free, is not going to choose an inferior academic institution over Lehigh simply because it's free."

For the moment, Villanova was not seriously exploring moving its program to the Patriot League, though the possibility of that discussion somewhere in the future felt a bit like the elephant in the room to those who favored scholarship football on the Main Line. Luckily, the university's current profile as a part of the Big East at least supported the argument that being affiliated with different types of schools was no great tragedy either.

"It comes up from time to time," said Randazzo, referring to the Patriot League discussion. "Some of the board members feel that that's where we should be, with those kinds of schools. Until you bring up basketball. Then they change their minds."

Villanova made its three-hour trek to Lewisburg fully comprehending the importance of coming back to the Main Line a winner. The losses to New Hampshire and Richmond had for entirely different reasons been like punches to the gut, and if the Wildcats didn't hit back against Bucknell, the fight was going to be, for all intents and purposes, over.

Talley's team was in a tenuous position as far as the playoffs were concerned, but they hadn't given up the postseason as a goal either. It would take six straight wins to end the season in order to make it happen, and the Cats could not afford to slip up, but the Bucknell tilt would be followed by home games against Rhode Island and William and Mary and a road trip to Towson, all winnable in their own way. If Villanova could find its way to 6-3, the final two games, against James Madison and Delaware, would at the very least be meaningful.

If he wanted his team to get to mid-November with a shot, Talley knew he was going to have to make some significant changes.

He'd seen enough of Adam James, who had four extra points either missed or blocked through five games, much too high a number for a team that wasn't scoring touchdowns with great regularity. Talley didn't have confidence in James's field goal leg beyond about 35 yards either, and he thought freshman Joe Marcoux, who had been impressive on kickoffs, represented a better option in that regard. James would still be the punter, but when Talley brought him in to tell them that the team would be using Marcoux on placements until further notice, James bristled.

"It pretty much pissed me off, because it is my senior year and I thought I've had a pretty good run at it," said James, who wasn't going to allow himself to shoulder the blame for the missed kicks. "They all got blocked right up the middle, in between the guard and center, and we finally got that straightened out."

James thought the coaches were pinning the struggles of the special teams on him in a less-than-equitable fashion, and he expected all his hard work for the team in the past four seasons to be at least acknowledged, if not rewarded.

"When they name out, 'It's the last go-round for all these guys,' I've never been mentioned the whole season. The only time they talk to me is to tell me to speed up my get-off time. I put up with a lot of crap. This is the first year I've had a long snapper that could actually get the ball to me. My [punting] average has been worse because I'm running behind my head catching balls, punting from like 30 yards behind the line of scrimmage, but still getting them off. Killing my average every game, but doing it for the team, never once said anything about it."

The kicker was at least somewhat aware that the coaching staff was unimpressed with his attitude, but he said that his seeming lack of fire was a misunderstood element of his personality.

"If I miss a field goal, I don't go and beat my head against the wall or something like that, which I think they would rather me do. But that wouldn't be good, because it would get me totally out of the game. In high school I used to have a lot more emotional reaction to different stuff, but as I've matured I've learned that it's not productive for me at all as a kicker. You have to be able to learn to control your emotions."

The James conversation wasn't the only awkward repartee that Talley would have leading up to the Bucknell game. Darrell Adams, the preseason All-America defensive end who was poised to lead the defense in 2005, had been a disappointment as the season neared its midway point. After starting the season off with a sack in the Rutgers game, Adams had been slowed by an infection against Northeastern, which in turn caused him to miss the Penn game. Adams hadn't been much of a factor in the 28-point loss to New Hampshire or the previous week's defeat at Richmond, and Talley was concerned not only with the fact that his tri-captain hadn't been himself but was also worrying how Adams's average play had affected his status with the NFL scouts.

Talley pulled Adams aside during warmups, reminding him how important he was to the fabric of the team and how vital the next six games would be to his future in football.

"He said, 'Your stock's kind of dropping as far as what you what you want to do for next year,'" recalled Adams. "'Now that you're healthy, it's go time, you've got to be Darrell Adams again. You have to reestablish who you are. You don't have two or three warm-up games to get this thing rolling, you've got to turn the switch on now.'"

Adams, one of the most coachable and overall most pleasant players on the team, respected Talley's approach and took his words to heart. "To hear that coming from him was definitely a boost," said Adams. "Coach T always tells you the truth, he's an honest man. To have that perspective up front is definitely helpful. I wasn't being the difference-maker that I knew I could have been."

Sensing that his team lacked leadership, it was during the Bucknell week that Talley had initiated a "Keepers of the Flame" society on his team. The Keepers of the Flame, which included captains Adams, Dieser, and Hulea, but also extended to players who were established and respected, like J. J. Outlaw, Allyn Bacchus, and Christian Gaddis, were supposed to make sure that the rest of the team was focused on its responsibilities and to serve in a leadership role. Talley's message to the Keepers of the Flame was that if the Wildcat players didn't take ownership of this team right now, the season would be lost, and that it was the responsibility of those who put on the uniforms, not the coaches, to make sure everyone was invested in the task at hand.

Talley hoped that the players understood his point, but he was unsure about how a group of players who seemed to become increasingly and frustratingly dispassionate with every loss was going to respond to the changes, if at all.

Talley and his coaching staff seemed less tense than usual prior to the Bucknell game, with the shaky quality of the opponent probably having much to do with that demeanor. Also lending to the good vibes was the setting. Bucknell's Christy Mathewson Memorial Stadium, named after the former Bucknell student and New York Giants right-hander, was a thirteen thousand-seat facility with a classy brick façade around the perimeter of the field and the name of the university spelled out in a large garden of hedges behind one of the end zones. It was a perfect stadium for most I-AA schools, and apart from the press box area and small locker rooms (Villanova's newly renovated press box was probably the best in I-AA), it was a much nicer facility than Villanova Stadium.

Talley sensed that with his players hungry for a win, there wasn't much that he needed to say to motivate them. After reminding his kickoff and punt returners to respect the stiff wind that was blowing on this sunny October afternoon, he took all of four sentences to sum up the big picture.

"Get on these guys early. It's a one-game season, it's what happens inside the big rectangle today at 1:03, guys. We've played hard, we've worked hard. Keepers of the Flame, let's get it going."

The flame would begin burning early, and for perhaps the first time all season, would remain lit for sixty minutes.

Bucknell would get the ball first, and would manage just one first down before the drive stalled. After the Bison punted, it would take but one play for the Cats to establish their dominance. Lining up on the left side of the field, J. J. Outlaw took Frank Jankowski's handoff and swept around the right end, dashing basically untouched 63 yards for a touchdown. The first PAT attempt of Joe Marcoux's career sailed through the uprights, and it was 7–0. This was going to be easy.

Bucknell would punt on its next drive, and Jankowski, playing just forty miles from his home in Berwick, drove Villanova close enough for Marcoux to kick his first field goal as a collegian to make the score 10–0 in favor of the Cats. It was the first significant lead Talley's team had held since the latter stages of the Northeastern game in Week 2.

The Wildcat defense would give up a couple of first downs to the overmatched Bison on the next drive, but after the home team got bogged down near midfield, the quarterback Ross bluffed running a play before punting the ball. Bucknell really was asking Ross to do everything, it seemed.

Four plays after Ross's pooch, Jankowski connected with Outlaw for a 74-yard pass play that got the Wildcats all the way down to the Bucknell 13, and moments later, on a third-and-goal play, Jankowski sneaked in for a 1-yard touchdown. Seconds into the second quarter, Villanova had a 17–0 lead, and their talent advantage was patently obvious. The Bison got on the board with a 42-yard field goal later in the second half, but Villanova answered right back with a five-play, 46-yard drive that culminated in a TD pass from Jankowski to Dieser from 6 yards out. As the Wildcats trotted to their locker room, the scoreboard at Mathewson Stadium read 24–3 in favor of the visitors. Villanova needed this, desperately.

Talley implored his players to finish the job, though there was little doubt that something less than a one-hundred-percent effort in the final thirty minutes probably would have been enough.

"In our sixth game of the year, let's develop the maturity that we need to make a run. Let's manage this game. You know anything can happen in the second half. They're gonna kick off, be ready for onside kicks. They're behind, so they can only run the ball so many times. At some point the kid's got to pull the ball up and start throwing it. So be ready for that, don't give them anything cheap. Stay in the game, physically and mentally. You're doing a great job on both sides of the ball. We could not ask for a better half. We got our penalties down to two penalties in the first half. Two. Let's make it zero in the second half."

Talley was sure to remind his charges what had happened against Bucknell one year prior, when the Bison had rallied from a 20-point deficit to cut the lead to six in the latter stages of the game.

"Let's manage this game in the third quarter and kick these guys off the field," said Talley. "Last year, we went out with our head up our ass and then fought for our life in the fourth quarter. Do not do that. Do not do that. Let's get the maturity we need, let's stay positive, work together, and let's go get 'em."

Villanova more or less called off the dogs in the second half, just as Rutgers had done for them in a similar situation back in Week 1. Jankowski threw a third-quarter pick inside the Bucknell 30, but he came back the next drive and threw another TD pass to Outlaw to increase the lead to four touchdowns, 31–3. On that same drive, running back Moe Gibson, who had not been a major factor in the game plan for weeks due mainly to the team's scoreboard deficits and the struggles of the offensive line, had made impressive runs of 22 and 50 yards en route to his first 100-yard day of the season. Once his friend Outlaw crossed the goal line again, it was all over but for the shouting.

Later, Jankowski would find Dieser for just the second time all game, and the completion went for a touchdown to extend the lead to 38–3. The Bison would have the final word, when the one-man team that was Ross rushed for a meaningless 16-yard touchdown with twenty-one seconds to play against Villanova's second-string defense, but that play did little to diminish the satisfaction of the Wildcat players and staff.

It had been a breeze for a team that needed a positive moment in a big way and had been looking for a win to reestablish some confidence heading into the season's second half.

The initial returns on Talley's changes had all been positive. Marcoux had kicked well, making all five of his extra points and a field goal. Adams had bounced back and made an impact, notching a couple of tackles behind the line of scrimmage and breaking up one of Ross's rare pass attempts. The Keepers of the Flame had taken on a noticeable leadership role, though admittedly, that stance was made a lot easier by the circumstances of the blowout win. Bucknell was not a very good team, but that wasn't going to keep anyone, least of all Talley, from cherishing the victory.

"Congratulations on a really fine win, you guys did what you had to do and you did it as well as you could possibly do it," Talley told the team before heading across the field with Jankowski to answer questions from a handful of assembled reporters.

In the press conference, the head coach praised his sophomore quarterback, who threw for 234 yards and three touchdowns while throwing just five incomplete passes, and he also credited the Cats' superior team speed as a factor in the easy victory.

By the time Villanova's busses returned to campus, many of the university's students had seen the Wildcats' football score scroll across the television. They weren't going to be welcoming the football team back to campus with any type of reception, because those types of things just didn't happen at Villanova and because the decisive nonconference win over a lesser opponent didn't deserve such adulation.

But if the school's student body had less awareness of the victory than usual, a glance at the calendar on the wall could offer a strong indication why. It was October 15, which meant there would be meaningful activity in The Pavilion, Villanova's on-campus arena, this Saturday. Basketball practice had begun in Wildcat country.

10

COMING HOME

By Week 8 of the season, and with a record of 3-3, every remaining contest on the 2005 schedule held major importance for Villanova's football program. But the Wildcats' October 22 matchup with Rhode Island had significance beyond the vagaries of playoff and championship implications. It was homecoming weekend at Villanova, a time for alumni to return to campus and reminisce about their experiences on the Main Line, while getting perhaps their lone glimpse of the football team's work during the 2005 season.

The game, scheduled for 3:00 Saturday afternoon, was at the center of the weekend's festivities and was to be preceded by an alumni family picnic on Saturday and the men's basketball team's "Hoops Mania" event on Friday night in The Pavilion. All points on the homecoming itinerary were supposed to lead up to the football game, but whether the Villanova–URI matchup or the basketball practice was the most-anticipated event on the schedule was a matter of debate.

Either way, it was good to be home for Andy Talley and his Wildcats. The month of November, the final one of the regular season, was but ten days away, and the fact that Villanova was appearing in its own stadium for only the second time all year was not lost on the head coach. As much of a joyous homecoming as it was for the VU alumni, the football team was also delighted to be reacquainting itself with its friendly confines after four straight games on someone else's turf.

Homecoming always brought with it its own brand of excitement for the players and coaches, and the pageantry surrounding the 2005 game heightened that sense of anticipation. Brian Westbrook, Villanova's most famous football alumnus of the moment, would be returning to the university to participate in a jersey-retirement ceremony. The presence of one of the Philadelphia Eagles' most visible stars was expected to increase media interest and attendance at Saturday's game. After Dean Kenefick sent a Tuesday press release announcing the retirement ceremony, the *Daily News* and the *Inquirer* had run stories on the matter. Kenefick wasn't surprised that the papers had picked up on his release. It was an Eagles story, after all.

The football program would also on Saturday be celebrating the twentieth anniversary of the 1985 team, Talley's first at the university and the one that had reintroduced the sport on campus. Around forty players from that team would be returning for a Friday night dinner at the home of Dave Pacitti, a freshman offensive tackle on the '85 club, and they would also be honored with a pregame reception in the west end zone. Under Talley's leadership, the school had also put together a twentieth anniversary DVD for each returning player, including old TV clips and highlights from that season as well as a miniature replica helmet and plaque given to each.

It was a testament to Talley's ability to build relationships with his players that so many would attend, coming from all parts of the country to share in the experience. The head coach made it a point to establish a rapport with his players from the moment they walked onto campus, nurtured those relationships throughout their four- or five-year stay at Villanova, and regularly checked in with them long after they were gone. Whether they had been stars, significant contributors, or walk-ons, a vast majority of Talley's charges left Villanova feeling good about their experience, a fondness for their alma mater that the head coach valued greatly.

Talley knew that disgruntled groups of players weren't going to go out of their way to sell the program via word of mouth, and they also wouldn't be among those inclined to offer the donations that were so vital to keeping Villanova competitive. The footage of the 1985 team was striking, and not only because of Talley's relative youth and the overall smaller size of the players. A glance at the video also reflected a much different energy surrounding the Villanova program than what existed twenty years later. The Wildcats played just a five-game schedule in 1985, with all of the contests coming against Division III or junior varsity competition. But excitement over the program's return, and the expectation of greater things to come, led each of Villanova's three home games, as well as the spring football intrasquad scrimmage, to be sold out. Footage showing Villanova supporters tailgating prior to games could have easily been mistaken for video shot on a normal Saturday at Penn State or at Pitt.

That type of enthusiasm had diminished at some stage in the twenty years that followed, and the buzz had by 2005 reached a point where most of Villanova's alumni were indifferent to the prospects of returning to campus for homecoming. A number of factors that were well beyond the university's control had led to this gradual erosion of excitement, including the natural evaporation of the novelty surrounding football's return and the competition that Villanova football now faced from the dozens of college games dotting the television landscape on a typical Saturday.

But major decisions that Villanova had made in regard to football in the previous two decades were part of the prevailing attitude toward the sport as well, most significantly the decision to keep the program at the I-AA level, and also the banning of large-scale tailgating on campus.

These factors were the ones that Bill Nolan read and heard most often in respect to the alumni's general ambivalence toward football. Few were able to gauge the sentiments of Villanova's alumni, particularly the sports-loving contingent, better than Nolan, the administrator of the university's most widely read unofficial Internet message board at Vusports.com. Nolan had been around Villanova athletics basically his whole life, since his father, Bill, a 1957 graduate of the university, had brought his son along to basketball and football games as a child. The younger Nolan matriculated at the university as well, graduating in 1996, soon after which he launched Vusports.com as a part-time pursuit. The enterprise grew in stature during the Internet age, and Nolan, probably more so than anyone outside of the football office or athletics administration, was by now in a position to hear unfiltered opinions from alumni on a daily basis.

As a long-time loyalist of both the university and the football program, Nolan had fully formed and well-educated opinions on the attitudes toward the sport at Villanova. "I kind of group Villanova alumni and fans in general into three categories," said Nolan. "The first category, the category that I fit in, my father fits in, a bunch of guys who use our website fit in, and that's just people who will go to Villanova football games because they like football, and they think Villanova, whatever level we play in, plays a pretty good brand of football and it's a pretty exciting game to go to. For that group, if we're in the Patriot League or the A-10 or in the Big East, we're going to go to games. We just like to go.

"The second group is a group of fans who would go to Villanova football games, but would only go to Villanova football games if we were at a I-A level and played a I-A-type schedule. That doesn't necessarily mean you have to play a Miami, Florida State–type I-A schedule, but nonetheless play a I-A schedule.

"And then there's a third group which are people who might or might not be basketball fans but are alumni of the school who just don't care about football. They'd never go to a football game, or maybe they'd go once every ten years."

For the latter two of Nolan's three categories of alumni, it was the presence of the behemoth basketball program, which for decades had participated at an elite level, that had long left Villanova football in the shadows. These groups couldn't connect with the schools the Wildcats were facing on the gridiron, ones that didn't have the same type of brand identity that their alma mater had achieved via its hoops program.

"I think the casual Villanova fan, from a basketball perspective, gets very excited about being able to play UConn, being able to play Georgetown, being able to play Notre Dame," said Nolan. "Whereas it's tough, and nothing against these schools because they're fine schools, but Maine, UMass, Northeastern? With the exception of a school like Delaware, which is a natural rivalry or maybe William and Mary, Villanova, I don't think, has a lot in common with the other schools that are on its football schedule."

According to Nolan, the Big East was considered the major leagues, and Villanova's current level of football was something that most alumni considered to be far short of that plateau.

"I don't know if I'd call it a stigma, but I do think it creates an environment where people at a Villanova or a Georgetown believe their schools athletically are at a higher level then the other schools they're competing against on a football basis. So if you're competing against a UConn, you're competing against a Louisville, you're competing against all those schools in basketball, you go up against Dukes and UNCs for recruits in basketball, and in football you're going up against Colgate and Hampton and the other I-AA schools, I do certainly think that that has some impact."

The success of the Villanova grid program at its current level was a moot point to many Wildcat supporters. When the 1997 team was ranked No. 1 in I-AA, the residual disappointment from the recent decision not to move to I-A had a counterproductive effect to the positive feeling created by that success. In 2002, when the Cats reached the national semifinals and made an exceedingly rare appearance on national television, the unfamiliarity of the competition the program was facing underlined what the anti-I-AA throng at Villanova considered to be a minor league association.

"From a Villanova basketball fan's perspective, there's just so many things that come into play that actually bias fans against the product," remarked Nolan. "I think more fans turn on the game and say, 'Where the hell is McNeese State, and who the heck are they?' I think that's what the bigger problem is, what the heck does Villanova have to do with McNeese State? There's not a lot of association with some of the schools you play.

"You could make the same argument that 'What does Villanova have to do with Florida in basketball?' But I think Villanova fans, rightly or wrongly, associate themselves as being a major university and think about as ourselves as a peer of BC or a peer of Georgetown or a peer of Holy Cross, which even though it fields I-AA football, is a national college. They don't really associate ourselves with McNeese State or Appalachian State. That's not taking anything away from those institutions, but it's just the perspective that Villanova fans have. That's one of the real big things that goes against us.

"Most of the people I encounter respect Villanova's performance given its I-AA affiliation. Having said that, I think a big chunk of people look at Division I-AA football and associate it with Division II or Division III football. There are still a lot of people who believe it's an outstanding brand of football and it's a heck of a lot of fun to watch. The reality is, Villanova playing Delaware is a heck of a great game, but I think we're certainly in the minority [in feeling that], and I think if you look at the attendance figures, it would show that.

"I think it's a shame that more people haven't had a chance to see guys like Brian Finneran, Brian Westbrook, Curtis Eller, Chris Boden, Brett Gordon, guys like that, or a Ray Ventrone. It's a shame that more people haven't had a chance to watch some of these guys play because they look at it and say, 'Division I-AA football is not the same, it's a lower quality.'

"There's a disparity between the level of play and the level of interest. Are we beating Notre Dame? No, we're not going to beat Notre Dame. At the same time, that ESPN Thursday night football game that's the Mountain West Conference against some other team, to me there's not that much of a difference in that quality of play and what you see at the I-AA level, but there's a big difference between how many people are watching those games."

In addition to the lack of name cachet and level of competition that Villanova's football association wrought in the eyes of certain alumni, the shifting sands of the collegiate conference landscape were also an element of concern to Villanova supporters.

Of the six conferences that made up the BCS, the Big East was the only one containing core members that were not part of the football makeup of the league. In addition to Villanova and Georgetown, five institutions—DePaul, Marquette, Providence, Seton Hall, and St. John's—did not field I-A football programs, and an eighth school, Notre Dame, was an independent part of the BCS but was not required by the league to play a Big East football schedule.

There had been widespread speculation in Big East circles that sooner rather than later, the eight football members of the Big East—Cincinnati, Connecticut, Louisville, Pittsburgh, Rutgers, South Florida, Syracuse, and West Virginia—would break off from the eight nonfootball members, leaving Villanova's basketball program in a "Catholic school" league with like-minded universities but also diminishing its conference strength and recruiting power, not to mention the overall image of the university. It was this thinking that led some Wildcat supporters to consider I-A the attractive option for the football program, regardless of whether the program could achieve success at that level in terms of wins and losses.

"Relative to the population that participates in our forums, I think the percentage of people that say we should go I-A is large," explained Nolan. "I would say it's probably a majority, probably in the 40 to 50 percent range, that say we should go I-A football. There are a lot of those folks that say that because they believe it would protect our basketball program. And there's a lot of folks out there whether they're in category one, two, or three, who at the end of the day associate Villanova with basketball and would argue that you need a I-A football program in the coming years to protect your basketball program with our ability to be in the conference."

In addition to concerns about the level of play and the political climate, many average Villanova fans, along with some current students on campus, felt little connection with football at the university because of the absence of what had long ago become one of college and professional football's foremost rituals: tailgating.

Tailgating at Villanova was confined to one small parking lot behind the football stadium by 2005, and consumption of alcohol was monitored closely by VU public safety. The university had more than a decade ago become concerned with the potential consequences of the excess drinking and vandalism that went on at the tailgates, and while that may have been the prudent move from a legal and societal standpoint, football games at Villanova were no longer the social event that they had been prior to the enacting of the policy.

"My perspective has been and always will be," said Nolan, "that a real big reason for [the lack of interest] is for a school like Villanova, given some of the other challenges of I-AA football, there's no tailgating allowed for students. And I can't necessarily blame the school, because tailgating encourages drinking and bad things happen with that. Be that as it may, for kids who are college kids to go out on a Friday night and get up for a Saturday morning game when you're playing against Maine, there's nothing in the tailgate to get kids out who aren't really big college football fans. Because there's no tailgating, there's nothing sort of social about it per se. So kids will just sleep in late, 12:00 rolls around, they'll turn on ESPN and watch "Gameday" and they'll start watching Penn State or the Michigan game or the Ohio State game, or in Villanova's case a lot of times, the Notre Dame game rather than the Villanova game. My perspective is if they had tailgating and they had sort of a more social outlet for students, I think more students would come to the game and it would be better-attended from a student perspective.

"When Nova brought back football in '85, tailgating was allowed. For the first four or five years, every Nova football game was sold out, packed, and tailgating was a big scene. Students tailgated, young alumni tailgated. And there was absolutely something about its novelty, that they were bringing back football, that was big and was sort of attractive, but I also think the game day activity that you see at a Penn State or a Michigan, where it's an event, also made people come back."

But the university clamped down on tailgating in the late 1980s, allowing widespread tailgating only at homecoming, before totally banning it in the main parking lots in 1993.

"You combine the [I-AA concerns with the] fact that there's no tailgating, which makes it less of an event then you see at I-A schools, or frankly other I-AA schools that have tailgating. It becomes more than just 'Hey, its a football game,' and there's a lot of Villanova alumni that don't want to spend a Saturday watching Nova play any one of those schools that I mentioned, unless there's something else that kind of makes an event of it.

"I think if you looked at the attendance of Villanova football from students and alumni you'll see a pretty strong correlation between tailgating and their attendance."

A Vusports.com forum topic that Nolan started relating to football gave rise to all of the usual complaints about the direction of football at the university. One poster typified the elitist attitude of many Villanova alumni.

> I drive down from North Jersey for every basketball-related event because our basketball team is big time, playing in the best college basketball conference in the country. However, our football program is not big time. I try to make it down for a couple of games a year & will go see them if they are playing local (i.e., I went to the Nova-Rutgers game last year). However, it's hard for me to get really pumped up about playing James Madison. Now, if we were playing in I-A, I'd drive down to Nova with a keg in the back seat ready to party! I believe when we played Temple downtown at the Linc a few years ago attendance was very good.
>
> I just think the level of competition is what attracts people. If the university is making decisions based soley [*sic*] on the current attendance at I-AA games they have a serious flaw in their formula (in my opinion).

Another fan showed that even Villanova's current base of football supporters had their reservations about the level, not to mention the game-day atmosphere and media coverage.

> I love the excitement and pageantry of big time IA football and as much as I have enjoyed traveling each year to SEC/Big 12/Big

> 10 and other sites to take in huge games, I would love to have a team of my own to be on the big stage. I still follow our team very closely and make three or so games a year, but being it is I-AA, outside the game itself, there really is not much excitement for a game/weekend. No buildup in the papers/media for a big game (maybe a tad for a UD game), no large scale tailgating, no throngs of coeds in the stands cheering loudly and genuinely, no national TV exposure, no bowl games in warm weather in the winter, no big recruiting battles, etc . . .

And as on most public forums, there was widespread misinformation being bandied about by some posters. To wit, a forum participant swung and missed on the financial and gender equity ramifications of a move to I-A, wasn't sure how far Villanova advanced in its last trip to the postseason, and was unaware of what other Big East schools fielded the sport.

> We already have a solid base of a football program to start with. It's not like we don't have a football team. We need to add what, 20 more scholarships & rent out a stadium? Even if you have to take a major loss the first few years you do it for the benefits down the road! As far as the argument made by the opponents that "We made it to the National Championship game & still no one showed" the answer to that is quite simple. There's your proof that no one gives a sh*t about I-AA football. Guess what, if you make it to the championship game & people still don't go you know what that means? People will NEVER go. As a result, either upgrade to I-A or close up shop!!
>
> By the way, it is just my opinion but I have always felt that I-AA football exists as an insurance policy. The school does not want to go I-A unless it has to. HOWEVER, I believe if push comes to shove & the choice is given "Either move to I-A or join a new A-10 for all sports that we will ultimately make the move at that point but only if we are forced to." I think by keeping I-AA around it keeps Nova as a Top choice for moving up to I-A. We are certainly better than

> the other Catholics schools in this regard. If we absolutely had to I think we could. If some of the others had to, it would be much more difficult. Hell, does Seton Hall, St. John's & Georgetown even have a football team?

One thing was clear by the afternoon of October 22, and it wasn't the sky. Autumn was here.

The remnants of Indian summer had held on in the Northeast well into October, but on this day, it appeared that it was time to give up that ghost. The temperature was in the low fifties at Villanova Stadium, but with torrential rainfall and the wind blowing at ten to fifteen miles per hour, it felt much colder than that. In other words, the exact opposite of the type of weather that anyone associated with the university would want to see on a homecoming Saturday.

Thousands of alumni, not to mention their families, would stay away from Villanova's homecoming festivities due to the weather. Others would attend the alumni picnic in the weather-resistant indoor Pavilion, but weren't about to sit for three-plus hours in the rain, wind, and darkening sky above the football stadium. Athletic department officials estimated that five thousand fans had packed the basketball facility for Friday night's "Hoops Mania" event, and though twice that number could have been expected on a sunny homecoming Saturday at Villanova Stadium, given the conditions, the football game would be lucky to match Friday night's attendance numbers.

Talley was upset that the day honoring the 1985 team was such a washout, and as was always the case in such circumstances, he was concerned that the wet conditions were going to hinder his current squad's offensive game plan. Still, the head coach was cautiously optimistic that Villanova was going to pick up the win and move to 4-3 on the year, with the quality of the opponent, Rhode Island, lending itself to that positive outlook.

Rhode Island was annually one of the Atlantic 10's worst teams, as the football program had long lacked both the facilities and overall support to achieve any sustained success on the gridiron. The Rams hadn't won a conference title or been to the playoffs since 1985 and had posted just three winning seasons in the nineteen campaigns since that postseason appearance. It looked like URI was traveling down the same losing road in 2005, as Tim Stowers's team had followed a 3-0 start with four consecutive losses, including a 53–9 manhandling at New Hampshire the week before. The team's triple-option offense, similar to the one Bucknell had employed against Villanova seven days prior, was struggling, and Talley felt confident that his team was up to slowing down that style of attack.

What's more, Villanova had historically owned Rhode Island. The Rams were 1-12 all-time against the Wildcats, with their only win coming during the last of VU's three-year string of losing seasons in 1995, and they were 0-7 at Villanova Stadium. The last time Rhody had come to the Main Line, in 2002, they had left as 45–3 losers. There was suitable reason to believe that even in the bleak conditions, the home team was going to have a pleasant late afternoon and early evening.

In the home locker room beneath the stadium, the players gathered round. After Father Hagan led the team prayer, a different figure than Talley stepped toward the players to address the team. Brian Westbrook had been invited by Talley to speak to the club, and whether through his words, high profile, or impeccable Italian suit, the NFL star managed to captivate the group. Westbrook was a reserved and shy person by nature and had never been extremely comfortable when it came to public speaking, but when his alma mater or his former head coach called on him, he generally responded. Westbrook talked briefly about his own career at Villanova, told the team that he had seen signs of greatness in watching them from afar in recent weeks, and implored them, above all, to play hard on every play. When Westbrook had finished speaking, the players exited the locker room with a collective purpose. For the members of the team, especially the younger ones, Westbrook's presence in their home stadium would seem to have an inspirational effect. At least for a time.

With the weather hardly helping matters, both offenses took a while to find their footing. The Rams and Wildcats exchanged punts on their respective opening drives, and Rhode Island's second march stalled at the Villanova 30-yard line when the Cats stood firm on a fourth-and-one play. Frank Jankowski drove his offense past midfield but threw an interception that handed the football back to Rhode Island at the URI 22. Rhody would run its triple-option deep downfield, reaching all the way to the VU 3-yard line, but again the defense held, and Rhode Island settled for a field goal to make it 3–0 late in the first quarter.

Moments later, the Wildcats would give the homecoming crowd, announced to be 5,109 but probably closer to 3,000, something about which to cheer. On a reverse play similar to the one that had burned Bucknell in the early part of the previous week's game, J. J. Outlaw took a pitch from Jankowski and darted 66 yards all the way down to the 1-yard line. On the next play, Moe Gibson powered into the end zone for his first touchdown of the season, and after Joe Marcoux's extra point, the Cats led 7–3.

For a while, it appeared that the home team would take control, just as most everyone had expected. Following a stalled Rhode Island drive, Villanova backup running back Aaron Jones blocked a punt out of the back of the end zone for a safety to make the score 9-3. After acquiring the ensuing free kick near midfield, it took Nova all of three plays—a 13-yard run by Gibson, a 21-yard pass from Jankowski to Chris Polite, and a 17-yard dash to paydirt by fullback DeQuese May—to record their next touchdown. Less than a minute into the second quarter, Villanova led 16–3, and there was every reason to suspect that the visiting Rams would recede quietly into the night, just as they had so many times before in similar situations.

But on this moist and unpleasant day, things would not be nearly that easy for Talley's team. Rhode Island would respond and score on its next drive, as fullback Joe Casey burst through the line for a 13-yard touchdown run. When Villanova's next series went nowhere, Adam James had his subsequent punt blocked deep in Wildcat territory, and the kick was converted just three plays later into a short TD run for URI quarterback Jayson Davis. A 13-point lead had morphed into a 1-point deficit, 17–16 in favor of the Rams, in a little over three minutes' time.

On the Villanova sideline, what was quickly sinking in was that the Bucknell game had not been an acceptable primer for Rhode Island and their option attack. Davis and Casey were much more talented, not to mention more sure of themselves, than the Bison's offensive principles had been and were capable of chewing up chunks of yardage if the Wildcat defense failed to find its focus. In addition, Jankowski and the offense were going to have to do what they hadn't for most of the season—match their opponent score-for-score.

The Wildcats moved the ball quickly after getting it back, with Jankowski leading his unit to the Rhode Island 37, but the quarterback fumbled following a blindside sack on a third-and-eight play. On the very next snap, Davis slipped through a hole and rushed 40 yards to the Villanova 8-yard line, and the defense failed to prevent URI from reaching the end zone two plays later. The score was now 24–16, and the Wildcat defense, much like it had against New Hampshire, was allowing yardage and points at a rate that suggested Mark Reardon's group had lost the plot.

But in a much-needed encouraging sequence, Jankowski and the offense actually picked up the defense in a critical position. Needing a score to help stem the tide, the quarterback led the attack on an 11-play, 68-yard drive that consumed more than four minutes and culminated in a 2-yard touchdown pass from Jankowski to Matt Sherry in the back of the end zone. On two separate occasions during the drive, Jankowski completed third-down throws to keep the team moving, and even stood in and absorbed a jarring late hit that resulted in an important roughing-the-passer penalty. With less than a minute remaining in the first half, Villanova had taken back a portion of the precious momentum, and if the defense could figure out the Rhody option in the second half, this game was going to be theirs.

The 24–23 halftime score indicated that the game had been a run-and-shoot-type affair. But Rhode Island didn't shoot, they just ran, and they were doing so with complete effectiveness. With Talley committed to the Westbrook jersey retirement on the field, the assistant coaches and players were left to do most of the talking, or in this case scolding, at halftime.

Linebackers coach Sean Spencer, whose unit had struggled reading the Rhode Island option, took note of the 62 yards already piled up by nondescript Rhode Island fullback Joe Casey, screaming, "You're making this guy look like he's fucking Bronco Nagurski." Like that of Spencer, Reardon's voice raised to a high-decibel level when addressing his unit, as he lectured his group about their lack of individual discipline.

As for the players, Sherry laid out the big-picture context usually addressed by the head coach, alluding to the team's playoff prospects when reminding the players, "This second half is our season."

But the biggest halftime noise would be an admonishment by tri-captain Brian Hulea, who found a perfect opportunity to make an example of an underclassman.

Standing at his locker near the center of the Villanova locker room, reserve safety Marco Radocaj began removing his shoulder pads. Radocaj scarcely if ever played, and with the wind bearing down and the rain having soaked through his jersey, the sophomore had started the process of warming his shivering body by putting a dry sweatshirt on beneath his game shirt. It was a perfectly logical thing to do in normal society, but in a football locker room, where any hint of a lack of toughness was heretical to the winning cause, Radocaj was about to get an earful.

"Take that fucking sweatshirt off," Hulea screamed. "You've got to be fucking kidding me. We're trying to win a fucking game and you guys are worried about being cold? Fucking horrible!"

As Hulea ranted, out on the field, perhaps the finest player ever to wear a Villanova football uniform was experiencing a somewhat muted and extremely damp celebration. Barely visible beneath a group of giant golf umbrellas, Westbrook, his family, and his college head coach listened as local TV personality Don Tollefson read the star running back's list of college accolades. Forty-one school records. Nineteen conference records. Five NCAA marks. Three All-America citations. Winner of the Walter Payton Award as I-AA's top player. A résumé deserving of honor, if ever there was one. And while the applause wasn't going to be anything close to deafening in light of the small crowd, the appreciation from those Villanovans who were present to hear of what Westbrook had accomplished at the university seemed genuine.

But as Westbrook left the field, the stands at Villanova Stadium began to empty at an alarming rate. Even in a one-point game, many of the fans had seen enough. They had gotten their glimpse of NFL greatness and weren't going to sit through this mess any longer than they had to, even if there was a future pro star or two about to take the field in the second half. Homecoming had become more of a "Homegoing" for the modestly sized audience.

Talley retreated briefly to the locker room following the Westbrook ceremony, admonishing his players for the lack of toughness in a similar fashion to Hulea, and soon after, the players and coaches reemerged from the locker room into the rain and wind before a sea of empty seats.

Any positive effect that the tongue-lashing conferred upon the team by its tri-captain and coaching staff was likely wiped away to some degree by the defection of the crowd. The Wildcats went three-and-out on their first drive of the second half, with Outlaw dropping a pass that would have extended the march on third-and-eight. The drop was the normally sure-handed Outlaw's third of the game. To compound the problem, James had his second straight punt blocked, setting Rhode Island up in Villanova territory. Two plays later, Casey, whom Sean Spencer had flippantly compared to Bronco Nagurski just moments earlier, rushed right through three lines of Wildcat defense, Nagurski-like, for a 40-yard touchdown.

It was impossible to imagine a worse sequence to open the second half, as the offense, special teams, and defense, in that order, all contributed to Rhode Island establishing the second half tone and taking the momentum right back from Villanova.

Jankowski and the Cats again answered, however, putting together another long drive, extended when the quarterback hit John Dieser with a 20-yard pass play on third-and-two from midfield, and ended when Gibson rushed for his second touchdown of the day, on fourth-and-goal from the 1, minutes later. With 8:29 remaining in the third quarter, the score was 31–30 in Rhode Island's favor.

Though it seemed that the game was about to get wilder, the pace would slow considerably as the third quarter continued. The teams traded punts before Rhode Island got close enough to kick a 29-yard field goal to extend the lead to 34–30 near the end of the third quarter. Following that score, Moe Gibson returned a kickoff inside the Rhode Island 10-yard line, potentially setting up the go-ahead touchdown for the Wildcats, but a block in the back by backup receiver Anton Ridley negated the nice return. Talley was livid with Ridley, and understandably so, getting right in the sophomore's face and reading him the riot act upon his return to the sideline.

As the fourth quarter began, and needing desperately to pull his team out of deep rut in its own territory, Jankowski again embarked on a three-and-out, which following a James punt would set Rhode Island up with prime field position in Wildcat territory. Now it would be the defense's job to come up with a big play, but it wouldn't. Rhode Island moved the ball down the field at a painfully deliberate pace, never breaking a long run or deep pass play, but getting 3 or 4 yards at a time and burning nearly five minutes off the clock.

When Davis finished off the drive by rushing for a 1-yard touchdown, URI had pushed its lead back up to double digits, 41–30, with the clock reading just 9:46.

Desperate for a score, Villanova instead went three-and-out yet again. The VU defense tightened up to give the Cats the ball back near midfield with 6:48 to play, but a promising drive ended seconds later when Chris Polite, who had already made a couple of key catches on the day, fumbled while attempting to stretch the football for a few extra yards at the Rhode Island 15. The Rams recovered, and on the first play of the subsequent drive, Davis slipped through another gaping hole in the Wildcat defense and dashed basically untouched for an 85-yard touchdown.

Much like at Richmond, a close game had gotten out of hand late in the going. Rhode Island would sprint to its locker room as a 48–30 winner, scoring its first win in eight tries at Villanova Stadium, ending a four-game losing skid, and ruining what had become a disastrous homecoming for the Wildcats on several fronts. With its fourth loss of the season in the books, Talley's team could pretty much forget about the playoffs, the earliest the school had been effectively eliminated from that picture since 1998, and they could also wave goodbye to the prospect of even a share of the Atlantic 10 title. As if those indignities weren't enough, the Cats had given up 430 rushing yards, a new record for a Villanova opponent on the ground.

Talley was clearly shocked at the turn of events, and though he said little to his team in the deathly quiet and morose locker room, his embarrassment about the loss, and frustration over the turn the season had taken, were building as he climbed the steps to face the assembled media in the makeshift press conference area housed on the second floor of the press box. His team had just relinquished its postseason chances, and had done so against a perennial Atlantic 10 bottom-feeder, on its own home turf, during Homecoming, with the great Brian Westbrook, not to mention the 1985 team, looking on from the stands.

Kenefick, who coordinated the head coach's press conferences, had often remarked to media members how well Talley handled himself following losses. Talley always answered reporters' questions with honesty and insight, no matter how frustrating the defeat, and he seemed to have more of a philosophical, big-picture approach to both life and football than most in his position. Wins and losses were extremely important, but weren't the end-all, be-all, which fed into Talley's general even-keel demeanor after defeats. But the toxic combination of circumstances surrounding this loss had changed the normal chemistry within the man who had fathered the current era of Villanova football. Talley's flame would emerge with a flicker, until eventually, it would become an inferno.

"We turned it over twice," began Talley. "Frank throws an interception, which is a bad throw and not one that we want. And at a time when we need a catch, Polite fumbles the ball. But that's what happens on a day like today, you figure you're going to have a couple here and there. This game was so out of control that any turnover was going to hurt us more, because we weren't playing the way we were capable of playing in terms of supporting our defense. We did not support our defense with a quality offense, we just simply didn't. And if we do that against William and Mary, they'll put a hundred [points] on us."

Though at this stage, Talley clearly seemed more aggravated than usual, his postgame vitriol was of the routine variety for a head coach coming off a tough setback. His mood would worsen, however, and Frank Jankowski would soon become the object of Talley's disaffection.

"I felt with Marvin Burroughs we would be heard from during the season," remarked Talley. "We have to try and continue to get this kid, Frank Jankowski, prepared better, or make a change. The change I would make [would be] to go to a freshman, where we would have to really limit the game plan, and I don't know if we can compete in the league by doing that.

"We keep wishing that it's going to happen with Frank, and hoping that it's going to happen. He's in his first year of playing, so we're going to live with some mistakes, but we regressed, and he regressed, against not the world-beating defense of the league. There are better defenses in the league. So we have to decide whether we're going to stick with him, but he's just not seeing what we need done, or go to the freshman and roll the dice. If we do that, you sort of send a message to your seniors that it's over, and I don't want to do that either. So I'm stuck here trying to make this decision of what to do. But I can't come off the field like this every Saturday, knowing we left tons of points on the field that we should have had."

Jankowski had certainly not played well against Rhode Island, and there was no reasonable argument to be made to the contrary. Though he had made some good throws, engineered some decent drives, and his numbers (22 of 38 passing, 194 yards, 1 TD, 1 INT, 1 lost fumble, 3 sacks) did not signal an unmitigated disaster, just as had happened in the Richmond game, Jankowski had not been able to put the offense on his back in the fourth quarter to win the game. Chris Boden and Brett Gordon had both done that a great deal beginning in their sophomore seasons, and Marvin Burroughs, to a lesser degree, had been known to do the same.

But from an objective point of view, and even factoring in the accountability that a college quarterback must have in order to be successful, heaping so much responsibility on a sophomore quarterback making his sixth collegiate start was not entirely fair. Perhaps sensing this, Terry Toohey, the team's veteran beat writer from the *Delaware County Times*, attempted to change the subject, asking Talley about Rhode Island's record-setting rushing effort and the defense's inability to come up with consistent stops. For the most part, the head coach was not biting on Toohey's angle.

"That's what they do, they run the ball. I think they're maybe in the top three in the country in rushing, they certainly lead the league in rushing, they don't throw the ball at all. They're going to have 380 or 400 yards every game. The big thing is, don't give them the big plays that they had with [Davis] at the end of the game."

Talley would then make comments that he would almost immediately regret, comments suggesting that Jankowski's play had had negative ramifications for not just one game, but for the entire season. As his words bounced off the walls of the second floor of the Villanova press box, the coach's relationship with his starting quarterback would be forever fractured.

"We anticipated that we were going to be a team that scored 35 points a game offensively, and I felt we were a defense that was going to give up the high twenties. That's the way I looked at the season. And if we had our quarterback, that's what we would be doing, we'd be outscoring some people . . . We'd have won this game, we would have won a couple of others, maybe two. We might have won the Rutgers game. If Marv had not broke his arm we could have made the score 24–14 and then anything can happen, but that's just wishfully thinking."

Anyone who followed Villanova football closely had to hear Talley's words and cringe, not only for their impact on the young quarterback, but also for the coach that had let the emotions of a difficult day get the better of him. Talley loved his players, and with that love naturally came disappointment from time to time, but to the detriment of the head coach, Jankowski, and the team, his disappointment had manifested itself publicly. The Rutgers game had been 24-6 when Burroughs was injured, and Jankowski had played well in his place, a fact that Talley had heralded to both his team and the media immediately following that Week 1 defeat. Now it would seem that the head coach was attempting to write a revisionist history of not only that loss but of the entire season, which most everyone who knew Talley knew was not really in the head coach's nature.

Just as Toohey had tried to change the topic of conversation moments before, another media member jumped in and succeeded in affording Talley the opportunity to deflect some of the blame onto the equally inept special teams. Which may have been good news for Jankowski, though the same couldn't be said for the already battle-scarred punter.

"Adam James was horribly slow, horribly," said Talley of his punter, who had suffered two blocked kicks and nearly sustained a third. "And then on the other punt, the kick had slipped out of his hand, and that's how he kicked the thing end over end. He sure doesn't look like a fifth-year punter. Our whole special teams operation on a wet day [was] really, really sloppy."

And that was it.

Talley rose from the press table, descended the stairs, walked silently through the locker room past his players, by now in various stages of undress, crossed the tunnel leading to the field, and went into the football office. He sat down at his desk, lit up a cigar, and in a haze both literal and figurative, simmered down as the pain of defeat gave way to acceptance and a sense that the season wasn't over, not by a long shot.

With four games remaining, Talley began plotting how to make his next press conference a more pleasant affair, make his postgame cigar taste a little sweeter. A little more like the taste of victory.

11

THE PROSPECT

Andy Talley began the week of the William and Mary game with an apology.

Soon after making his "If we had 'our quarterback'" statement on Saturday night, Talley had felt bad about his statements regarding Frank Jankowski. While he may by now have truly believed that Burroughs could have been more consistent than Jankowski and perhaps won Villanova a couple more games, revealing those thoughts to a group of reporters was not the right move, Talley now realized. The head coach brought Jankowski into his office and admitted that he had yet to cool down from the difficult loss, and he shouldn't have said what he said. He told Jankowski that he still had confidence in him, still believed they could win some games, but that he had to cut down on the turnovers if the team was going to win.

For his part, Jankowski had only been vaguely aware of Talley's statements in the first place. He didn't read the newspapers, whether things were going well or going poorly, so everything he knew about Talley's Saturday night monologue came second-hand from friends or family. The quarterback was hurt and confused by the statements, but believed that Talley honestly regretted his words and prepared to move on to the business at hand.

The head coach had decided to apologize to Jankowski only after consulting with his coaching staff. Talley had been serious about letting the true freshman, Antwon Young, push Jankowski for the starting job, but the idea went over like a lead balloon with Villanova's offensive coaches. Young was too raw, both physically and mentally, and while it appeared that he could be a good player down the line, there was no way he was prepared to face William and Mary, the ninth-ranked team in all of I-AA.

The fact that Talley had even opened the door to the prospect of Young playing was an argument against his CEO-style role within the program. Had he been in the trenches with Young during drills as Sam Venuto and Mark Ferrante were, he might have been more hesitant to suggest that the freshman was ready to be the starter. To Talley's credit, however, he wasn't going to spend much time arguing with his coaches just because it was within his power to do so. And so it would be Jankowski until further notice. As Talley was issuing a mea culpa to his starting quarterback, Dean Kenefick was busy issuing the regular spate of press credentials for Saturday night's home game against William and Mary. Just as in each of the Wildcats' home games to date, included in that mix were passes for a handful of pro scouts. Three NFL scouts would be present this week, and while the trio would take at least a passing glance at wideout J. J. Outlaw and linebacker Brian Hulea, their main focus would be the tall defensive end wearing number 90, Darrell Adams.

Adams's year had been a disappointment, and he and the coaches knew it. His knee and elbow injuries, when they hadn't kept him off the field altogether, had at times turned him into simply an average player. In the second half of the Rhode Island loss, Adams, though generally healthy, often wasn't even in the game, a fact that would have been unthinkable heading into the season. With only four games left in a season that likely would not be ending with great team success, Adams needed to concentrate his attention on finishing strong from a personal standpoint. He was big, fast, and strong with great potential, but wasn't such a can't-miss prospect that he could afford to play poorly down the stretch, and he was going to have to catch someone's eye.

It was going to be more of an uphill battle for Adams to reach the next level than it would have been for a similar player at Penn State or Notre Dame or even Temple, but it wasn't as if he had to go knocking on doors to sell his wares. NFL scouting in 2005 was an exceedingly meticulous process, and there had been enough small-college success stories in the league over the past two decades to ensure that franchises would come out to watch a possible diamond in the rough at a non–football factory like Villanova. Brian Westbrook and Brian Finneran had thrived as NFL starters in the past decade, and the fact that the Cats had placed some other recent players like Ray Ventrone, Terry Butler, and former cornerback Clarence Curry on NFL rosters suggested that "the league" had woken up to the talent present at the I-AA school.

That Villanova football players had made it at the next level had to be encouraging to Adams, and the precedent of stardom set by other former I-AA standouts was another mark in his favor. Jerry Rice, out of tiny Mississippi Valley State, had been one of the best players in league history despite a college career spent in relative obscurity. Walter Payton, top three on any list of the NFL's all-time greatest running backs, had played his college ball at (then-Division II) Jackson State, a school in the I-AA Southwestern Athletic Conference. More recently, one-time I-AA quarterbacks Steve McNair (Alcorn State), Kurt Warner (Northern Iowa) and Rich Gannon (Delaware) had all started Super Bowls or won league MVP awards. As for defensive ends that Adams could pattern himself after, the Giants' Michael Strahan (Texas Southern) and the Chiefs' Jared Allen (Idaho State) were among the league leaders in sacks at this very moment.

I-AA players were rarely considered elite pro prospects, many times for the very same reasons that they had become I-AA players in the first place. Perhaps an inch too short, a fraction of a second too slow, or a few pounds underweight, and once on the NFL radar screen, always perceived to be "raw" or "a project" due to what was often unfairly viewed as an inferior level of both coaching and competition at the I-AA level. But what many scouts loved about I-AA and other "small school" prospects was a generally stronger work ethic than their I-A brethren.

Because they hadn't been groomed for pro stardom during their college careers, I-AA players often had less of a sense of entitlement, tended to work harder, and were more coachable at the next level.

Adams fit this description to a T. Like Strahan, Adams was the typical I-AA late-bloomer, a player who never received any type of meaningful interest from the top football programs because of his small size and a lower-tier high school program. Dimensions and high school pedigree weren't the only factors that Adams had overcome in developing into an NFL prospect.

Born September 16, 1983, in Jamaica, New York, a rough-and-tumble section of Queens, Adams had been the only child of a teenaged mother, Brenda, and an absentee father whom Adams never knew. Adams and his mother moved to the Long Island suburb of Bayshore when he was young, and an attraction to sports, particularly basketball, quickly formed.

Adams played football with the other kids in his neighborhood, playing organized ball for the first time in the seventh grade, but being tall and reed-thin growing up, he looked much more like a basketball forward than a football player. At Islip High School, basketball was indeed Adams's strength. A two-time all-league basketball player and an all-county choice as a senior, Adams also set the Islip school record for rebounding. Football, meanwhile, was an offseason pursuit that hardly brought with it any great status on Long Island.

"I catch flak all the time, New York football's not very good," said Adams. "We were a decent program, we went 6-2 my senior year, went to the playoffs. We were primarily a run team, we ran the option, the whole trap series, very basic. We competed, though we were twenty-two guys deep, so every guy played, everybody went both ways. It was fun."

People at Islip may have considered Adams to be a basketball player first, but since he wasn't being seriously recruited on the hardwood and given his size, speed, and aggressiveness, Islip football coach Joe Patrovich thought he might have in his midst a diamond in the rough on the gridiron. It was that feeling that led Patrovich to get in contact with Joe

Trainer, Villanova's defensive coordinator at the time and the school's recruiter for the New York metropolitan area. Trainer would not normally have been scouring Long Island for football talent, but Patrovich made his raw defensive end and center sound intriguing.

"[Patrovich] says, 'Joe, I got this kid, he's only 210 pounds but I think he's going to be big,'" remembered Trainer. "So I go up and see him, and he's 6-5, he's 210. I'm like, 'Man, this kid's big.' [But] he's thin too, Islip's not a football power, and Long Island football's not real good. But the thing I liked about him, he played center and defensive end, so he wasn't one of those kids who was afraid to mix it up and wanted to play receiver and D-end. As gawky as he was at center, he would mix it up, he would pass protect, he'd stick his nose in it. So at that point I thought he had some toughness about him. Then I went up and saw him play basketball, and this guy's dunking, he's chasing loose balls, he's on the floor, he's running the court. I said at that point, 'We gotta get this kid, and just pray to God he gets bigger.'

By now midway through his senior year of high school, Adams was a newcomer to the recruiting process, and the quiet Long Islander's lack of both interpersonal and football polish along with his less-than-prototypical size concerned Talley greatly. Adams showed up on his Villanova visit weighing just 212 pounds, not even big enough to play linebacker in some Atlantic 10 programs, and his ability to make conversation with Talley did not come naturally. Trainer was beginning to think he might lose the potential jewel he had just unearthed.

"Because he's not being heavily recruited, he doesn't know how to play the game," said Trainer. "Most kids, they have a coach that's in their ear saying, 'Hey, make sure they're recruiting you.' For kids who you're recruiting that have a lot of stuff going on, they like the process, they know what to say. Basically they're playing you as a recruiter.

"So here's this kid, he's wide-eyed, he's kind of soft-spoken, he's not real schooled up, and he visits in December. I'm thinking, 'I want to get this kid locked up before anyone else gets on him,' because somebody's going to take this kid. And ironically enough, Jerry Azzinaro, who was at Syracuse at the time, he had him scheduled for like a January twenty-ninth visit, which in I-A means you're the backup's backup. All they're doing at this point is saying that if the board falls apart four days before the signing date, maybe they try to place you in a prep school or something. And the only other school that's talking to him is Fordham, and [then–head coach] Dave [Clawson] and [then–defensive coordinator] Dave [Cohen] are good friends of mine.

"[To Cohen], I said, 'Dave, the head man's not crazy about him, what do I do?' He's like, 'Dude, if I was at Delaware, we'd be fighting for this kid.' I thought he was a winner, and in my ten conversations and four visits with him, I really thought he had a passion for the game."

Trainer, one of Talley's best salesmen as a recruiter, ultimately won his head coach over just as he had many a prospect. And Adams, more grateful than most for the opportunity he had been afforded, began working to make Trainer's faith in him pay off. After coming into camp during his freshman year weighing 222 pounds, Adams bulked up to 244 while redshirting and was beginning to look like a player who would see the field sooner rather than later. While absorbing a full-scale crash course in the intensity of the college game, Adams lifted, watched, and learned.

"I wasn't very highly recruited coming out of high school, so Villanova was like USC for me," said Adams. "I was a question mark coming in, I was undersized, didn't have a lot of football experience. I just worked my tail off in the weight room and elsewhere, learning the technique and taking to coaching.

"I knew I wasn't ready to play. And being that I wasn't a star, it wasn't a big ego trip for me. It was like, 'I understand this is my role on the team, to be a scout-team player, to give the offense the best look I can, and to get better myself. Redshirting that year really helped me out a lot. I took it as an opportunity rather than a knock."

Finding the right role models on the team also aided the young defensive end's progress. Adams buddied up to fifth-year defensive tackle Willie Lewis, who taught the youngster the necessity of competing on every play, no matter the situation, and not to expect to be celebrated for it.

Adams also learned to fit in on campus, which had been among Talley's chief concerns when he had shown tepid interest in recruiting the Long Islander. Once at Villanova, the skinny defensive end blossomed socially just as he had physically.

"You knew he was a nice kid, and to this day I still love talking to him because he's such a positive source of energy," recalled Trainer. "But I didn't know he was going to be as outspoken and kind of gregarious as he was when he showed up. And I think Villanova did him a lot of good too, because it really gave him a chance to be in an environment that was kind of nurturing, and at the same time he was able to forge an identity."

Trainer had seen hints of Adams's burgeoning maturity even when visiting him on Long Island as a highschooler. "Honestly, Darrell was kind of on his own. His mom was there, but he was going to make decisions. In that respect, he's a bit of an old soul. From a decision-making standpoint, he's been making them for a long time."

As a redshirt freshman in 2002, Adams played in thirteen games as part of a three-man rotation with Terence Taylor and Jamil Butler at defensive end, recording four sacks for the team that reached the national semifinals. He continued getting better as part of that rotation in 2003 and 2004, earning All-Atlantic 10 first-team honors in both seasons. During his junior year, with Taylor and Butler having emerged as senior leaders, Adams shifted to defensive tackle, where he thrived, recording forty tackles with ten tackles for loss and recovering five fumbles.

All the stars seemed to be aligned for a big 2005 for Adams, and Talley and the Wildcats needed the defensive end to assume the leadership role that he had earned via his play, but to date, things had not gone nearly according to plan. In the offseason, Trainer had left Villanova to become the head coach at Millersville, and Adams's position coach, Clint Wiley, had left the staff to take the helm of a prep school team, defections that had had a profound effect on Adams's demeanor. Then came the spring, when knee surgery had left the preseason All-American on the shelf, placing an abrupt delay on both his on-field development and his vital role within the leadership structure of the team.

"The spring was probably the start of the hardest calendar year of my life to date," reflected Adams. "Having the surgery, missing the spring, not being able to lead a young team on which I was supposed to be the premiere guy. Not being on the field every day, in the grind, was definitely stressful for myself and for my teammates.

"And then losing my two best friends as far as coaches were concerned was another adjustment I had to make. I was in a funk for a while. Coach Trainer was my recruiter, and he was also like my number-one fan. He always mentioned NFL from day one, he knew things I didn't know. As a coach, he could see the talent. And then Coach Wiley was like my big brother, I mean we were tight. It was like big brother, little brother–type stuff. And when they left at the same time, all the air was out of my system, because I had lost my whole [recruiting] class too."

Adams had not been a hundred percent to start the season, as the knee problems that cropped up again during August practices greatly diminished his effectiveness on the field. After it looked like he had turned the corner on the knee injury, Adams began suffering with an elbow injury after taking a hit against Northeastern, an ailment that caused an infection eventually requiring surgery and forcing him to miss the Penn game. The senior had come back and played well against Bucknell but had been ineffective the next week against Rhode Island. To date, Adams had just one sack, way back in Week 1 against Rutgers, and the NFL scouts who had come to watch him had been far from mesmerized by his play. As the William and Mary game beckoned, Adams knew he was running out of opportunities, and had to pick up the pace both for his team and for himself.

"This is not the way I imagined my fifth year going," Adams reflected. "I had to battle back all summer, recovering, rehabbing, and getting ready for summer camp. And then I get into camp and I have a couple of run-ins with the knee. I'm missing more time. Have to deal with a young team that I hadn't had a opportunity to lead in the spring, then in come twenty, thirty freshmen I have to deal with. So it's like all of this is being thrown at me at such a fast pace, I'm going to have to get this thing rolling. It didn't turn out the best possible way it that could have, as our record shows. It's definitely been a rollercoaster season. Not the way I planned it to be."

Adams knew things weren't going especially well, but neither he nor Talley believed it was impossible for the captain to turn his season around as November approached. Westbrook and Finneran, the two finest players of Villanova's I-AA era, had both overcome obstacles to make it at the next level, and though Adams's situation was different, logic suggested that facing up to his difficulties with a similar degree of determination might just yield similar results.

Westbrook, the NFL Pro Bowler, had received exactly two scholarship offers for football coming out of DeMatha Catholic High School in Hyattsville, Maryland, one from Richmond, the other from Villanova. An untimely knee injury suffered while starring at point guard for the DC-area school had scared the major recruiters off, and even Talley was left unimpressed with Westbrook's high school tape. The 5-foot-9 Westbrook, whom legendary DeMatha basketball coach Morgan Wootten once referred to as the best point guard he had ever coached, was still being recruited by lower-level Division I schools in basketball, but he felt that when healthy, football was his best sport. Stan Drayton, who recruited Westbrook to Villanova, convinced Talley of Westbrook's skills just as Trainer had done concerning Adams, and months later, Westbrook had not only won the head coach over but had won the starting running back job midway through his true freshman year.

As a sophomore, Westbrook topped that feat, becoming the first player in college football history, at any level, to amass over 1,000 rushing yards and 1,000 receiving yards in the same season. At the time, the feat was so rare that only one player at any level of football, Roger Craig of the NFL San Francisco 49ers, had ever accomplished it—and in sixteen games, not the eleven that Westbrook had. But months after achieving that milestone, Westbrook reportedly slipped on a patch of ice while walking on campus and tore his ACL. As he sat out the 1999 season, observers both inside and outside the program wondered whether he would ever regain his explosiveness, questions that were promptly answered when Westbrook rushed for more than 1,200 yards, caught 59 passes, and scored 22 touchdowns the next season. As a senior, Westbrook would score 29 TDs, win the Walter Payton Award as I-AA's best player, and break the NCAA all-divisions record for all-purpose yards with more than 9,500. Had he been at a BCS school, Westbrook likely would have been a first-round draft choice, but with his injury history and hailing from I-AA Villanova, the undersized running back had to settle for being the Eagles' third-round selection. It was all downhill thereafter for Westbrook, who had become a vital component in the team's offense and had just signed a lucrative new contract.

Finneran, meanwhile, had managed to star in college despite becoming a father early in his freshman year and a husband following his sophomore season. On his first day of summer camp as a freshman, Finneran informed Talley that his girlfriend had just gone into labor in California. The receiver would be sent home to attend to the mother of his child before returning to the team prior to the start of the season. Eventually, Finneran would bring his young family to the Main Line, get married, and add another child before his days at Villanova were through. At nights after practice, when most of his teammates were carousing, Finneran was in his off-campus apartment changing diapers as his wife worked a full-time job. Whether in spite of or because of the pressures of fatherhood, the wideout developed into one of the top players in Atlantic 10 history.

But even given his 6-foot-5 frame and dominance at the I-AA level, the 1997 Payton winner was passed over by all thirty NFL teams during the seven rounds of the 1998 draft due to a slow 40-yard dash time, and he was cut in training camp in the summer prior to the '98 season after signing a free agent contract with the Seattle Seahawks.

It wasn't until he went to the Barcelona Dragons of NFL Europe in 1999 that pro teams began taking an interest in Finneran, who ranked in that league's top five in all receiving categories. It was the Eagles who would sign the former local star next, and Finneran would make the active roster on head coach Andy Reid's first team, only to spend most of his season on the inactive list after dropping a key pass in a one-point Week 1 loss to the Cardinals.

With his professional future very much in doubt, Finneran would find a role in Atlanta, as head coach Dan Reeves brought him on as a fifth wide receiver and special teams player. Finneran's playing time would gradually increase to the point where he was a key starter and the favorite target of quarterback Michael Vick on a 2002 Atlanta team that went 9-6-1 and reached the playoffs. By now, Finneran was an established pro in the midst of his seventh season as a Falcon.

These were the type of feel-good, against-all-odds stories that Adams hoped to be able to reflect upon someday, and though he hadn't performed as well in his senior season as had Westbrook or Finneran, the defensive end believed himself talented enough to eventually reach the same professional plateau. As for all of the players from Villanova and elsewhere who hadn't realized their NFL dreams, Adams was too positive a person to allow himself to think very long about them.

To a degree, the pressure was off for Villanova. The playoffs were no longer a realistic goal, so the Wildcats could concentrate more on playing well than on the ramifications if they didn't come away a winner. Saturday night's game with William and Mary wouldn't serve as homecoming or have any other significance attached to it. It would just be another game. They could just play.

But even considering the relatively low stakes, Villanova was desperate to record a win. The Rhode Island defeat had been a major embarrassment, perhaps a signal to some outsiders that the Wildcats were actually one of the league's weakest teams, closer to the bottom of the Atlantic 10 hierarchy then the top. Losing to William and Mary at home would reinforce that perception and would also drop the Cats to 3-5, meaning they would have to win their last three just to salvage an above-.500 record. Villanova had posted just one losing campaign since 1996, a 5-6 mark in 2000, when the team had started strong before succumbing in each of its final four games. A loss to William and Mary would put Talley's team in danger of plumbing the depths of 3-8 for the first time in a decade.

The prospects for avoiding that morass didn't look particularly good.

Villanova's three wins to date were a squeaker against Penn of the Ivy League, a blowout of Patriot League cellar-dweller Bucknell, and the long-forgotten early-season victory over Northeastern, which by this, the final weekend in October, was 1-6 and sinking like a boulder.

William and Mary, on the other hand, had been cruising. The Tribe, which had been to the national semifinals in 2004, was currently 5-2, with one of those losses coming to I-A Marshall, and was ranked No. 9 in all of I-AA. Though Jimmye Laycock's team had, like Villanova, been stunned by Rhode Island a few weeks back, they had recovered by drilling New Hampshire, then No. 1 in the nation, by a score of 42–10. With four straight victories in their rear view mirror, William and Mary looked primed to make another serious run at the postseason.

Laycock and company couldn't have been too intimidated about the next opponent on their schedule. Villanova hadn't posted anything resembling a marquee win since beating Temple at the beginning of the 2003 season, and the program's last truly attention-grabbing victory in the conference was notched by Brett Gordon's final team against Delaware at the end of the 2002 season.

But as usual, Talley was loath to engage in any type of defeatist thinking on the eve of the contest. Villanova–William and Mary games were almost always close, with three of the last four having been settled by eight points or less. The Wildcats rarely had trouble scoring points on the Tribe either, having scored in the forties in four of the last six meetings. And perhaps most important, Talley knew that his players respected William and Mary and wouldn't be overlooking them as they likely had Rhode Island. W&M was one of Nova's truest rivals, another private, academically oriented school against which Villanova often recruited and was always determined to beat.

Talley stressed the importance of the game in his Friday evening address to the team, challenging their resolve, desire, and toughness in the wake of the Rhode Island loss.

"William and Mary is coming in here about as arrogant and abrasive a team as you can play," Talley began. "And they truly believe they're going to kick our ass. And I'm telling you right now, this is a stand.

This game's a stand. A lot of players around here this week are concerned about how much some of us really care about where we are right now, and what we're thinking about. There's genuine concern. So if there was ever a game to put our three things together—defense, special teams, and offense—this is the game. Put the stupid penalties away. Let's see a defense that's going to turn the ball over, and get after people, smack [William and Mary running back] Elijah Brooks around, let those quarterbacks try to come out of that pocket. An offense that's going to get after it. Special teams that are going to be as serious as a heart attack. Let's break a punt return, let's break a kick return, let's block a punt, let's have our kickers and punters play well, meaning a full game. A full game."

After being dismissed for the night, the players looked forward to the approximately twenty-four hours of rest and relaxation they would be receiving, a rare window of leisure in the midst of the grueling schedule of the regular season. The 6 p.m. kickoff, without question, offered the Wildcats something of an advantage. Villanova's players could recharge their batteries while going through a manageable game day routine, while William and Mary would probably be anxious and would run the risk of growing stale while whiling away most of their daylight hours in a hotel.

That situation wasn't the only intangible working in favor of the Cats. For once, Talley was not going to have to put his skills of meteorology to the test. The temperature would be in the high forties at kickoff, and though there was a noticeable wind, there was no precipitation in the forecast. For Jankowski and the offense, that was a godsend.

The Wildcat players and coaches never could have predicted yet another heaven-sent element, which revolved around the state of mind, and pregame approach, of William and Mary's players. Perhaps searching for a measure of enthusiasm after their day of lethargy, some of the members of William and Mary's team came onto the Villanova Stadium field in an overly vocal manner. As the squads went through their typical pregame drills and warm-up routine, the Wildcat players couldn't help but hear some of the Tribe players chanting, shouting, dancing, showing more emotion than most opponents would. This type of exuberance did not sit well with the home team, which saw the Tribe's pregame show as being indicative of disrespect for the hosts.

Suddenly, after weeks in which their emotional Richter scale was stuck at flatline, Villanova's players had come to life. The scene in the locker room before the game was as raucous as a Wildcat locker room, home or away, had been all season. This was a group of guys who looked like they wanted blood.

"They think they're just going to fucking roll the ball out and fucking score points on us?" screamed Brian Hulea. "That's fucking bullshit. Kick their fucking sorry asses all over the field."

John Dieser also chimed in. "Don't let them fucking act cocky like this, let's go! Special teams gotta set the tone, man. From the first play, special teams. The first fucking play, hitting people."

Picking up on the emotional state of his players, Talley seized the opportunity to crank the intensity up. This is what he had been looking for all year.

"I've been here twenty-one seasons," began Talley. "I've never seen anyone come on our field and talk trash like that. EVER! Twenty-one seasons, never saw anybody walk on our field and start that bullshit.

"We haven't beaten a name team in two years. We have not beaten a name team in two years. In fact, to have a team like William and Mary come here, desecrate our field, is unbelievable. I talked to you yesterday about the flame, those guys are trying to stomp it out before the game. Now it's time for you to play with emotion for four quarters. For four quarters! That's not asking a lot. If you love the game and you care about it and you want to get this thing turned around, you start today. Right now, now's your opportunity. Let's get it."

The cry Villanova's players let out following Talley's speech was one heavily dosed with vengeance. As the team flooded out of the locker room and onto the turf, Darrell Adams summed up the situation.

"Better be ready for a war today, baby," shouted Adams.

Had it actually been a war, William and Mary would have been tempted to reach for the white flags at several points during the proceedings. After the teams traded punts on their respective opening drives, Jankowski led a crisp, nine-play, 94-yard touchdown drive to make just about all of the five thousand or so in attendance forget about the Rhode Island debacle. Jankowski was 5-for-6 passing on the drive, including a 47-yard toss to Dieser and a 15-yard TD on a slant to J. J. Outlaw for the touchdown. With 4:49 to play in the first quarter, Villanova led by a 7–0 count and was brimming with both confidence and intensity.

William and Mary, meanwhile, had trouble sustaining anything offensively for the entire first half. Laycock's team drew close enough to get on the board on the drive that immediately followed the Villanova touchdown, but Tribe kicker Greg Kuehn missed a 39-yard field goal. When the Wildcats committed a pair of second quarter turnovers—a Jankowski interception on a tipped ball and a DeQuese May fumble—William and Mary failed to convert either into points. And in the second quarter, moments after Kuehn had his second field goal try of the game blocked by Matt Costantino, Jankowski began another methodical march down the field.

Moe Gibson started it off with a 13-yard run, which was followed by a 15-yard personal foul on William and Mary to get the Wildcats to midfield. Jankowski would do the rest, completing three of his next four passes, including a 20-yard toss to Dieser and a 14-yard touchdown strike to Anton Ridley on the very next play. Joe Marcoux's point-after made the score 14–0 with just over two minutes left in the half. William and Mary would reach as far as their own 45-yard line on their final drive of the first half, but Adams, Hulea, and the stiff Villanova defense again held their ground. As the teams retreated to their respective locker rooms, the number nine team in the country had been manhandled, shut out no less, by a VU club that had looked lifeless just one week prior.

"Amped" was the word to describe the scene in the Villanova locker room as the team awaited the second half. They hadn't won a championship, or even a game, in the first thirty minutes, but for a group of players in desperate need of some sustained success, it felt that way.

The Cats had done exactly what Talley had asked during his Friday speech. All three phases of the team had played well, and even more significantly, they had done so with an intensity seemingly lacking for most of their previous seven games. "They woke up a sleeping giant," Adams insisted, and his emotion carried over to his coordinator.

"They ain't nothing but a bunch of hairy-ass fucking hillbillies," said Mark Reardon of the players from the Williamsburg-based school. "Let's knock them the fuck out. Give them your best shot right out of the gate. Bring it the fuck on!"

Talley, knowing that he didn't have to say much to a team that was this hyped up, spoke only briefly while trying to rein in their focus. "They came out and acted like hot dogs and disrespected us, and look what happened to them," boasted Talley. "Now, get ready for sudden change, because their coach is over there kicking their ass. They're playing like crap, and you guys are playing great. You gotta come out and play great in the second half because they're going to play great. Beat 'em."

Talley's Cats would not let up, not in the slightest. William and Mary's first drive of the second half ended in a punt, following which Jankowski and the offense made their job look easy yet again. On a drive that began at the Villanova 12, Moe Gibson ripped off 20 much-needed yards to keep the clock moving. Jankowski went a perfect 4-for-4, hitting giant pass plays to Ridley for 19 yards, to Outlaw for 22, and finally, to Dieser, who was having a monster game, for a 22-yard touchdown. It was 21–0, and Talley's team was dominating.

The VU defense forced another three-and-out, and the offense was again on the move, tearing up 71 yards in just four plays, including a 28-yard pass from Jankowski to Dieser and a nifty 30-yard touchdown run for the suddenly explosive Gibson.

With 5:58 to play in the third quarter, Villanova led by a count of 28–0. The Cats were obviously going to get their first win in a long time against a "name team," and it was going to be a convincing, message-sending victory at that. Jankowski had just led three consecutive impressive scoring drives, exactly the kind of consistency that Talley and Venuto had been searching for, and the defense was as stifling as it had been all season. When cornerback Rodney Badger intercepted a Jacob Phillips pass on William and Mary's next drive, Talley and his coaching staff even began contemplating getting the reserves some playing time.

Just before the end of the third quarter, that thinking would change, however. While working deep in his own territory, Jankowski dropped back to pass, was pressured, and threw wildly into the arms of William and Mary linebacker Trevor McLaurin. After catching the ball at the 14-yard line, McLaurin rushed to the end zone to get William and Mary on the scoreboard for the first time. The score was 28–7 after Kuehn kicked the extra point, and while the touchdown was disappointing for a Villanova team that looked like it would have a realistic shot at a shutout, with a twenty-one-point advantage near the end of the third quarter and with the defense playing its best game of the year, the TD wasn't causing anyone on the sideline to hyperventilate.

The Wildcat attack would sputter a bit on its first two drives of the fourth quarter, with the big lead clearly sapping some of the unit's urgency. But all was well, since William and Mary's offense continued to struggle, having punted on their only drive since the interception return. After getting the ball back with 8:44 to play following an Adam James punt, William and Mary and its offense was simply looking for progress in the form of its first positive moment of the game.

The Tribe would get way more than it bargained for. A roughing the passer call on Adams helped the Tribe move the football to midfield, and four plays later, Phillips found wideout Josh Lustig with a 37-yard touchdown pass. The offense's first score of the game had come 52 minutes and 19 seconds into the contest, but it had cut the score to 28–14 with 7:41 to play.

Again, the tightening of the score was disappointing for Villanova, but one more sustained drive would effectively end any suggestion of an amazing comeback. That sustained drive would indeed be delivered by Jankowski. On two separate third-down situations, Jankowski came through, completing a 24-yard pass to the indefensible Dieser and scrambling for 11 yards on a third-and-six moments later. Venuto sprinkled some Gibson runs in among the pass plays, with the senior running time off of the clock in large chunks. After getting down to the William and Mary 20 with 2:19 to play and a 14-point lead, the Cats were a third-and-five conversion away from icing the game. Even if they failed to pick up the first-down yardage on the next play, a made Joe Marcoux field goal from a modest distance could push the Villanova lead to three insurmountable scores.

During a timeout, Talley and Venuto considered their options. They could make the conservative call, which meant playing for the field goal, or put their money on Jankowski's hot hand and look to get the first down or better. The call in this situation was Talley's, and noting how well the offense had moved for most of the game, he went with the bolder, fan-friendlier option.

Jankowski dropped back, looked to the right side, felt the William and Mary blitz, and fired off a pass in the direction of Dieser. At the last possible instant, William and Mary's James Miller jumped the route, stepped in front of the receiver, and sprinted untouched for an 80-yard touchdown as the Tribe sideline reacted in exultation. Jankowski had not read the coverage properly, and upon his return to the sideline, Venuto dressed the quarterback down. For Venuto, Jankowski, and everyone adorned in Villanova colors, an unthinkable reality was setting in. A game that had been all but conceded to the home team just seconds ago was now a seven-point affair. As they recoiled in horror at the events, Talley and his team peered at the scoreboard. William and Mary still had all three of its timeouts, and there was 2:05 to play, a virtual eternity given the circumstances.

Could William and Mary possibly steal this game? It seemed entirely possible. The Wildcats caught a break on the next play, getting the football back near midfield when an onside kick attempt drifted out of bounds. Not wanting to risk another turnover from Jankowski, Talley and Venuto went conservative all the way on the next drive, much to the chagrin of the remaining crowd at Villanova Stadium. Three straight runs from Moe Gibson netted a total of 5 yards, and James was on to punt with 1:44 to play. James's kick was a beauty, dropping softly inside the 10-yard line before Adam Clements downed it at the William and Mary 3.

Had Talley known on Friday night that his team would be holding a seven-point advantage over the ninth-ranked team in I-AA with 92 seconds remaining and that his opponent had 97 yards of field left to conquer in order to tie, with no timeouts, he would have been overjoyed. Had he been told that Villanova had outgained William and Mary to that point 540 yards to 194, yet the Tribe still had a reasonable opportunity to tie the game, his attitude might have promptly changed from joy to incredulity.

Still, Villanova had the upper hand, and Reardon, as well as everyone in the stadium, knew that William and Mary had to pass if it wished to tie the game. Reardon sent in his nickel package, employing an extra defensive back and his best pass-defending linebackers to defend against William and Mary's multiple–wide receiver set. On first down, Phillips hit Lustig on a 12-yard pass play that got the offense to the William and Mary 15. So far, so good for the Tribe. But after hurrying to the line and taking the next snap, Phillips floated a throw on an out pattern to the left side of the field. Badger, who had read the play immediately, tipped the football into the air once, batted it again while reaching for it, and finally caught the ball before sprinting 15 yards to the Wildcat end zone.

This time, it was Villanova's turn for a sideline eruption. After being swarmed by his teammates, Badger got a giant bear hug from a waiting and relieved Mark Ferrante. Though the celebration would be tempered by the fact that they had very nearly given the game away, the Cats had done it. A 14-point win over a Top 10 team was not something to take lightly. Talley's heart rate slowed to a normal pace, and for the first time in six weeks, the head Cat walked into Villanova's spacious home locker room to address a winner.

"Here's the deal, you just beat the number nine team in the country, and they beat the number one team in the country, 42–10," said Talley. "Villanova football came back tonight with what Villanova football's about. Treasure it. Embrace it. Feel it and remember it. And love it. Because we're going to take it into next week's game. That's a typical A-10 game. Give, take, you're never out a of a game, you gotta keep playing. Sometimes we make a couple of mistakes, sometimes they make a couple of mistakes. The coaches have never given up, we care so much you don't even know. Good job tonight."

The players smiled. They would embrace it, and they certainly would enjoy it, some in a different manner than others on this still-young Saturday night. And one week after his last emotionally charged press conference, Talley this time had a chance to be positive when he met with the media.

"I really feel like we have finally turned the corner, and we're back to playing Villanova football," began Talley. "That's the big thing, we have not played Villanova football all year. And we talked on Friday about keeping the flame alive. The flame is flickering. We haven't beaten a name team in our league in I don't think two years. And there were a lot of doubters out there, and we have worked hard with this group, and they responded today. Took out a number nine team, and I mean really, the score was not indicative of the game. We played a dominating game today on both sides of the ball. Our players came to play, they were ready, they were coached up, they knew what they were doing, and they just executed beautifully. Except for a couple of bad mistakes by Frank there with the interceptions, I thought we were really in control of the game all day."

Despite his satisfaction over the win, Talley still wasn't going to let his quarterback's errors slide. Jankowski had thrown three picks, including two that were returned for touchdowns, to a great degree offsetting any encouragement that could be gleaned from his 325-yard, three-touchdown performance. Later in the press conference, Talley was asked a direct question about Jankowski, and he managed to strike something of a conciliatory tone.

"Except for the interceptions, he really played extremely well for us, and hit some big plays. And that's what you have to do to [score] in the thirties, and I think if he does that we're okay. The one interception that was kind of tipped around is really kind a ticky-tack interception, but the one at the end there was really bad. In a tight-knit game it could have cost us the game. But we had enough firepower today, Moe had 179 yards rushing, Johnny [Dieser] had 182 in the air, and we had a lot of big-play stuff today, so we were really able to overcome it. And our defense, they were only able to score one touchdown on our defense."

Talley was flanked at the press conference by two seniors, Gibson and Dieser, along with junior safety Allyn Bacchus, who had posted a huge outing with nine tackles, a sack, and three pass breakups. With those players looking on, Talley then said something that while honest, forward-looking and realistic, had to damage the psyche of his seniors and would also wash away any reparations that had been made in his relationship with Jankowski over the previous week.

"Our year really is next year," said Talley. "I thought with Marvin, if Marvin had been our quarterback this year, we might have had a shot, because maybe we could have played like this earlier."

For Gibson and Dieser, there would be no next year, at least as far as football was concerned, so Talley's musings didn't ring with the same encouraging undertones that the head coach had undoubtedly intended. Whether or not either believed, as Talley had again suggested, that the year could have been different with Burroughs at the helm of the offense, those two players and their fellow seniors had to feel on this victorious evening that they could at the very least be winners during the final month of their college football careers. And whatever his hurt about the failure of the campaign, Jankowski's erratic play, or his feelings about 2006 and beyond, Talley, who had just completed a brilliant job of coaching on this night, thought his team had turned the corner as well.

"It was the best we've played. It was crisp, hard, fast football and I think it's a sign of things to come," said Talley. "With a young team, I just hope we improve."

12

OUTLAW IN CHARM CITY

For Russell McKittrick, the end of the line was here. As he sat in Andy Talley's office, the sophomore defensive end knew that he had screwed up for the final time and was about to pay with his spot on the football team.

On Sunday night, roughly 24 hours after the victory over William and Mary, McKittrick had partaken in an installment of an ongoing ritual with some friends, along with a group of girls from the women's soccer team, an event that had come to be known as "Sophisticated Sunday." Each of the participants would get dressed up in their best clothes, go to someone's dorm room, drink, play drinking games, and hang out. It was all somewhat innocuous fare as far as college partying was concerned, but for McKittrick, who was taking medication and was a major risk to miss class on his most clear-headed day, such festivities were dangerous.

McKittrick hadn't intended for his Sunday night to get out of hand. He figured he would just have a couple of drinks, but somehow the evening had gotten away from him.

On Monday morning, with the coaching staff and several of his teammates monitoring his every move, McKittrick had been unable to rouse himself for class, instead spending the day sleeping off a hangover. Meanwhile, several other student-athlete participants in "Sophisticated Sunday" were openly discussing the previous night's fun around the athletic department buildings, and by Monday afternoon, Talley had been briefed on the situation by a concerned member of the athletics staff.

Talley knew that McKittrick's moment of reckoning was here. He had seen the final warning sign he cared to see and was now certain that neither he nor anyone else at Villanova could help the player. The head coach made a phone call to McKittrick's mother in Oregon (his parents had moved back to the Pacific Northwest after McKittrick finished high school), and told her what he wished to do. He wanted to withdraw McKittrick from all his classes immediately and put him on a plane home, where he would receive the psychiatric help he obviously needed and get his act together. Liz McKittrick agreed with Talley's assessment.

Talley left the door open to McKittrick's possible return for spring practice, just as he had done for Dave Dalessandro the year before, but Talley wasn't nearly as hopeful that McKittrick would return as he had been with Dalessandro. McKittrick's problems obviously went beyond drinking, and Talley was not willing to bet that there was a quick-fix solution that would get his troubled defensive end back to campus in short order.

When Talley confronted McKittrick with his findings and his plan of action, the player put up faint resistance, but he knew by the tone of the head coach's voice that the decision was final. He would remain on campus for the rest of the week to get any remaining affairs in order, and would be permitted to stand on the sideline for the team's upcoming game at Towson, but would head back to Oregon thereafter.

The developments saddened Talley, who was not accustomed to failing when it came to finding a path toward success for his players. Now more than ever, the head coach was concerned much more for the person than for the football player. Like a parent dealing with a child, Talley hoped that this extreme course of action would have a positive effect on McKittrick.

"He has trouble making the connection of consequences," said Talley. "'If I do A, B will happen, if I do B, C will happen.' And now he's lost the thing that he loves the most. If there's anything that will save him, that'll do it."

McKittrick wasn't the only player that would soon be experiencing a homecoming, although J. J. Outlaw's return to familiar surroundings would be much happier than would McKittrick's. The trip to Towson would give Outlaw a chance to head back to the Baltimore area, where he had been a two-sport star at Mount Saint Joseph High School, for the first time as a college player. Most of the receiver's family would be in attendance at Johnny Unitas Stadium on Saturday afternoon, as would a good number of Outlaw's friends.

Unfortunately, Outlaw's father, John, would not be able to make it to the game, but he had a pretty solid excuse for missing the upcoming gridiron exploits of his only child. The elder Outlaw had just begun his second season as an assistant coach with the NBA Charlotte Bobcats and would be seated on the bench when the team played host to the Boston Celtics on Saturday night.

J. J. Outlaw was used to his dad not being at games, though John Outlaw had made every contest that did not directly conflict with his own work schedule over the years. Since the younger Outlaw had been on earth, his father had been well traveled, pulling up stakes and moving from Denver to DC to St. Louis and now to Charlotte. Not seeing his father for extended stretches had become second-nature to the senior wide receiver.

"It's just sort of the way my family is. When I was six, my dad went out to Denver ahead of my mom and I. He was out there for a year when he was working with the Nuggets, and my mom and I would go visit. Then he was back in Maryland a year before my mom and I joined him, to work with the Wizards. When he got the job down in Charlotte, he was down there a year before my mom went. My mom always had to stay around and tie up the loose ends with the house or with me. He was around, and we talked every day, but him being away was just normal for me."

J. J. Outlaw took those absences in stride, just like seemingly everything else in his life. It didn't take long for an outside observer to marvel at how this twenty-one-year-old college kid seemed to carry himself like a pro, from his refined pregame rituals to the way he interacted with the media, coaches, and officials, to his occasional prima donna moments. Being brought up around professional sports had obviously rubbed off on Outlaw, and mostly in a good way.

"I tried to pattern myself after [former Nuggets forward] LaPhonso Ellis, coming up as a young guy. You can go back and look at any tape of LaPhonso, going back to the first year he was drafted, he never once complained about a referee's call, no matter how bad. It was very powerful, and it was a good message that you don't always have to argue, you don't always have to fight, sometimes it will be a lot easier if you just smile and go about your business. Even in the media, he was always pleasant."

Outlaw did not have much media to contend with at Villanova, but when he did speak to reporters or was interviewed as part of the Wildcats' radio broadcasts, he seemed very much at ease, unlike many of his teammates who were fidgety and uncomfortable around the press. When the *Delaware County Times* spoke to Outlaw, it was if he were sitting down with *Sports Illustrated*.

"No matter what level you're on, if the media is interested in you, you should always be professional," said Outlaw. "I think you should answer all of their questions intelligently, and speak intelligently. Because you've seen where the media can kind of tear a career down, and I've seen the good, the bad, and the ugly when it comes to interviews or the way a player handles the media, or vice versa. It can be devastating, and I've seen it happen to good people . . . if you respect them, they'll respect you."

One former NBA star Outlaw saw struggle with the media was Rod Strickland, the journeyman point guard and antihero whose off-the-court headlines, including DUI and domestic violence charges, never seemed to jibe with the person the young and impressionable Outlaw knew. The growing sports star was much more affected by Strickland's work habits and sense of style than any villainy that may have been portrayed in the press.

"I liked how tough he was, I liked the fact that after games he would go and lift weights," remembered Outlaw. "That says a lot, especially in this day in age in professional sports. I just liked a lot about Rod. He was a smooth guy, he dressed well and was very professional when he was leaving the games. You never saw Rod without a suit on. And he gave me my first bottle of Jean Paul Gaultier cologne."

But it wasn't just his father's work associates Outlaw had to look up to when he searched for role models in the world of pro sports. The decade that John Outlaw had spent as an NFL cornerback was a subject with which the son was clearly fascinated.

"I never got to see him play," lamented J. J. "That's something I would have liked to have seen. We have some old reel-to-reels and some old tapes and stuff like that. Every now and again on the old episodes of NFL Films I'll catch a glimpse, or he'll be on there."

The fact that his father had made it to the top in two different forms of professional sports might have given the indication that outsized expectations would have been heaped upon Outlaw from an early age, but the wideout insisted that though he was attracted to athletics, he never felt that he was being steered toward following in his dad's footsteps.

"He really didn't push me," Outlaw said of his dad. "He never had to. There was not a time that I ever thought about giving up sports, there was not a time that I ever thought that I was burned out. It was my life and I think that because he saw that I was so enthusiastic about it, he didn't have to push me. All he had to do was support me."

Nor did the younger Outlaw worry that coaches, teammates, or other outsiders would expect more of him because of his lineage. "I never felt any pressure, not at all," said the receiver. "I always knew that I had to work hard but I never felt any pressure. I always looked at it as a blessing, almost like cheating a test. I knew I wanted to get to this point, and I was on the inside of professional sports. So I had all the answers, the rights and wrongs, what to do, what not to do. I didn't need anyone to tell me what coaches were looking for. I knew how to treat people around the office because my dad had been that person. I knew how to treat kids around the office, and how to treat kids out in the public, because I was the kid always running around the players asking for autographs. I just looked at it like a blueprint."

Outlaw was quick to credit not only his father's influence, but also that of his mother, Linda, for helping to lead him on the path to success. "My mom was at every single game," recalled Outlaw. "She was the enforcer. She was the one that was quick to call my coaches and tell them that I wouldn't be playing for a few games if I didn't have my grades right. She was the one that did all the punishing and everything like that. My family, I think we had a really good balance."

Not surprisingly, Outlaw grew up excelling in both of the sports that had been part of his father's professional vocation. In fact, as a youth, Outlaw actually found a way to blend the two.

"Football and basketball, those are the two sports that he loved, so those became the two sports that I fell in love with," said Outlaw. "I can remember my dad built me a basketball court in our backyard, and I would dress up in full football gear, go out and shoot baskets. I'm talking about helmet, shoulder pads, and everything. Being an only child, sometimes you do stuff just to keep yourself occupied, but to me that was fun. And it was normal."

It was in Denver that Outlaw first became involved in youth football, playing in the 7 to 8 age group as a six-year-old and nurturing his love for the sport that his father had played professionally.

"I remember I was at this elementary school," remembered Outlaw. "We had just moved to Colorado, my dad was working with the Nuggets. And this lady called my dad early one morning and said, 'We're having our football team, and we just don't have a lot of kids that want to come out and play, because they're young, and the organization needs an age group for this year.' The lady called my dad because her son was actually going to be on the team, and he had suggested that I play. So my dad just volunteered me right there. He knew he didn't have to ask me, I'd be jumping at it."

That the diminutive Outlaw had a rare talent was immediately apparent. "In Colorado I was the only black kid on the team, so I kind of stood out. I was real fast and at that time I was really small. My career from when I started, I was the smallest kid, to growing and becoming one of the biggest kids, to being in college and being one of the smallest again, it's almost gone full circle. My mom told me to get out and run, and just don't let them hit you."

After taking the Denver basketball and football youth leagues by storm, Outlaw and his family relocated to Columbia, Maryland, midway between Baltimore and his father's job with the Wizards in DC, when the youngster was in the eighth grade. Though he was an unknown in Maryland, Outlaw quickly got people's attention, at least in one sport.

"[Local coaches] had never seen me play football, football was over by that time," said Outlaw. "When I first moved back to Columbia, there was this basketball league called CBA—Columbia Basketball Association—and this was as 'rec ball' as you could get. Everybody had on the same t-shirt, and everybody had on the same white CBA shorts. You could only play three quarters, and the coach wouldn't start me so I could play the last three quarters. I just kind of took over the league. It got to the point where I stopped playing after about the third or fourth game. My coach said, 'You shouldn't be playing here,' and he sent me down to play for Mount Royal."

Mount Royal was perhaps the best AAU basketball team in Baltimore, and Outlaw held his own in a league that included future stars like NBA All-Star Carmelo Anthony. It was while playing hoops for Mount Royal that Pat Clatchey, the head coach at Mt. St. Joe, noticed Outlaw and convinced him, in consultation with his parents, to attend the Xaverian Brothers high school located in West Baltimore. No one at St. Joe knew about Outlaw's football prowess until he arrived during freshmen year, and the teenager was frustrated to discover that some of his classmates already had predetermined roster spots on the JV and varsity teams. Outlaw would have to play most of his first high school season on the freshmen team before being moved up to JV at the end the year.

Outlaw was good enough to make varsity as a sophomore, and it was obvious that he had arrived when in his first game at that level, he scored on a 92-yard touchdown catch against Severn High School.

From there, the wideout was off and running. "We ran a four-wide receiver offense, and I played the slot, just like I'm playing here. I really have never changed my position."

It wasn't long before Outlaw would start receiving interest from college recruiters, though those schools were calling more because of his talents as a point guard on the hardwood than as a pass-catcher and kick returner on the gridiron, a situation that did not sit well with the player.

"Because I had been playing varsity since I was a freshman in basketball, I actually had more basketball scholarship offers than I did for football. A lot of your mid-majors—Quinnipiac, Wagner, Coastal Carolina, Central Connecticut, Northeastern—were interested. I didn't even start getting football letters until I was a junior. I was on varsity [football], and there were kids that were on JV getting letters before I did. And I thought that was crazy, I had never really heard of that. It really pissed me off."

That sense of consternation, and the style of the highly successful and visible NFL Baltimore Ravens, prompted Outlaw to make his decision about which sport to pursue at the collegiate level. He would follow his father down the gridiron road.

"I decided I wanted to play college football in my junior year of high school, in homeroom. I was reading an article in *ESPN Magazine* on Ray Lewis, Shannon Sharpe, and Rod Woodson after they had won the Super Bowl, and I decided I wanted to play in college."

Now Outlaw would have to find a college football program willing to offer him a scholarship, and also one that could properly use his talents. The wideout, who was being seriously courted by some low I-As and many of the better I-AA programs, had some familiarity with Villanova's football program, as his high school coach, Mike Working, had coached with Sam Venuto's brother, and former St. Joe standout receiver Shaz Brown had attended the Philadelphia-area school. In speaking with Venuto for the first time, Outlaw liked his sales pitch, or lack thereof.

"Coach Venuto came down, and there was something about him that

I kind of liked," recalled Outlaw. "He didn't come down with any media guides, he didn't come down with any pictures of the stadium, any highlight films, anything. He just came down wearing a leather coat and said, 'We throw the ball to our slots a lot, look what Brian Westbrook's done, he's getting ready to go to the league, and we run a lot of the same stuff you run now in high school.' I had always worried about how long it would take me to get a college offense down. And when he said they do a lot of the same stuff, and my position wouldn't be changing, I liked my opportunity here. I thought I would have an opportunity to come in and play right away."

The Westbrook connection was a huge selling point for Outlaw, who chose Villanova over Atlantic 10 schools like UMass, as well as low-level I-A programs like Bowling Green. "I was real impressed with what a guy like Brian Westbrook had done here and the type of success that he had here. And Coach Venuto really broke it down and said that I could be doing a lot of the same things he did—running the ball, catching the ball, special teams and different things like that—so I kind of saw myself in that mould. Obviously he was a lot stronger than I am, but we're both around the same height, so I kind of felt like they would do some of the same stuff with me that they had with him."

It was immediately upon arriving on the Main Line that Outlaw realized he would have a lot of work to do if he wished to become a productive college football player. Having underestimated the level of player he would be competing with at Villanova, the only thing the flamboyant young wideout would be receiving for a while would be a painful dose of reality.

"I really expected to be a contributor right away," said Outlaw. "I didn't expect to come in and miss a beat, but I soon realized that these freshmen that I'm playing against now, even in freshmen camp, were some of the best players that I had ever seen. I was like, 'Wow.' Then the rest of the team came back, and it was crazy. I had never seen the game move so fast, and I had never seen guys that were this strong and this intense before, or coaches that were this intense before. I kind of struggled in training camp, and they decided they were going to redshirt me."

Fellow incoming freshmen Marvin Burroughs and Moe Gibson, who had quickly developed into two of his best friends on the team, adjusted more quickly to the college game than did Outlaw, and much to the Marylander's chagrin and envy, they were placed on the travel squad to start the 2002 season.

"I was pissed, because we were roommates, and Marv was traveling because he was a quarterback, and Moe was traveling because he was the backup kickoff returner," remembered Outlaw. "The first week, when they went to Rutgers, I drove up to the game with Chris Polite, but it killed me. I was basically preparing myself to sit out the whole year, bitching and complaining because I had to prepare myself, and Marv had to listen to it. Then we came back home against Maine, and in pregame warm-ups, [former VU receiver] Brian White pulled his hamstring. I didn't play against Maine, but the very next morning when we came to Sunday workouts, they told me they were taking me out of redshirt against New Hampshire."

Outlaw would actually start against UNH but would struggle to grasp the offense and played mainly on special teams as a freshman. "I didn't know the offense," said Outlaw. "They only put me in for things that I knew how to do. The thing that got me was I had spent all of training camp trying to learn this offense, and I'm thinking that once I learn this offense, I'll be good, not knowing that the offense is going to change every week depending on what team we're playing. So while I was trying to grasp the base of this offense, everybody else was moving on from week to week, putting in new stuff, taking out stuff. I was a few steps behind, I'm not going to lie to you."

But Outlaw would catch up as a sophomore, blossoming quickly into one of the team's most useful offensive and special teams weapons. As a sophomore, Outlaw amassed over 700 receiving yards, was second in the Atlantic 10 in all-purpose yardage, and was named first-team all-conference. As a junior, Outlaw scored eight touchdowns and was again an all-league choice.

And now, Outlaw was having his best season as a collegian, already having recorded sixty-one catches and scoring eight touchdowns through just eight games. The circumstances were a tad bittersweet, since the team was having a subpar year and Burroughs was not on the field to share in his friend's continued emergence, but as always, Outlaw was projecting a positive demeanor. Unlike his teammate Darrell Adams, it looked like Outlaw had improved his pro stock as a senior, and the notion that he had a chance to become a second-generation NFL player was becoming more realistic with each passing week.

"Going to the next level, it's something that I think about all the time, I'd be lying if I said I didn't," admitted Outlaw. "I try not to pay too much attention to the scouts. Sometimes you're in practice and you're conscious of where they are, but I try not to think about that too much. I think about it a lot more now that I only have three games left in a Villanova uniform. Hopefully I have a chance to play after that."

And this Saturday's game represented another good chance for Outlaw to impress the scouts, though the trip to Towson obviously had more meaning for the player than had the year's first eight contests.

"My mom will be there, my aunts will be there, my friends from high school, a lot of whom haven't seen me play since high school, will be there, a few ex-girlfriends," joked Outlaw. "It will be a lot of people, a lot of support. Some people get so up for these games that they go out and bomb, so I want to just keep an even keel, not get too high about it, just approach it like any other game. But the fact of the matter is, I'm going up against a lot of dudes that I know, that I've grown up with in basketball and football, a couple of guys that I work out with in the summer. It means a lot to go home. I don't think anything's better than going home."

Apart from the Russell McKittrick episode, the week leading up to Villanova's trip to Towson was a positive one, with the victory over William and Mary finally providing the Wildcats with a measure of long-desired and concrete proof that they could play with just about anyone.

The day after the win, the Atlantic 10 honored Allyn Bacchus as its Defensive Co-Player of the Week, the first such honor for the blossoming junior safety.

On Monday, Bacchus's teammate, Darrell Adams, was chosen to play in January's Las Vegas All-Star Classic, one of a handful of postseason events held for players who had exhausted their eligibility to showcase their wares to pro scouts. The selection to the event took some of the pressure off of Adams in his final three games, since a good week in Vegas would probably mean just as much, if not more, than what he or his team did on the field down the stretch.

Along with the personal accolades, there was a general sense around the VU football office that the team had finally gotten things rolling, and there were even some whispers that if the team could win out, and some other dominoes within the league and around the country fell the right way, a playoff spot was attainable. The NCAA had the year before slightly altered its selection criteria for the 16-team postseason field, eliminating the long-standing three-loss dividing line and allowing a team that had seven Division I (I-A or I-AA) wins to be considered as an at-large entry. Villanova currently had four Division I wins with three more contests to play. Matt Dougherty, I-AA's national beat writer for *The Sports Network*, the media entity that compiled the weekly Top 25 poll, listed the Wildcats forty-third on his forty-four-team list of teams still alive for the playoffs.

It was a long shot, especially with difficult tilts against James Madison and Delaware looming on the horizon, but at this point, hope was hope.

With the Rhode Island implosion still framed large in their rear-view mirror, the Cats couldn't afford to look past any opponent, but on a list of league teams for which Villanova had respect, Saturday's foe, Towson University, would have ranked at or near the bottom. The Tigers were in only their second year in the conference and were still in the midst of a transition from the Patriot League to the Atlantic 10. They had finished 0-8 in league play the year before, including a 41-6 rout by Villanova on the Main Line. The Baltimore-area school had obviously improved in 2005, having begun the year at 5-3, including an attention-grabbing win against Delaware, but ugly defeats against teams VU had already beaten, such as Northeastern (56-41) and William and Mary

(44-13), strongly suggested that they were not quite in the Wildcats' class at this stage.

When Talley perused the Tigers' roster early in the week, he noticed a handful of those dreaded I-A transfers (none of whom were making a serious impact), but otherwise he was excited about the prospect of facing a freshman quarterback, Sean Schaefer, as well as the many weak links on a defense that was giving up more than 40 points per game in league play.

"I think we're going to score a lot of points on them," predicted Talley, adding, "I think we're going to beat them, I think we're better than they are, but it won't be a walkover like last year." To that end, Talley was hoping his team would be as ready for the Tigers as Towson undoubtedly would be for them following last year's 35-point thrashing. TU was also coming off a bye week, another mildly disturbing fact for the head coach and his inconsistent group. "It'll just be interesting to see which team shows up," said Talley. "The one that beat William and Mary, or the one that played against Rhode Island. I really don't know. It's the most bizarre group I've ever been around. But maybe we're a team you don't want to play in the last three games."

Talley's uncertainty about his club's direction still had much to do with the quarterback. "Frank was awesome [against William and Mary], but he did enough to get us beat," Talley confided. "I mean, two going back for picks? Holy shit. He's still playing loose enough to hurt you. I guarantee I'm not calling any damn pass plays when we're trying to ice the game."

When game day finally arrived, the word "ice" was not on the tip of anyone's tongue, as the weirdly warm fall weather continued for the Wildcats. The calendar read November 5, and the temperature as Villanova went through its pregame routine at Unitas Stadium was seventy-six degrees and humid. Why, Talley pondered, was it never like this for home games?

The climate shift was among the head coach's talking points when he gave his pregame speech in the locker room that was located one flight down from Towson's old-school AstroTurf playing surface. "The key today will be in the following categories," Talley began. "No turnovers. No penalties. Watch the heat today, stay hydrated in the game, it's going to get a little warm out there. You're going to have to play hard into the second half here. They played toe-to-toe with William and Mary for a half and then folded in the second half. Really important today that we play at the same level from Saturday night. Can we reach back up there and be who we are?

"One thing about this football team that I've noticed is that you guys usually are what you are. When we weren't doing so well, we'd go out and not do so well. Special teams wouldn't do so well and we'd be fighting for our life. Now all of a sudden, we play a world-class game. Let's be who we are. Let's play the way we know how to play."

Talley's last statement had been unintentionally ambiguous, for this team was just as well-versed in how to play without emotion, purpose, and concentration, perhaps more so, than it was in playing at the world-class level it had displayed for the first forty-five minutes of the William and Mary game.

And if last Saturday had represented Villanova's version of Dr. Jekyll, on this balmy afternoon the Wildcats would spend the next three hours playing the role of Mr. Hyde. As in "run and hide."

Actually, the coin flip went quite well, as Villanova won the toss and elected to receive. But the first play from scrimmage, a 3-yard loss on an option pitch to native son Outlaw, was the first hint that the Cats' day would for the most part come up tails. Jankowski led one first-down drive before the offense stalled near midfield against the league's lowest-ranked defense, then Adam James came on to punt. Following the snap by Mason Frakes, Towson's Josh Corle busted through the Villanova line, blocked the punt cleanly, picked up the football at the Wildcat 28 and ran the rest of the way for a touchdown as the small assembly of approximately four thousand applauded.

On two previous occasions, against Rutgers and New Hampshire, Villanova had given up early big-play touchdowns and ended up on the wrong side of blowout losses. The team would search in vain for a way to avoid a similar scenario this week.

After the VU offense again went three-and-out, James got his second punt of the day off cleanly, but it was returned 22 yards into Villanova territory at the 43. Seven plays later, Towson fullback Kerry Miles barreled into the end zone for a 1-yard touchdown run. Less then seven minutes into the game, the Cats were already down 14–0.

Four plays into the next Wildcat drive, Jankowski was intercepted by Towson's Allan Harrison. Though the Villanova defense held, the offense was on the turf all of three plays before Jankowski was sacked on a blindside hit at his own 21-yard line and fumbled, yielding the ball to the Tigers with another short field. And Towson kept its foot on the gas, much like Villanova had done against William and Mary the week before, taking four plays before getting into the end zone again on a 1-yard QB sneak by Schaefer. It was 21–0, and somewhere, Matt Dougherty was revising his list of I-AA playoff hopefuls.

Each of Villanova's next two drives ended in punts, and Towson upped to its lead to 24–0 on a short field goal midway through the second quarter. The Wildcats would finally answer on their next drive, going 74 yards on ten plays in less than three minutes and finishing up with a 3-yard touchdown run by Moe Gibson. But the era of good feelings would be brief. Joe Marcoux's ensuing extra-point was blocked, and on the second snap of Towson's next drive, Schaefer lobbed a pass deep down the middle of the field to wide-open receiver Marcus Lee, who trotted 84 yards for another easy touchdown.

Villanova safety Terrance Reaves had blown the coverage on the play, and Talley, feeling the strain of the deficit, upon Reaves's return to the bench unleashed a soliloquy of f-bombs on the safety that would have made Richard Pryor blush. It would be a while before Reaves would see the field again.

The Wildcats' next set of downs began in a promising fashion, as Jankowski hit freshman Phil Atkinson on a 38-yard pass play, then came back on the next snap and completed a toss to Chris Polite for 22 more yards. With just over two minutes to play in the half, Villanova was at the Towson 17-yard line, well within striking distance of a positive moment to end an awful first thirty minutes of play. If they could get a touchdown to cut the score to 17 or 18 points, the Cats could regroup at halftime with an eye toward getting back in the game. They had been down by 17 to Penn, they reminded themselves, and had found a way to win that one.

But that type of thinking meant putting the cart well before the horse for this Villanova team. The Wildcats backed up 5 yards after a false start penalty on first-and-ten, and Jankowski's next two passes, both intended for Outlaw, fell incomplete. After a timeout so the offense could draw up a play on third-and-fifteen, Jankowski went back to pass, was again leveled on the blind side, this time by blitzing safety Marcus Edwards, and fumbled. In yet another rerun of the same bad movie, Tiger defensive back Trent Covington picked up the ball at the 30 and ran 70 yards in the other direction as the Wildcats, once again, gave futile chase.

Moments later, Villanova ambled stone-faced to the locker room trailing, stunningly, by the count of 38–6. Even in their wildest nightmares, the Wildcat players and coaching staff hadn't dreamed of this scenario. Just seven days after playing their best game of the year, they had failed to show up in suburban Baltimore.

The halftime demeanor of the coaching staff was easy to predict, though no amount of ranting and raving was likely to have a profound effect on a game that had gotten this out of hand. The normally reserved Venuto gave it a shot though. "We gotta block!" Venuto screamed at his offense. "Up front! On the perimeter! We've gotta throw accurate passes, and know where we're throwing the ball! That's football! It's blocking, it's passing, it's catching, and we didn't do shit in any of those categories!"

Talley's tone was anger as well, laced with noticeable tinges of astonishment and bemusement. "We did about as much as we could possibly do in the first half to give the game away," Talley analyzed. "At best, the game should be 17–13. Our turnovers have been so absurd that they're totally ridiculous. Then we add in a busted coverage and a cheap touchdown, and all of a sudden they have 38 and we have 6. So the reality of it is, we've been embarrassed. Probably one of the top two or three most embarrassing halves I've ever had at Villanova.

"So I say to myself, 'Is that indicative of our football team, is that the way we play, could we be that bad?' Jesus, I don't think so. I don't think so. You have put no pressure on them at all. I asked for no turnovers, I asked for no penalties, we get fucking turnovers and penalties right off the bat."

Having diagnosed the myriad problems, the head coach offered his second-half directive, which included some forceful words for the turnover-prone quarterback that Talley was giving serious thought to pulling from the game at any moment.

"There's only one thing you can do when you're in this situation," said Talley, "is get your ass back up on the field and play your ass off. That's all you can do. You might have to play better then you've ever played in your life. I need aggressive hard-nosed football from our defense. We need some turnovers. Offensively, I need technique, assignment-conscious football. That's what we need. Frankie, you need to get your head out of your ass, and throw the football downfield. Alright? And read what they're doing.

"If you want to win this game you have to count on us playing a terrific second half and them making some mistakes, which they will. Okay? They will make some mistakes, you have to take advantage of them. Now, where are we going to go? We only have one place to go, men, and that's up. So keep your poise, hang together, and let's get back on the field and see what we can do."

Talley's team did play slightly better in the second half, but not nearly well enough to make a game of it. The defense continually kept Towson out of position to score, thanks to more inspired play by guys like Brian Hulea and Allyn Bacchus, but Venuto's offense just couldn't sustain any momentum.

Their first two drives of the half netted a total of 24 yards, until near the end of the third quarter, when Jankowski gave the team a new set of downs with a 20-yard completion to Outlaw on third down. Three plays later, on third-and-ten, the quarterback launched a 58-yard bomb to Polite to get VU back on the board, but true to Villanova form on this day, Marcoux's subsequent point-after try was blocked and picked up by

Towson's Davon Telp, who promptly went the length of the field for an ultra-rare defensive 2-point play.

When Villanova next got the ball back, just four plays and thirty-five seconds into the drive, Jankowski was intercepted again. Mercifully, his day was over. Antwon Young would play the rest of the way, completing 3-of-5 passes and leading the team's second-string to a touchdown over Towson's second unit in the closing minutes.

But Young's play was hardly a silver lining, just an incidental part of a 40-19 bloodbath that had been in the home team's control from start to finish. Now more than ever, Talley was at a loss to understand what made his players tick on the football field. Every time he allowed himself to exhibit any faith that they had turned the corner, the club seemed to throw the bus sharply into reverse and back it straight over a bridge.

Talley's demeanor when he spoke to the team in the otherwise silent visitor's locker room was no longer one of frustration. Instead, it was resignation. "The only lesson that you need to learn is this," said Talley. "You must show up at 1 o'clock in the afternoon, at 6 o'clock at night, at 7 o'clock at night, at 12:30, and at 1:30. Those are the times that we play football in the Atlantic 10. And you have to be ready for every single encounter. It is obvious to me from the scoreboard, the way we played, that this football team in this room does not know how to get ready for a game, any game. Because if you take a look at us right now, we are about as inconsistent a group of people . . .

"You can't tell me we can go from what we did last Saturday night to this. Did you look past Towson? Did you not think, at 5-3, they were a team that could do what they did to you? It's bad enough you handed them the game. So I'm not going to beat you up, I'll have more to say tomorrow, but the reality is that our football team, this edition of Villanova football, is not ready to play college football every Saturday. You guys decide to play when you want to play. When you don't want to play, this is what you have. Let's get on the bus and get the hell out of here."

Though some familiar with the situation might have been bracing for another postgame media conference skewering of the starting quarterback by the head coach, Talley instead betrayed a sullen calmness when he spoke to the press, exactly the kind of approach that Dean Kenefick had marveled at for the past decade. Talley made no specific mention of Jankowski, instead assigning team-wide responsibility for the mistakes.

Seated to Talley's right at the press table, red-eyed and with head bowed, was J. J. Outlaw. Outlaw's stat line was his weakest of the season—8 offensive touches, 33 yards, and zero memorable plays—and had been formed before a large group of hometown friends and family that desperately wanted better for the ebullient senior in his personal homecoming game.

Asked about his disappointing personal performance by a Baltimore-area reporter fishing to formulate a local angle, Outlaw sounded like Father Hagan leading a postgame blessing. "It's a tough loss because it's at home, but sometimes when you take a loss like this you've gotta kinda put things in perspective. I was able to have a lot of family and friends who I hadn't seen in a while come out, and when I'm done here I'll shower up and get a chance to go and chat with them before we head back up."

Schooled from years of watching diplomatic pro press conferences, Outlaw was also careful to remain detached while praising Villanova's opponent. "We may have taken Towson lightly, but at the same time we understand that they're a good team. You don't beat the teams that they've beaten, Delaware and everyone like that, compete like they've competed, if you're a bad team. My hat goes off to them, they played a great game."

Just before rising from the table and moving slowly toward the showers, Outlaw, with two games remaining as a collegian, whispered a statement designed to reassure the media, his head coach, and himself that despite the day's events, the sun would indeed rise tomorrow. "We'll bounce back," Outlaw said. "It'll be alright."

13

REACHING FOR THE TOP

It was eight o'clock on this Friday morning, and much like every normal Friday morning on every normal college campus, there wasn't much commotion at Villanova during this time of day. On the easternmost point of the campus, just outside of the stadium and locker room, the sound of the football team's three rented coach buses idling could be detected, but the future occupants of those vehicles were making scarcely a murmur as they prepared to board.

Dressed identically in their navy blue Nike Villanova warmups, the players, some of whom had been up late on Thursday night doing exactly what typical college students do on Thursday night, shuffled like zombies to their assigned busses. Most would spend the remainder of the morning sleeping, listening to music, studying, watching the movies that Brian Hulea had picked out for the ride, or some combination of all four.

The trip from Villanova to the campus of James Madison University was an especially long and exceedingly boring one, a five-hour sojourn if the traffic cooperated. The town of Harrisonburg, located in the Commonwealth of Virginia's northwest corner near the West Virginia line, was the destination of the team's longest road trip of the year, too close for the team to make air travel an efficient or economical choice, but not a close or comfortable voyage by anyone's standards.

As rough as the journey would be, a large portion of the team's players would soak in the experience for everything it was worth. Fifteen players, including the three captains and other Keepers of the Flame like J. J. Outlaw and Moe Gibson, would be embarking on their final road trip as college football players. They peered out their windows as the buses slowly pulled away from campus, considering just how quickly the past four of five years of their lives had rushed by.

To a lesser degree, the quality of Saturday's opponent was on the minds of the players. James Madison had won the I-AA championship the previous season, the third Atlantic 10 team in a seven-year period to capture the national title. But unlike the wealth of respect USC or LSU or Ohio State had been afforded in I-A, a national champion in I-AA didn't automatically garner the same type of feeling from opponents. Some of the freshmen hadn't even realized JMU was the reigning national champ before Talley had made mention of the fact following a practice earlier in the week.

Because of smaller squad sizes and stricter scholarship limitations, coupled with the fact that loose transfer rules assisted losing programs in becoming winners quickly, it was difficult for I-AA teams to sustain the momentum necessary to build a dynasty. James Madison had been the eighth school in nine seasons to win the I-AA championship, and as the 2005 season neared its conclusion, it did not even appear that the Dukes would get an opportunity to defend their title in the postseason. With two weeks to go, JMU was 5-4 and barely clinging to the final rung in the weekly Top 25 poll.

In addition to their opponent's mediocre season, Villanova was not giddy with anticipation over facing the defending national champion because there simply wasn't that much national prestige that went along with winning the crown.

In light of I-A's system of bowls and computer rankings, I-AA was the highest level of college football to determine its champion in the manner that most fans desired, namely on the field, but several factors kept the playoffs from making a ripple with the general public. I-AA was not consistently covered as a national entity by the media, meaning the deeper the tournament went, the less enticing many of the matchups became for fan bases or would-be television viewers. Villanova had experienced this firsthand in 2002, when their "final four" matchup was in Lake Charles, Louisiana, against McNeese State, a school that a vast majority of Villanovans had little awareness of and even less identification with. While the prospect of winning a national title was a nice inducement that most I-A schools had already relinquished by the end of September, a large portion of I-AA fans still related better to and were more likely to attend or watch conference or regional rivalries.

The structure of the tournament was another problem. Because of the way the calendar fell, the first of the I-AA playoffs' four rounds, which included eight of the tournament's fifteen games, was always played on Thanksgiving weekend. First-round attendance suffered for that reason, as making on-the-fly plans to attend a football game on a weekend normally reserved for family pursuits was not easily done. Most students were absent from campuses as well, which also negatively impacted the gate.

Attendance difficulties were a major reason why most I-AA administrators denounced the playoffs as a money loser, but they weren't the only bottom-line mark against the setup. The NCAA required universities that had a chance to be included in the sixteen-team field and wished to host a playoff game to submit bids for the first round, quarterfinal round, and semifinal round prior to the bracket being revealed on the Sunday prior to Thanksgiving. Only the championship game was played at a neutral site, with the other fourteen contests unfolding on the campus of one of the two participants in each game. The minimum guarantees required by the NCAA in 2005 were $30,000 in the first round, $40,000 in the quarterfinal round, and $50,000 for the semifinal round.

Large state schools with sizeable fan bases like the University of Montana or the University of Delaware would scarcely blink before submitting the bids, since such schools could count on good crowds throughout the tournament, but an institution like Villanova, which had struggled to put five thousand in the seats when it last hosted postseason games in 2002, was between a competitive rock and a financial hard place.

Universities could choose not to submit a bid and send a message to their hardworking players and coaching staffs that financial solvency was more important than giving the football team its best opportunity to win, or they could guarantee the necessary financial figure and risk piling more thousands of dollars onto a football budget that was already seven figures in the red. In 1991 and 1992, to Andy Talley's chagrin, Villanova had not submitted bids to host playoff games and had lost close first-round tilts at Youngstown State in both years. In 1997 and 2002 Villanova had hosted a total of four postseason contests and had lost money on all four.

Villanova athletic director Vince Nicastro estimated that it cost the university a minimum of $20,000 to put on a home football game, a figure that included the employment of game staff, campus police, grounds crew, and custodial staff, as well as the printing of programs and marketing efforts and providing food and beverage for the media, officials, game staff, and opposing teams. This financial commitment, plus the NCAA-mandated guarantee, minus the small dollar revenue gleaned from ticket sales, netted big-time losses for the school. In '02, when the Wildcats defeated Furman and Fordham in playoff games on campus, Villanova had dropped roughly $33,000 even before it had boarded its flight to play McNeese State in the semifinals.

Nicastro was among those who had been forced to grapple over the postseason question. "The great thing about the playoffs is that you get a national championship determined on the field," said Nicastro. "It's exciting, it's unbelievable, but the business model just doesn't work. It's counterintuitive. You figure the more you win, the easier it should be for you, and in the real world of I-AA, the more you win, the less we're bringing in. And it's disheartening. You want to be really successful, but you have this business model that becomes almost a disincentive."

Traveling during the playoffs was not a cheap alternative, either. The NCAA defrayed expenses for a travel party of 125, but if a school wished to do the things typically done in big games—bringing extra administrators, coaches' wives, band, cheerleaders, etc.—it was up to the school to figure out a way to foot that bill.

For budget-conscious administrators at most I-AA schools, those financial realities represented a disincentive for reaching the postseason or advancing in the tournament, if a team was able to get there. Despite the democratic ideal and overall competitiveness of the tournament, presidents, athletic directors, and I-AA conference commissioners rarely sung the public praises of the I-AA playoffs, and some in that group had thoroughly investigated more cost-feasible postseason alternatives such as one-off bowl tie-ins or conference championship games. One of I-AA's most visible leagues, the SWAC, had given up its automatic postseason bid some years back, preferring to keep its network-televised Bayou Classic between Southern and Grambling in its normal Thanksgiving weekend slot due to financial considerations, and also adding a league title game in lieu of I-AA playoff participation. Also choosing not to be a part of the playoffs was the Ivy League, and though that decision had much more to do with the elitist thinking of Ivy presidents than financial concerns, the stance was another piece of the puzzle in terms of the I-AA playoffs' struggle in building brand identity.

A number of coaches were wary of the I-AA playoff format as well, since up to a month of valuable recruiting time could be wiped out, dents were leveled against the football budget that were likely to be felt on the back end, and it was a difficult tournament to prepare for and win.

To make matters worse, the championship round was played in a city, Chattanooga, which had been the site of the finale since 1997 mostly because it was the only place that had shown serious interest in hosting the game. Chattanooga was a decent location because it had a nice, new stadium and was a relatively short trip for many of its likeliest participants, such as those from the Southern Conference and the southerly programs of the A-10, but the local community didn't support the event, and the fan bases of many of the schools that reached the title game weren't too moved about traveling to a minor-league town where the temperature would be in the fifty-degree range just a few nights before Christmas. In 2004, when JMU won the title, the biggest story deriving from the game had been about the recently laid playing surface at Chattanooga's Finley Stadium, which was scarcely playable and was being uprooted in giant clumps. Players from both teams, JMU and Montana, told reporters that the field was the worst they had ever been on, and much of the ESPN-viewing audience was left to scoff at the low-class trimmings of what was supposed to be I-AA's finest hour.

Even the one thing that could always be counted on to give the I-AA playoffs greater credibility when contrasted with the I-A system—the fairness of the postseason structure—had come under fire in the most recent decade. In 2002, the group of I-AA athletic directors chosen to select the field had politicked to keep an obviously deserving at-large program—Wofford College—out of the tournament. In 2004, the exact same fate had befallen another school, Cal Poly. In 2003 it appeared that the bracket was manufactured to undeservedly allow Montana, with the most sizeable and loyal fan base in I-AA, to host additional playoff games ahead of teams that had earned the right to do so by posting better seasons (Montana lost its first-round home game, rendering the manipulation useless).

With very little media outcry over the process due to a general lack of media knowledge of I-AA's national picture, certain members of the selection committee were left to promote their own agendas when bracketing teams without any fear of being called on the carpet for their actions.

The utopian ideal that I-AA's sixteen-team playoff field represented was, by 2005, more like a flawed aristocracy, with enough corruption and dollar-sign thinking at the highest levels of power to make a comparison with the arcane BCS system truly befitting.

Not that Villanova's players and coaches could have cared in the least about the ills of I-AA's postseason structure at the moment. By mid-November, the Wildcats would have been happy to simply be part of the playoff discussion, but after the Towson loss, that talk had officially been muted.

The current group of seniors had been either true or redshirt freshmen when Villanova had last qualified for the playoffs. John Dieser,

Moe Gibson, J. J. Outlaw, Darrell Adams, and Adam James had all been significant contributors during the playoff run. Brian Hulea, who had been a starter for most of that season, missed the '02 postseason due to a bout with mononucleosis.

But by next year, there wouldn't be a single player left in the program who had been active when the Cats lost to McNeese State in the 2002 semifinals. After making the playoff field five times between 1989 and 1997, Villanova had been there just once in the seven seasons since—once in eight seasons by the time 2005 eventually careened to a close. The competitiveness of the Atlantic 10, as James Madison could attest, had much to do with the Wildcats' inability to reach the postseason on a regular basis. Every A-10 team apart from Rhode Island and new member Towson had made the playoffs in the past five years, but none had made it more than twice over that span.

This year, there was just one postseason lock in the Atlantic 10, and that was New Hampshire, which had gone 4-1 since beating Villanova and was sitting at 8-1 with two weeks to play. Also looking to be in decent shape was UMass, which was 7-2 after throttling Delaware the week before. The Minutemen were at I-A Army this week, which would be a tough game in which to prevail, but they would finish up with a winnable contest at Hofstra.

If the league was going to get a third playoff entry, it would probably come from a surprising place: this week's Richmond–Towson game in suburban Baltimore. Towson was 6-3 after beating Villanova, and after whipping up on the Wildcats and taking down Delaware earlier in the season, the Tigers looked to have a reasonable shot to win their final two. Also peaking was Dave Clawson's Richmond team, which was 6-3 and in the midst of a five-game winning streak that had begun with its fourth-quarter comeback against Villanova. If Clawson could beat Towson and William and Mary over the final two weeks, the former VU coordinator would be back in the playoffs well ahead of schedule, with a program that had already clinched its first winning season since 2000.

Most head coaches would be hesitant to admit being interested in other league games, but Talley, who had coached in the conference longer than any other current A-10 head man, was not afraid to scoreboard-watch. By midweek, he was telling people that he thought Towson would win on Saturday, and while the Tigers' recent 28-point throttling of Villanova probably had much to do with the prediction, those who heard it couldn't help but wonder if the pick was rooted in at least a touch of anti-Clawson sentiment.

Clawson, at thirty-eight years old, had made a meteoric rise and looked poised to hit the big time—I-A—sooner rather than later, and there was suspicion, though completely unsubstantiated, that perhaps Talley was envious of that position more than he had let on. Talley himself had flirted with a couple of I-A jobs during his tenure. New Mexico had courted him seriously prior to the 1992 season, but Talley didn't feel that he fit in with the southwest and didn't have a blueprint for winning there, so he opted to remain at Villanova. He had previously interviewed with Rutgers as well but never felt that he was a serious contender for the job. Not seizing on those flirtations, coupled with Nova's decision to stay at I-AA in the mid-90s, gave rise to a sense of regret that Talley would express at his weakest moments.

Back in 1991, when media reports began to surface that Villanova would investigate moving into the Big East, Talley had been quoted in a local newspaper story, saying, "I'm forty-eight years old and I want to be a I-A head coach."

Now sixty-two, he knew he was in a good situation at Nova, but he often wondered whether he could have been a star at another level instead of being a very successful though nationally anonymous coach in what most considered to be "small college football." Clawson was nearing the crossroads that Talley had once seriously pondered—and some of those closest to the coach suspected that it was difficult for Talley to root for Clawson wholeheartedly because of a sense of envy over his former assistant's situation.

Mike Kern, who had covered Villanova for the *Philadelphia Daily News* since the mid-eighties, considered the course that the longtime Wildcats head coach had charted. "Andy's always had this impression when Division I[-A] jobs come up, whether it be Maryland, or Temple, this job or that job, 'I'd be right for that job,' always looking to move up, which I understand, that's what I-AA guys do," said Kern. "And I said to him one time, 'Andy, did you ever think the worst thing in your life is you're going to coach at Villanova for twenty-five, thirty years, you're going to have a great record, playoffs, whatever, and they're going to build a statue of you when you leave?' It's not the worst legacy in the world.

"If Andy had taken the New Mexico job fifteen years ago, that [current Texas A&M coach Dennis] Franchione took, or if Maryland had ever approached him, or some of the programs he thought he might have worked at, who knows what would happen? Would Andy Talley be Dennis Franchione? Maybe. I don't have the answer to that. But I do know that where he's been for the last twenty years, and what he's done there, starting from nothing. They've been successful. They've been a national program. They've been to playoffs. They've been close to winning championships. They had the number-one season. They had two players of the year. Whatever you think of Andy—and I know opinions vary—there's no way you can look at his body of work with the Villanova program and say that it's been anything but very successful. And I think there's a lot to be said for that.

"People say, 'It's only I-AA.' And even though Temple has been bad for a long time, they're still Division I[-A], and it still tends to overshadow what a I-AA does in this town, because it's not a I-AA town. If Villanova were where Georgia Southern is, maybe it would be taken a different way."

Whatever his thoughts about his or Clawson's career arc, Talley was desperate to get Villanova back in the playoff mix in short order, and during Friday night's team assembly in one of the hotel conference rooms, the coach showed the 1997 and 2002 highlight films to map out the direction in which he wanted the players, especially the young ones, to head. Only a handful of team members had seen with their own eyes people in Villanova football uniforms achieving sustained success, and Talley knew that if the Wildcats were ever going to reach the pinnacle again, his players would have to visualize that success. In that regard, the highlight films represented a powerful visual, and one that the head coach hoped would put the team in the right frame of mind on Saturday against James Madison.

Though JMU was a long shot to reach the postseason, Villanova's players and coaches knew the Dukes were a solid program on their worst day, and beating James Madison on the road would help wash away last week's humbling at the hands of Towson. If any Wildcat was feeling a bit of an inferiority complex over facing the defending national champions, James Madison's sterling football facilities were hardly going to cure them of that sense.

The defending national champions had just built a gorgeous $10 million football facility, the Plecker Athletic Performance Center, which included a 7,000-square-foot weight room with state-of-the-art equipment, a 5,000-square-foot sports medicine facility, a full array of coaching offices and conference rooms, spacious locker rooms, and an academic support facility with a brand new computer lab.

Temporary stands had also been added to JMU's playing facility, Bridgeforth Stadium, which raised capacity to fifteen thousand, a deluxe video board was brought into replace the old scoreboard, and Virginia governor Mark Warner was reportedly set to earmark another $10 million of the state budget for a considerable expansion and renovation of the stadium within the next two to three years.

I-AA schools tended not to spend in this manner if they were planning on remaining I-AA schools. Though university officials were mum on the subject, James Madison's upgrades screamed "I-A move," with a shift to a non-BCS league like Conference USA seeming more than plausible down the road. In the meantime, Talley and the other head coaches in the A-10 would have to try to figure out how to remain competitive with a school that was adding important recruiting enticements by the score. As if Villanova needed another obstacle with which to contend.

As he walked the field prior to the game, Talley enjoyed the sixty-degree Virginia weather but was more than a little concerned about how his team would come out. He had been stunned by what had occurred at Towson, and James Madison was undoubtedly a better team than Towson.

Talley and Sam Venuto would also be unveiling a new system at quarterback. Barring anything unforeseen, like consistently strong play from Frank Jankowski, true freshman Antwon Young would get a chance to lead the offense on every third drive. JMU was a heck of an opponent for Young to face in the first meaningful action of his career, but with nothing beyond a winning season left to play for in 2005, the coaching staff had to start thinking about the future. With that in mind, some game snaps might be good for the freshman.

In his pregame address to the team, Talley reinforced Friday night's message about Villanova's proud football tradition and asked the players to carry that sense of pride onto the field against JMU.

"We talked last night about our lineage, about where we're from and our pedigree," began Talley. "This is what has been bred. This team, 2005, depending on how you want to approach the game today and how you want to play, can be as good as any of those teams were. Any of those four championship teams, six playoff teams, you can be as good as them on any given day. You just gotta decide if you want to play.

"You got a packed house, you're playing against the defending national champion. If you read the Harrisonburg paper this morning, Villanova looked like they were the little sisters of the poor. Leading us to the slaughter, that's what they think, that's what people think of you. That's what the writers think about you, that's what their coaches think about you, because they feed the writers, and that's what their players think. You have a great opportunity to get it done today . . . so knock people down and play the way we know how to play. We've got a chance to have a great win today. Let's do it today."

In an approach dissimilar to the Towson game, Villanova showed up looking like a team that was interested in getting it done. On the first drive of the game, Jankowski played like a quarterback desperate not to allow Antwon Young to see the field. The sophomore engineered an efficient 11-play, 72-yard drive, complete with a third-and-long pass play to Outlaw to keep the drive alive and two long completions to

Dieser to get the Wildcats inside the 5. Moments later, a short run by Moe Gibson put Villanova on the scoreboard first, and Joe Marcoux's point-after made the score 7–0.

JMU, still clinging to its playoff hopes, answered quickly. Nova had a chance to send the Dukes three-and-out, but on a third-and-eleven play, quarterback Justin Rascati hit wideout Ardon Bransford for a gain of 47 yards. The Dukes continued to drive before running back Alvin Banks scampered in for a 12-yard touchdown. That quickly, it was 7–7.

But the Wildcats refused to wilt. On the ensuing drive, Jankowski converted a pair of third-and-long passes to Dieser to put Villanova in position to score again. The drive would stall at the James Madison 24-yard line, but Joe Marcoux came on and calmly hit a 41-yard field goal to put VU back out in front, 10–7, in the latter stages of the first quarter.

The beginning of the second frame brought more good things, when a long JMU march was stifled after linebacker Bryan Adams forced a fumble, which was in return recovered by defensive tackle Brian Hentosz. But one play after converting his fourth third-down of the game, Jankowski dropped back to pass on first down, was hit, and lost the football straight up in the air. JMU's Justin Barnes intercepted the ball and brought it back to the Wildcat 23. Four plays later, the Dukes took their first lead, with Rascati hitting Casime Harris for a 3-yard touchdown pass to make the score 14–10.

The interception had hardly been Jankowski's fault, and the game was still a nip-and-tuck affair, but the coaching staff made good on its promise to play the freshman nonetheless. Young was about to see the first meaningful action of his career, but any spectator who blinked could have easily missed his presence. After Moe Gibson set the youngster up for success with a kickoff return all the way down to the James Madison 41, Young took his first snap of the day, attempted to hand the ball to Gibson on a stretch play, and mishandled the transition. The ball fell to the turf, where it was fallen upon by JMU's Clint Kent.

It was at that moment that Talley determined that Young wasn't ready, and that for all of Jankowski's shortcomings, it was the Berwick graduate that gave them the best chance to win. Young, whose mistake would be costly, would not see the field for the rest of the afternoon. Following the fumble, the Villanova defense failed to get the ball back on a fourth-and-two play on the series following the fumble, and four plays after that, Maurice Fenner bolted in for a 3-yard touchdown to up the Dukes' lead to 21–10.

The Wildcats hadn't played poorly over the first twenty-five minutes of the game, but in yet another chapter of a similar story that had played out multiple times earlier in the season, their two turnovers had been converted into 14 crucial points.

Encouragingly, Villanova didn't use its recent misfortune as an excuse to crawl into a hole as it had at Towson. Just before halftime, Jankowski executed another solid drive, getting the offense close enough for Marcoux to kick his second field goal of the game, from 34 yards out. As the teams retreated to their locker rooms, the fancy Bridgeforth Stadium video board read 21–13, JMU. The Wildcats were behind, but they were also in the football game against a very good team and had at the very least shown more life than they had the previous Saturday. There was hope, and that was worth something.

Rather than ranting and raving at the half, Mark Reardon used encouraging tones when addressing his defense, which had helped keep the game under control. Mark Ferrante was intense but espoused good vibes when talking things over with his offensive line, with his group breaking its meeting with a Ferrante-led cry of "Win this fucking game."

Talley's halftime speech also had a much different ring than had his embarrassed words at Towson. "I think you got their attention, men," he said. "I know you got their attention. Their coach is over there kicking their ass right now. They came out not playing hard, they played a little bit then they backed off, played a little bit . . . You guys have been on 'em. If it weren't for the two turnovers, we'd be ahead right now. So that's in the past, it's history. We're only down by a touchdown. We're in great shape, we couldn't be in better shape unless we were ahead by a touchdown.

"We're going to kick off. Define the game immediately. You gotta stop them, you gotta go in and punch 'em with a touchdown right off the bat. Anything can happen, we can win this game going way. Let me tell you something, they're not responding to the enthusiasm that we have on the football field. Keep your mistakes to a minimum, keep tackling hard. You guys are tackling great. You're tackling great. We're moving the ball up and down the field on these guys. So just hang in there, play a complete game. But we gotta define the game in this quarter, okay? Let's have a great half."

The Cats tried to gain control of the game the way their head coach had demanded, but instead it was their opponent that set to defining the second thirty minutes. On a crucial third-and-one play early in the drive, Fenner rushed for 27 yards. Later, on second-and-seventeen, Rascati tucked the football and ran 26 yards down to the Villanova 11. Two plays after that, Rascati plunged in for a 1-yard touchdown, and James Madison had their biggest lead of the game at 28–13.

With 10:50 to play in the third quarter, the game was certainly within reach, but it was lost on no one that JMU possessed one of the Atlantic 10's top defenses, and also that the Dukes had outscored Villanova by a 21–3 count over the last quarter and a half. This was going to be an uphill climb, but Talley's team had not conceded anything.

After getting the ball, Villanova went on a ten-play drive consuming more than five minutes of clock time, with Moe Gibson totaling 48 yards combined via the ground and air. But the offense sputtered at the James Madison 14, and Marcoux's subsequent 31-yard field goal try was blocked, robbing the Wildcats of much-needed momentum and confidence, not to mention precious time.

Hulea and the defense held on the ensuing drive, but Villanova's next march stalled right around midfield just as the fourth quarter began. The Cats got the ball back via a fumble forced by Hulea and recovered by Terrance Reaves, and another nice drive led by Jankowski got Villanova inside the JMU 10 near the nine-minute mark of the fourth quarter. A touchdown here and another stop by the ever-resilient defense would give the Cats a chance heading late into the fourth. But after advancing the ball to the 10-yard line, Villanova embarked upon a sequence that would sum up its season perfectly.

On second-and-two, Gibson ran straight ahead for 1 yard, and on third-and-one, another play to Gibson netted no gain. The game riding on the next play, Villanova called a timeout, with Talley and Venuto deciding to use 200-pound running back Matt Dicken to pick up the short yardage. Dicken powered ahead for the necessary yard, giving Villanova first-and-goal from the 8.

On first-and-goal, Jankowski threw incomplete to Matt Sherry. On second down, Gibson was stopped for no gain on another running play. Prior to third down, the Wildcats blew their second timeout in the span of 1:02, again trying to get the correct play called in an important situation. But Jankowski threw incomplete to Sherry again. On fourth down, he was pressured and tossed a third consecutive incompletion. A thirteen-play drive consuming nearly five minutes had again yielded zero points, and with the clock now reading 6:51, it was all but over. Villanova wouldn't get the ball back again until the 2:28 mark, following which another drive stalled, and JMU ran out the clock from there.

No points had been scored by either team in the final twenty-five minutes of the game, though the underdog Cats had seen plenty of golden opportunities come their way. Just like the previous week, Talley's team hadn't played well enough to win. But much unlike last week, they had played hard and with purpose, which is why the head coach sounded encouraged in defeat following the loss.

"First of all I look around this locker room and I see a lot of pain in faces, I see a lot of disappointed faces, and I see a lot of guys that are hurting right now," said Talley. "I see a lot of guys that played their ass off today and are hurting coming off a tough loss. I think we made a lot of progress today, and I'll be honest with you, I was very concerned about this football game after the Towson game."

The second-half attitude displayed by the team hadn't yielded a win, but it had at least convinced the coaching staff that its team still had desire. "To me, when we stopped 'em defensively a couple of times, and we got in there on fourth down, and we got it on fourth-and-short, I think we came of age, I really do," said Talley. "In the past, I'm not sure we would have gotten it. I just have to tell you right now, even though the seniors are leaving us in a game, you have no idea the progress that this team is making right now. We'll see rewards down the line. This is a football team now that I think you can take a lot of places, in a lot of venues, and win a lot of games. I didn't think that after last week.

"You guys played a good football team, a very good football team. A couple of turnover mistakes here and there, we could have won that game today, men. Okay, you can sit back and critique the game all you want, it's a very, very close game. As far as the head coach is concerned, and the assistant coaches, this is a football team that can go play anywhere in the country.

"This is a building block. For our seniors, our captains, I know it's a tough one, because it doesn't look like we can have a winning season, but we can beat Delaware. So just make sure whatever you're holding in your heart, you hold onto a little longer. You've got nothing to hang your head about men. Absolutely nothing, okay? Last week, let me tell you, I snuck out of the stadium. This week I'm walking out with my head held high because of you.

"I hope you looked up on the scoreboard when they introduced us: Freshman, sophomore, redshirt freshman, sophomore, senior, freshman. We've got a lot of young guys here. And I hope you're learning from the seniors that play in this program. This is difficult for them because they have a ring on their finger, you young guys don't have a ring on your finger. They know what it's like to be on the mountaintop, so this is tough for them, disheartening, and it's heartbreaking because they have one more left. The only thing I can tell you is, let's dedicate ourselves to making sure when those guys come into our stadium next week, we're going to say goodbye to our seniors and send them off with a great victory."

Hulea, who after an eleven-tackle effort against James Madison was within striking distance of Villanova's all-time career record in that category, appreciated the acknowledgment, but he didn't want to hear about building blocks or the good that might have come out of a losing effort. When he gathered his teammates for the final time in a visiting locker room, Hulea's message was clear.

"Do not be satisfied with losing," Hulea began. "It doesn't matter what your record is, how you play. Do not fucking be satisfied with losing. If I can fucking leave you guys with one thing when I fucking leave here, and I'm sure Dies and Darrell will say the same thing, not to fucking be satisfied. Next week come out and fucking kick Delaware's ass back at our place."

14

THE RIVALRY

The last thing Villanova needed heading into its final game of the 2005 season was another distraction. The school's "Senior Day" festivities brought with them their own set of routine-altering elements, as pregame warmups would have to be pushed back to allow twenty-one players to be honored on the field. Those players would be escorted onto the playing surface by their parents, and getting all of them in the stadium on time and organized was another detail to be considered by the players, coaches, and football support staff. Also, Mark Ferrante had invited a large group of recruits to Villanova Stadium for the team's home finale, since the big crowd that was expected for this week's game was a crucial part of the program's sales pitch to prospects. On top of all that, emotions would naturally be high due to the circumstances surrounding the seniors' last game, and the fact that it was a home game against archrival Delaware ratcheted up the tension to an even larger degree.

And now this. A Wildcat player came to Andy Talley's office in the middle of the week with information that the team's freshman long snapper, Mason Frakes, was engaged in activities on campus that represented a serious violation of team rules. After twenty-one years at Villanova, Talley's investigative skills on campus were practically Columbo-like, and just as he had known every detail of Russell McKittrick's extracurricular activities before the player's hangover had even worn off, it took Talley all of an afternoon to acquire corroboration on his tip about Frakes.

Unlike McKittrick and Dave Dalessandro, Frakes would not be placed in exile and given the option of returning to the team. In fact, Frakes's activities rose to a level that prompted the university to immediately terminate his affiliation with the school. The federal Student Privacy Act prevented anyone at the university from revealing the exact nature of Frakes' actions, leaving the players to make their own assumptions. The unsubstantiated rumor spreading like wildfire throughout the team was that Frakes's transgressions had in some way involved drugs.

Talley took firm and decisive action when it came to anything concerning drugs on his team. He had learned his lesson the hard way in the mid-nineties, when it came to his attention that there were several players in his then-struggling program who were engaged in either the use or sale of drugs on campus. After seemingly separating the bad element from his program, Talley had discovered on the eve of the Wildcats' 1996 playoff game with East Tennessee State that one of his senior leaders and perhaps the team's best defensive player had violated both team and university rules concerning drugs. Though he could have waited for the appeals process to play out, Talley immediately suspended the all-conference player for Villanova's biggest game in five years, as the Wildcats posted one of their weakest defensive showings of the season in a 35–29 loss.

From the time of that suspension to this alleged incident, almost nine years later to the day, drugs had not been an issue for the Villanova football program. And though he would never regret taking the necessary action against either player, just like in the '96 situation, the circumstances regarding Frakes were almost sure to make the Wildcats a weaker football team come Saturday. Though he had missed some blocking assignments earlier in the year (helping lead to Adam James's downfall as the team's kicker), Frakes was an excellent snapper, and the Cats had no one else on the roster that even remotely fit that description. Matt Costantino had struggled in the role earlier in his career, and the starting defensive tackle didn't want the part-time special teams job any more than Talley wished him to fill it. But the only other realistic option was Alex Koplin, a 200-pound walk-on receiver and honor student who risked getting blown off the football even worse than had the 230-pound Frakes.

The quandary was not one that Talley wanted to be devoting his time to prior to facing off with Delaware, of all teams. The University of Delaware was located just a forty-five-minute drive south of Villanova's campus, and despite the major differences in both the makeup of the schools and the passion of their football fan bases, the Blue Hens were the Wildcats' chief gridiron rival. The teams had been playing one another annually since the early 1960s, apart from the seven-year period in the eighties between the Catholic school's dropping of the sport and the year it joined the Yankee Conference.

In the two decades that the universities had been part of the same I-AA league, the rivalry had truly heated up. Early in his Villanova career, Talley had major trouble beating Delaware, then coached by the legendary Harold "Tubby" Raymond. Talley's Wildcats won just once in their first eight meetings, until in 1996 VU got off the mat with a 27-0 demolition of the Hens. Villanova would own the series through the end of the century, beating Delaware six times in seven years in games that were nearly always exciting and closely contested. UD had reassumed control of the series again in the last two years, winning by a field goal at Villanova Stadium in 2003 and holding off a late rally to take last year's game, 41–35.

Talley had little trouble stoking his own competitive fire for the Delaware game. The statewide following that the UD football team generated (a byproduct of the absence of I-A football and major pro sports in the state), coupled with the fact that Villanova was in fact the Blue Hens' biggest rival, had turned Talley into a genuine and legendary villain in the First State. Being outspoken and animated, not to mention small in stature and somewhat bookish-looking, helped widen the target on the head coach's back.

When *Sports Illustrated* did its year-long profile of the sporting passions and peculiarities of the fifty states in 2003, Talley's name was a close second to that of Dallas Cowboys owner Jerry Jones as Delaware residents' choice for "Enemy of the State." Before the 1992 game, UD linebacker Mike Bandish made headlines by referring to Talley as an "idiot" at the Blue Hens' weekly press luncheon (Bandish later retracted the marks and apologized). The same year, when Delaware reached the national semifinals and Villanova was downed in the first round, Raymond himself had baited Talley by sarcastically asking reporters, after the Cats' season had ended, how Villanova had fared that week.

Delaware fans, which comprised at least half of the crowd even in the years that the rivalry was played on the Main Line, shouted epithets, generally profane and often hilarious, at Talley from the stands. Talley also received a steady stream of hate mail from the state, some of it threatening and curiously racist (curious since Villanova typically had a similar percentage of minority players on its roster as did Delaware) in nature.

And while the worst of this correspondence unsettled and disturbed Talley, he privately admired Delaware's fan base, aside from the small number of lunatics, and he enjoyed much of the attention they paid him and his program. Talley didn't encounter a great number of passionate football supporters at Villanova, and it wasn't as if the fans at places like Northeastern or New Hampshire would ever care enough to shout hateful things from the stands. For a coach who reveled in even the suggestion of a big-time college football atmosphere, playing Delaware was about the most fun that Talley could hope to have all season, especially if he was on the winning side.

The head coach's feelings about the Blue Hens' football program, however, were decidedly more mixed. Talley had achieved a friendly respect with Tubby Raymond over the years, and even had a picture of himself and the longtime Delaware coach framed and displayed prominently on his office wall. But Raymond had retired prior to the 2002 season, and Talley didn't feel nearly as much natural kinship with his successor, K. C. Keeler.

Whether fairly or unfairly, Keeler had developed a reputation as something of a renegade at Division III Rowan University in New Jersey, building one of that level's most consistently strong programs in part by welcoming in large groups of transfers from Divisions I and II. Since arriving at Delaware, his alma mater, Keeler had done the same in taking advantage of I-A transfer rules, which did not force players to sit out a year if they moved down a level. The Blue Hens' first-ever I-AA championship, in 2003, had been fueled in large part by the efforts of Andy Hall, a quarterback transfer from Georgia Tech, and Shawn Johnson, a former All-ACC defensive end at Duke.

And while Delaware was doing nothing even remotely illegal or below-board by welcoming in I-A transfers, and Talley himself had even brought in a few transfers over the years, the head coach felt in his heart that what appeared to be an open-door policy at Delaware violated the spirit of college football and unfairly altered the competitive landscape of the league. The word was that Johnson, who had received an undergraduate degree from Duke but had used his one remaining year of eligibility in order to star for a winner at Delaware, had been enrolled at the university as a graduate student for the fall semester, and after his team won the national title in December, he was never seen on campus again. It was this legal recruitment of "hired guns," which had gone on at other schools in the Atlantic 10 as well, that galled Talley, whose recruiting practices had always involved bringing in players who were also interested in contributing to Villanova as students. Earlier in the season, Talley had received a phone call from A-10 commissioner Linda Bruno, gently reprimanding him for comments made on his weekly radio show, when he referred to UMass as "Transfer U." As he got older and became seemingly more bulletproof, Talley had become less hesitant to make such comments publicly.

As with most coaches in the league, Talley's relationship with Keeler was fine on the surface, but he clearly wanted to beat him, and beat him badly. Talley had sent Keeler a basket of cookies as a gesture of goodwill upon the latter's hiring at Delaware in 2002, but he had bristled when Keeler went on local television and sarcastically suggested that since he was unsure of the Villanova coach's motives in sending the gift, that he would test the cookies out on his dog. Talley was not amused, though any underlying ill will in his relationship with Keeler had simmered down since that time.

A spike in tension between the coaches was not expected this week, and the fact that this year's game was essentially meaningless, beyond the notion of bragging rights, had something to do with that relative sense of quiet.

After starting the year 3-0 and rising as high as No. 5 in I-AA, the Blue Hens had fallen like a ton of bricks, losing five of their next six games to stray far from their postseason pace of the previous two seasons and join the Wildcats near the bottom of the Atlantic 10's South Division standings. In fact, 2005 would mark the first time since the game was moved to the final week of the season in 1999 that the league title or playoff races would not be affected by Villanova–Delaware.

The big conference games of the day instead involved Richmond, which had pounded Towson by a 48–21 score the previous Saturday and needed to win at rival William and Mary on Saturday to make the postseason, and UMass, which had just been beaten by Army, 34–27, and would have to win at Hofstra to be considered for the playoff field.

Despite the dearth of national or conference implications that Villanova–Delaware held, there were positives, or more accurately the avoidance of negatives, that the winner could hang its hat on. With both standing at 2-5 in league play, the loser of the contest would clinch sole possession of last place in the Atlantic 10 South Division, an ignoble fate with which neither had been traditionally familiar. Villanova hadn't finished last since 1995, when it occupied the division basement along with Northeastern, and hadn't finished alone in the cellar since 1993. Delaware, which still had a shot at a winning season, had never finished last.

Beyond those storylines was the sentiment surrounding the seniors. No team in the country wanted to send its seniors, most of whom would be wearing a football uniform for the final time, out as losers. Talley knew that there was enough respect throughout the roster for guys like

Brian Hulea and Darrell Adams that he could use the last appearance of those players on the Villanova Stadium turf to provide an inspirational lift. So on Friday night, as he did every year, Talley gathered the entire team in a room on campus and gave all of the seniors a chance to address the team.

The tone of the speeches differed from year to year. Sometimes the players were emotional, sometimes they were lively and wisecracking, and in other years the speeches had combined both elements. With the 2005 season already having been stamped a major disappointment, Talley was expecting to hear some regret from what had to this point been one of his most difficult groups to understand or get through to.

Not all of the players were comfortable or compelling public speakers. Talley allowed all of the seniors, even those who still had eligibility in 2006 such as Marvin Burroughs, to address the team, and that sector of the group naturally had little to say. But there was some winning oration as well, which ran the gamut from light-hearted to heart-wrenchingly emotional.

The players had heard people like Hulea and John Dieser speak many times before, but John Angelo's voice was nowhere near as familiar to the assembled group. The coaching staff had taken a chance in recruiting the likable Angelo out of Youngstown, Ohio's Ursuline High School in 2001, after the linebacker had resisted the advice of doctors in playing his entire senior year with a severely broken hand in order to get a shot at a scholarship offer. Villanova had been the only school to offer Angelo, who came from a family full of former college football players and whose uncle, Jerry, was currently serving as general manager of the NFL Chicago Bears.

But as pedigreed a football player and pleasant a person as Angelo was, he was also considered by the coaching staff to be a "miss," meaning he hadn't developed on the field as anyone had hoped and wouldn't have been recruited if the program had to do it over again. Angelo had seen the field some in 2005 as a special-teamer and backup linebacker, but he was a senior academically and hadn't done enough to be asked back for his final year of eligibility.

Many players in similar situations had privately blamed the coaching staff or some other external element for their disappointing careers, but as he stood for the first and last time before his assembled coaching staff and teammates, Angelo was contrite. His eyes cast downward, speaking softly, Angelo thanked Talley for giving him a shot, thanked Reardon for allowing him to contribute for the first time in his career as a senior, and then directly addressed his teammates with an air of resignation.

"It's kind of tough when you come into a place, and you set all these goals for yourself, and you don't quite get there," Angelo confided. "But the friends I've made, the memories I have, that's something I wouldn't trade for any amount of playing time. And that's what Villanova football is to me, just the guys in this room."

When George Smith began talking, it appeared he would be covering the same emotional territory as Angelo. Smith was a walk-on quarterback out of St. Augustine High School on the South Jersey shore, an athletic player who had run the option during his prep career and never had a realistic shot of taking a collegiate snap. Smith had actually pulled a major upset by rising to No. 3 on the depth chart at quarterback at Villanova as a senior, running the scout team offense after Burroughs' injury had moved Antwon Young up to the No. 2 slot. Special teams coach Apollo Wright had also used him on the punt coverage unit. Smith, whose claim to fame on the team prior to getting onto the field was leading-man looks that were known to consistently turn the heads of Villanova's female students, made sure to publicly thank his coaches.

"I want to say thank you to Coach Talley for not only letting me walk on," said Smith, "but for building the program and making it what is. It means a lot to me. This program wouldn't be anything without Coach Talley and what he did. I want to thank Coach Venuto for putting up with me in meetings and everything, I appreciate that. I want to thank Coach Wright for getting me out on special teams, and with people who are a little bit bigger and more athletic than me. I appreciate you giving me a chance to get out there and try and contribute.

"Football has really helped me . . ." Smith paused, giving the indication that his emotions had gotten the better of him, before continuing, ". . . get more girls." The room erupted in the type of laughter that had not been present around the Villanova football team very often during 2005. When the players and coaches finally contained themselves, Smith continued his speech, deadpanning, "I'm serious." Another wave of laughter bounced off of the meeting room walls.

Smith would be a tough act to follow, but if any player on the team was going to make a run at his comic timing, it was Matt Costantino. Costantino was a former walk-on from Lynn, Massachusetts, who had worked his way into earning both a scholarship and starting position on the team, and his work ethic and bone-dry New England sense of humor made him extremely popular with his teammates.

Costantino, whose name was similar enough to tackle Mike Costanzo's that Talley routinely butchered it, started off by ribbing his head coach and made sure to allude to the unwilling reacquisition of long-snapper duties that he would be forced to complete on Saturday in Frakes's absence.

"I'd like to thank Coach T. Even though sometimes I don't know if you know my name yet, you usually get the initials right. I'd like to thank all the coaches. Coach Reardon, I'd like to apologize for all those hairs you lost. Coach Wright, I thought we were friends until yesterday. I'd like to thank Coach Daly for coming out, I think he did a great job this year. Coach Ferrante, it's been great. One-on-ones, that's one thing I don't think I'll miss, but I did win my last one-on-one."

Costantino's words then switched from cheerful gratitude to reflection and seriousness. "Any sport I've played, I've never been part of a championship team. And that's something every year, to start out a season, I always wanted so bad. And when I came to Villanova I heard about the '97 team that was undefeated. Freshman year, we went to the national semifinals, and I said at Villanova, this is the place that it's going to happen. We have the personnel and the players and the program to win a national championship.

"As time went on, a championship is something I wanted more than anything in the world. You don't come back in the summer, go through winter workouts, for nothing. You don't come back just because of the eleven games, you come back because you want to win a championship. That meant everything to me. And you know, I was thinking about it, if someone had told me before the season that you can either be a part of a championship team, or part of the Villanova football team that's going to go 5-6 . . ."

Costantino's voice broke and his eyes began to tear. There was no punchline forthcoming from the 6-foot, 275-pound senior, simply raw emotion.

"These coaches, the people in this room, the relationships you've made throughout your four years here are going to matter the most, and they're going to be the people that are around 5, 10 years from now when everything else has gone past. You're going to be talking about how you wanted to win that championship, and the 5-6 season that wasn't so good, but you're also going to be talking about the good times, and all the things that you've done in your four years that were some of the best memories you've ever had. I wouldn't trade that for anything, I wouldn't trade being on this team and being 5-6 for any other team in this whole nation."

As Talley had hoped, Costantino then turned his attention to the Delaware game.

"Tomorrow is our last opportunity to go out, and for me and a lot of these guys, the last stage of our four-year process here. And for you younger guys that haven't been there when we beat Delaware, it's one of the greatest feelings that I've had in my four years. And even though we've won playoff games, we've won some great games, beating Delaware, there's nothing like it. You'll know tomorrow when we walk off that field victorious. Let's go get 'em tomorrow, fellas."

It was hard to imagine the room getting more emotional, but then again, Brian Hulea had yet to speak. Hulea's words to the team during the season had been mostly of the run-of-the-mill motivational variety, the same type of attempts at inspiration that could be heard in most football locker rooms all over the country during the fall months. And while Hulea's play over the past four years said much about his sense of personal pride and passion for the game, it wouldn't be until this night, with less than twenty-four hours left as a football player, that Hulea let his teammates and coaches know exactly where he stood.

"When I came in here, I thought I was going to play right away," Hulea began. "I had offers from Division I[-A] schools, but I came here because I liked the atmosphere. And I got redshirted. For people who know me and my friends, there's nothing to us besides football. We're all football, that's all we are, and to not play . . . I said, 'I'm going to come back and work hard,' and I remember going into the spring, I looked at the depth chart before anything had ever happened, this kid named Randy Sims was ahead of me, and he hadn't played either. I remember Coach Trainer called me in the office and said, 'I know you're probably down because you're second on the depth chart, but these guys are better athletes than you, you have to work harder than everybody else. You can't get hurt, you can't miss a practice.' Besides my whole incident with mono, I haven't missed one practice since I've been here. I'll take that over four hundred and whatever tackles.

"Football means everything to me. I'm not a very complicated person, I don't think. This is my life, and it sucks that tomorrow I'll feel like something's getting stolen from me. I don't think there's a place in the NFL for linebackers who run 5.5 40s and bench 300 pounds. It hurts a lot.

"I have to pick the movies for the away trips, and in the movie Fever Pitch—I liked it, I watched it with my girlfriend, it talks about the Red Sox and stuff—there's a line, and it stuck with me so much. He was getting in a fight with his girlfriend about the Red Sox, and he said, 'Can you think of one thing that you've loved since you were nine years old?' I've been playing football since I was nine years old. I really can't believe that tomorrow, after that game, I'm not going to be a football player anymore. That's my whole sense of my worth, my whole sense of self-being. And I'm not going to have that anymore.

"So I just want to tell the younger guys, I know everyone here isn't all football, and football this and football that. We have guys on this team that have other stuff in their lives, but you guys have to make the most out of this sport. Because it's about playing with your best friends."

Hulea's words struck a chord with the players, not to mention the head coach, who completed his final Friday night speech to the team with his own most personal words of the season.

"Men, we've been through our trials and tribulations together," said Talley, "and I know we're disappointed, but hey, I'm right there with you. When Hulea talked about what he is in life and what he's going to be and where he fits in, I'm just like him. I've got nothing. Just this. That's it. Villanova football, that's what I am, that's how I perceive myself. I know it's sad, but it's true. Twenty-one years, that's what I do."

If the players and coaches left the room on this mid-November Friday night feeling a profound sense that they were part of something extraordinarily meaningful, it might have been difficult to sustain that sense as they walked across Villanova's campus and back toward the football facility.

The traffic on Lancaster Avenue and the surrounding campus streets was bumper to bumper. Villanova public safety was out in force directing traffic, and large groups of people of all ages, dressed mostly in their Wildcat gear, were walking toward The Pavilion, the University's on-campus arena. Basketball was officially tipping off its season.

In the small parking area located between the visitor's stands on the north side of Villanova Stadium, and The Pavilion, the school's oddly shaped brick and concrete basketball facility referred to derisively as "The Ski Lodge," a handful of tailgaters congregated. With beer cans or red plastic cups in hand, even with the temperature in the forties, many wore wide smiles as they awaited the arrival of game time, scheduled for 1:00 p.m. Much of this diehard Villanova contingent had been inside The Pavilion about fifteen hours prior, watching the school's fifth-rated men's basketball team whip up on Stony Brook, its overmatched competition, 78–35. It was tough to tell against such a weak opponent, but it looked like the hoopsters might be able to live up to all the preseason hype already heaped upon it in 2005.

Since making one of the more miraculous runs in the history of sport by winning the national championship in 1985, the fortunes of men's hoops had experienced peaks and valleys. Head coach Rollie Massimino resigned under pressure to take the UNLV job in 1992, and his successor, assistant Steve Lappas, spent nine mostly rocky years as the head coach on the Main Line. Since Lappas left in 2001, an exuberant and youthful head coach named Jay Wright, formerly of Hofstra, had resurrected the program's fortunes to a point where it was playing at an elite level once again, and interest in men's basketball at the school, which had always been high, was currently at an extraordinary level for this time of the year.

The Stony Brook game had been sold out, and the crowd of 6,500 in The Pavilion was wildly enthusiastic. The chant of "Vill-a-no-va" had begun before the team even emerged from its locker room, and the noise kept up throughout. In the Associated Press story chronicling the win, Wright was quoted as saying, "Our crowd set the tone tonight. I have never heard the chanting start so early before a game, and I could hear it back in the locker room. That was pretty neat. We live off of that energy and we very much appreciate it."

Andy Talley, who was standing on The Pavilion court two hours before kickoff of the Delaware game, wasn't expecting to experience quite the same level of home support on Saturday. Talley was wizened enough to use the presence of basketball as a recruiting tool on campus, and he would make sure that the top prospects the team entertained during the winter months would get to see a great Big East hoops rivalry like UConn or Syracuse. It wasn't that he was attempting to trick highschoolers into thinking that football had the same type of following, but he knew that if he could convince players that they would be attending a "big time" school, the I-AA label or the facilities or the sometimes weak football attendance might not mean as much.

Otherwise, as Talley addressed the large group of parents and recruits seated inside The Pavilion on this late Saturday morning, the sales pitch was an honest one. "It's not for everybody," Talley told the assembly. "The first thing we're emphasizing immediately when you come here is, it is an academic school. So if you're coming here to play football, you gotta turn around and go somewhere else, because that's not what we're interested in doing. We want to make sure you're coming here to get an education. If I know that, then you have a good shot to have a lot of fun and enjoy yourself. Secondly, it has to fit, you have to feel good about this place, you need to be a part of the fabric of this school. If those two things are there, then we're home free. We'll have phenomenal seasons and win a ton of games."

After Talley's brief address, he turned the proceedings over to Ferrante, the program's recruiting coordinator. Every player recruited by Villanova in the past decade dealt with Ferrante, who followed his head coach's lead in being brutally honest about the realities of the process.

"Here's the way I sum up recruiting, and I've been coaching the offensive line here since 1989," said Ferrante. "We're going to look to sign probably three linemen this year, that's the last meeting we had, three offensive linemen. Give me all the line film [the assistant coaches] like, I'll watch it all, and I'll narrow it to six guys. After that, it's nearly impossible to separate them, and it's probably going to be hard to get to six. Put those six names up on the wall, give me three darts and a blindfold, and the first three I hit, I'll take."

Ferrante's honest approach had the attention of all the parents, if not their sons. "Because really," he continued, "what do we know? We don't know enough. How many first-round draft choices in the NFL do they spend millions of dollars on researching, and pay millions of dollars to draft, that don't make it? There's a lot of 'em. And we can't bring you here, and put you in the weight room and test you, we can't get you on the track over there and have you a run a 40. We can only come see you once a week starting the week after Thanksgiving. We can see you three times in December and three times in January and then the signing date takes place."

Ferrante had stories to illustrate the inexact science that recruiting was. "I went to a school and there were two players that the coach recommended," he remembered. "One guy had ridiculous stats as a running back, the other guy was a good player at his position. I asked for a transcript, they sent me over to the guidance office. So I asked the guidance office about these guys, and the lady says positive things about both guys. But then out of the back room comes this gentleman who introduced himself as the athletic director, and had been there for thirty years. He said, 'Coach, I heard you asked for a transcript about Jimmy and Johnny.' And Jimmy was the one that had all the ridiculous stats and Johnny was the good player. And the guy said, 'One guy I'd put my thirty-year reputation on the line for, the other guy, not so sure.' Now I have a different perception of this one young man, and ended up not recruiting him. He went to a school in our league, and I'm like, 'This is great, he's going to kick our tail for four years, I probably made a mistake not offering this guy.' He went to that school, didn't play his first year, missed his spring practice because he was ineligible academically, got eligible over the summer and then left school in his first semester, second year. Had I not bumped into [the high school athletic director], I might have recruited that guy.

"Our class we graduated last year, we had eighteen guys in that class. Ray Ventrone was the last guy that we signed. He visited a week and a half before the signing date, by himself. We had all our other verbal commitments done. Ray Ventrone was from Chartiers Valley out in Western PA, he had a half-scholarship offer from Youngstown, and that's all he had. We had a scholarship still available, we brought him in, we met him, we liked his film a lot, so we offered him a scholarship and he accepted. He was the only true freshman to start for us that year in a class of eighteen. He was a three-year all-league player, and now he's on the New England Patriots practice squad. With Westbrook, it was us and Richmond, those were the only two people recruiting him."

The next Westbrook or Ventrone may have been seated somewhere before Ferrante, but at this stage, it was nearly time for a group who had listened to the assistant's anecdotes four or five years prior to be honored on the Villanova Stadium field. Due to the pregame senior ceremony, Father Hagan's customary blessing, along with Talley's words to the team, would have to take place about ten minutes earlier than usual and would be on the brief side. The head coach seized upon the message of Hagan's prayer, which had dealt with redemption, in outlining the cause ahead of the Wildcats on this day.

"This game, we're going to let it hang out, men, we're not holding anything back. We're going to come out flying, okay? We're going to play hard. It is the biggest game of the year for us, it's a chance, like Father said, for resurrection and the beginning of the era of next year. Let's send our seniors out of here the way they should be sent out of here. Let's make sure everybody who plays around these guys plays hard. And seniors, let's have the best game of your life today, what do you say?"

The seniors, who were to be escorted onto the field by their parents, would be the last to exit the locker room. As they milled about on the navy blue carpet, waiting for the signal to enter the tunnel, the intensity seemed a tad higher than usual, the emotions closer to the surface. The fact that most were about to play their last game had much to do with that feeling, but there was another reason for passions to be stirred. He wore number 17.

In uniform for the first time since his jersey was carefully lifted off seventy days prior was Marvin Burroughs, who would be honored alongside his soon-to-be-departed best friends, J. J. Outlaw and Moe Gibson. The presence of Burroughs was a bittersweet sight to behold. The Atlantic City native, who had during his two-plus-month convalescence developed into Talley's ideal of "our quarterback" despite never taking a live snap, had been throwing and running for the last few weeks, and looked to be as ready to run the offense as he ever had. But this Marvin Burroughs might as well have been a ghost. He hadn't been cleared to play, as another helmet to his still-healing left arm would have reset the progress he had made since September. Burroughs would represent Villanova as its starting quarterback again, but wouldn't do it on this day.

The small crowd on the Villanova side of the stadium offered polite, restrained applause to the outgoing seniors. Many who bothered to show up were all cheered out from last night's basketball game, and after all, this wasn't a group that had accomplished enough over the past four years to go crazy over. There had been no Atlantic 10 titles won by any active members of this group, and those two playoff wins back in 2002 had been more the work of Brett Gordon and his supporting cast than any of the current players who had competed as freshmen that year. The parents indeed looked proud, but apart from that, the pregame ceremony was treated with the same ho-hum acceptance that was usually applied to football at the university. This group had played hard and had won some big games, but they had failed to claim the hearts of Villanova nation.

Maybe today's effort would change their minds, though the first five minutes did not bode well for that prospect. After receiving the opening kickoff, Delaware began its initial march. Led by senior quarterback and University of Missouri transfer Sonny Riccio, the Blue Hens' multireceiver spread attack proved difficult for the Wildcats to get a handle on. Reardon's unit was keying on talented Delaware running back Omar Cuff, to the benefit of Riccio, who tucked the football and picked up a total of 38 yards on the game's first four plays. The Cats managed to bring up a third-and-one situation on the Villanova 24, but Cuff gained 2 yards to extend the drive. Two plays after that, Riccio chewed up a big gain all the way down to the VU 5-yard line, and Cuff did the rest, slicing through for a 3-yard touchdown on second-and-goal. The Delaware crowd, more restrained than usual given the circumstances of the game, cheered as the Blue Hens went ahead 7–0.

Villanova had been down by seven points or more seven times in 2005 and had rallied to tie or win exactly once, against Penn way back on September 24. In light of the ease with which Delaware had moved down the field on its first drive, there was little reason to expect today would be any different.

Frank Jankowski led Villanova down to the Delaware 36-yard line before two incomplete passes and a Gibson run for no gain forced an Adam James punt attempt. On came Costantino, whose first snap of the year was high but playable for James, who in turn got the kick off. Talley and the coaching staff let out a sigh of relief.

Upon getting the ball back at their own 11, UD attempted to establish Cuff, but got nowhere with that approach, netting minus 3 yards to turn it over to Villanova with good field position at the Blue Hen 35. The Wildcats threatened to give the football right back, facing a fourth-and-four moments later, but a 14-yard completion from Jankowski to Outlaw extended the drive. Outlaw would move the team inside the 10 with a 9-yard run on the next play, and fullback DeQuese May, who had missed the past two games with a high ankle sprain, returned with a 2-yard touchdown run two snaps later. Joe Marcoux's point-after sailed through, and the Cats were back in business, tied 7–7.

Talley's staff was encouraged. As the first quarter neared its end, this looked to be a game the Cats could compete to win. It continued to look that way as the second quarter began. On third-and-one from the Delaware 32, Villanova defensive backs Eugene Clay and Terrance Reaves stuffed UD running back Danny Jones for a 2-yard loss to apparently force a punt. But safety Kalise Cook was flagged for offsides on the play, instead affording the Hens an important first down. Delaware drove to midfield before facing another difficult third-and-eleven, but Riccio hit Armand Cauthen for 14 yards to reset the first-down markers again. Riccio would extend the drive another time on a third-and-four completion seconds later, and on the next play, the quarterback weaved through Reardon's defense for a 23-yard touchdown run. It was 14–7, and Villanova, which couldn't seem to make the big defensive play it needed, would again have to count on the offense to answer.

As it had so many times during the 2005 season, that call would go unheeded. Villanova's next two drives yielded a grand total of 11 yards, with dropped passes, runs to nowhere by Gibson, and heavy pressure on Jankowski conspiring to give the ball back to Delaware. Luckily, the Villanova defense was able to keep the score manageable, as Riccio and Cuff found little room to run. The Blue Hens were forced to punt on one drive and were stuffed on fourth-and-one on their next.

After getting the ball back at their own 21 with 4:15 remaining in the half, a sustained drive resulting in some points could send Talley's crew into the half with some momentum. And Jankowski led the attack in the right direction, passing for a couple of first downs and picking up another when Delaware was flagged for pass interference near midfield.

But a dropped pass by backup wideout Phil Atkinson on third-and-four forced the punting team to come out again with just over a minute and a half to play. It looked like VU would head into the locker room down seven, not the score they were looking for, but a manageable one nonetheless.

Just then, however, the most pressing fear of the day was realized. Costantino released his snap to James a fraction of a second too late. It floated over the punter's head and rolled threateningly toward the Villanova end zone. Dieser, one of a dozen or more players giving chase, jumped on the football at the 19-yard line. Delaware's sideline celebrated the good fortune, as Costantino, James, and the special teams walked dejectedly off the field.

Predictably, Delaware scored three plays later, as Riccio scored his second touchdown of the day from 6 yards out. The score would be 21–7 in the Blue Hens' favor as the teams headed to the locker room, and anyone who had followed Villanova closely in 2005 was probably already chalking it up as a loss.

Fiery halftime speeches hadn't done much to inspire the team this season, but several Wildcats gave it their best. With a Villanova Hall of Fame induction ceremony scheduled for the game field, halftime would be extended. Mark Ferrante would be the first to try and inject some new life into the home team. Unlike his previous tirades, Ferrante's tone would this time be gentle and businesslike, as he searched for an approach, any approach, that would get through to this group.

"We're handing it to them on a silver platter," Ferrante said. "Rally around each other. We can get this game, decide right now if you want this game. Alright? When Coach comes in here and he addresses you guys, and then we go out to the field, take that field with the most emotion you've had all year. We spotted 'em one, we can get that shit back without any problem. But if you start pointing and calling each other out, we're in trouble. Keep your composure, go out there and play a half that you've never played before, and we'll win this game if you decide to do that right now, collectively, together. Okay?"

Brian Hulea, whose words on Friday night had been so inspirational, was next in line to try and fire up the troops. Hulea laid out the plan of attack.

"Offense, you gotta go down the field and score," said Hulea. "We'll stuff 'em, get the ball, bang, score again, 21–21, it's anyone's game. Don't cower to these guys, men. Villanova–Delaware man, no one said this game was going to be easy. Let's come back and have the best come-back we've had all year. Just like Penn, we've done this before. This is our field, too. It's not anything they're doing, it's us. We just gotta turn it around. Balls out, man, everything you've got. Seniors, man, this is what you're going to remember, this half. Let's make it memorable, we come back, beat Delaware. Underclassmen, this is what you're going to have to think about the whole offseason, this half right here. Make the decision right now. Kick their ass, or get your ass kicked."

When it was Talley's turn to speak, he touched on several themes, all coming back to the same message: no matter what happened in the past, this game was far from over. "We're going to get the ball now," said Talley. "We need some people to execute what we ask you to do, and we'll be fine. We need some plays from somebody, some of these guys aren't making plays. We've had chances for plays, we're not making enough of them.

"Unfortunate set of circumstances on the punt snap, we knew that was a possibility and it happened, so we'll have to overcome that somehow. What would be very helpful is for us to score immediately and make it 21–14, and you're back in the game. We've been down to these guys before. There is a mentality at Delaware, they never know how many points they have to beat us by, they never know, because we've nailed them in the past so many times from behind. So you have to get back into the game, once you pump 14 in there, I'll guarantee you they'll start to think about, 'Uh-oh, here we go, how many points do we need, are they going to come back, are they going to beat us?' Eight minutes to go, about five years ago, we're down 21 points and blow them off the field. That's what they know about Villanova. So right now, you still have a chance, but you can't go out and screw around with them. You gotta play football the way we know how to play football.

Keep your hands in, come off the football, run your feet, get us some turnovers. If Riccio runs down the field, knock his ass off."

The extra long halftime afforded Talley the opportunity not only to motivate, but to vent. The bad snap had been extremely costly, and the head coach had gotten together with Apollo Wright and determined that they would try Koplin there in place of Costantino. The reasons that the Wildcats had been forced to use Costantino in that position at all were very much on Talley's mind with thirty minutes to play. The deposed Frakes had not been on the field, but his presence had been felt all too much as far as the team was concerned.

"Alex is going to snap in the second half for punts, alright?" Talley told the team. "Take the pressure off Matty, and then we'll have Matty snap on the extra points and field goals. This is what happens when we let shit in our program that shouldn't be there. We rely on somebody, and then in a situation when we have need, he's not here, because he's not worth being a part of us. And so who got hurt today because of him? Our team. You think twice about what you have to do when we bring kids in this program. You think hard about who you want to be part of this program. We're just going to have to make it up now. We put Matty in a shitty situation. Make it up, somebody make a play, get that touchdown back, let's learn from this in the future. This is a sacred place, I don't want any bums in this program. Come out and play our ass off the second half."

Before the third quarter kicked off, Sam Venuto and the other offensive coaches conferred on a change of pace offensively. The senior Gibson had received just five carries in the first half, and the coaching staff, knowing that Delaware would be looking for the Cats to pass, wanted to try its hand at establishing the run. On the first play from scrimmage, Gibson carried for 4 yards. Moments later, Gibson got the ball on back-to-back plays and reeled off rushes of 7 and 8 yards, respectively. Then, with the ball near midfield, the senior broke off his most important run of the year, finding a seam in the Blue Hen defense and rushing 40 yards down to the Delaware 11-yard line. After a pass interference call got the Cats down to the two, backup running back

Matt Dicken barreled ahead for a touchdown on the next play. Just as they knew they had to, the Wildcats answered. And once again, a touch of momentum was taken away from the impressive Gibson-led drive by a missed Marcoux point-after that kept the score at 21-13. Still, it was a ball game again, and Villanova seemed to be playing with a renewed sense of purpose. The Wildcat defense held on Delaware's next drive, stalling the Blue Hens and forcing them to punt soon after they had crossed midfield.

Jankowski took over at his own 5-yard line, needing to orchestrate a touchdown drive to get Villanova within a point or perhaps tie. Given the number of extended drives the offense had completed during the season, the notion of such a march was a long shot. It would also be the Wildcats' last best shot.

Jankowski completed a 12-yard pass to John Dieser for a first down, but two plays later, tackle Izzy Bauta was called for a false start that put Villanova in second-and-long. Then, the quarterback was swarmed under by a group including UD linebacker Keiandre Hepburn. On third-and-seventeen, a Jankowski screen pass to May netted nary a yard. James punted following a good Koplin snap, but the Blue Hens capitalized on their good field position to kick a field goal and make the score 24–13.

Needing a score to keep pace, the VU offense failed again. A 25-yard pass play to Outlaw was negated by another penalty on Bauta, this time an illegal shift. Villanova punted. Hulea and the defense got the offense the ball back early in the fourth quarter with the game still within reach, but deep in his own territory, Jankowski was hit and fumbled, giving it right back to Delaware just 19 yards shy of the Villanova end zone. Two minutes later, Riccio scored his third touchdown of the day.

It was 31–13, or, in other words, over. As the successful point-after sailed through with 10:46 to play, much of the Villanova contingent was on its way to the parking lot. Most had yet to start their cars when on the first play of the Wildcats' next series, Frank Jankowski threw his seventeenth interception of the year on a tipped ball intended for Outlaw. Many listened to the radio call of Villanova announcers Joe Eichhorn and Ryan Fannon four and a half minutes later, when Jankowski was sacked and lost his seventh fumble of 2005. A select few were still listening when on a fourth-and-one play from the Villanova 6, Riccio broke through the Wildcat defense and scored his fourth touchdown of the day.

Another close game had gotten out of hand. The scoreboard would read 38-13 as the season finally, at long last, ticked away. It was the most one-sided loss to Delaware that Talley had ever endured and the biggest blowout that the series had seen since Nova's 27–0 shutout of UD in 1996. The only good to come out of this day was Hulea's thirteen-tackle performance, which made him Villanova's all-time leader in stops. Otherwise, it was a disaster, a game that the seniors, not to mention the recruits in the crowd, would be able to remember in only negative terms.

Little did the seniors know when they had walked off the field following the William and Mary game three weeks earlier that they had tasted their last victory wearing Villanova uniforms. Little did they know that a season that had begun with such promise would decompose into the rubble of a 4-7 finish, the worst mark for the program since a 3-8 showing in 1995.

Afterward, the tears flowed freely in the locker room. There would be no more yelling and screaming in this space for another nine months, and no more yelling and screaming here from guys like Brian Hulea, John Dieser, and Darrell Adams ever again. By the time Talley would gather his team for his next pregame words of wisdom, there would be new leaders and new voices, and the group assembled on this Saturday, five days before Thanksgiving, would be viewed as one that failed to measure up to the standards that had been set at Villanova over the previous two decades. And that was sad. Because there were some good players, some dedicated and outstanding coaches, but ultimately, this was not a team that could figure out how to consistently win football games.

Talley knew it, and his final speech to the 2005 edition of the Villanova Wildcats sounded like a eulogy for a deceased person who had never quite lived up to his capabilities in the course of a long, mostly miserable, existence. Talley had suspected it would be an uphill climb as early as the New Hampshire game, and he and the coaching staff had been incredulous about the mindset of the team right up until the end. On the eve of the game, even in the midst of some emotionally charged speeches, some seniors had explicitly stated that the Delaware game was no more important than any other.

By the looks of the small crowd at Villanova on this Saturday, the team's fan base had felt exactly the same way. And so in his recap to the team, Talley addressed the sins of the past while looking toward the future, throwing down the gauntlet for those who would remain Wildcats.

"First of all, I'd like to thank Father Hagan and all the coaching staff, all of the assistant personnel, Tom, Reggie, everybody that helped the team and was behind us," said Talley. "I want to thank the seniors for four of five years of some great football, I appreciate everything you guys have done for our program and you will be missed.

"I will say just a couple of things with regards to the Delaware game. You noticed there is a sign up on the wall with the date of the game. I thought last night the game was taken a little too lightly, frankly. I'm not going to say anything more about it. So you guys who are going to play against Delaware in the future, let me tell you something, it is important, it's very important.

"Not the kind of season we wanted to have, very disappointing for everybody. The thing that you can do right now is, seniors, gather up the great things that you have, take them with you into the next life. We'll be behind you one hundred percent. For you underclassmen, understand the feeling that we have right now. Understand what we went through this year, the dysfunction, the dissatisfaction, the mistakes that were made, and know that we will be back stronger than ever, because it will happen.

"We will meet when we get back from the Thanksgiving holiday on that Tuesday, and at that time, get ready to tie it down. Because you will have a coaching staff that will come after you harder in twenty-one years than any coaching staff that I've ever had. We will be watching every move you make, we'll be coaching everything you do, we will be demanding. So if you decide to stay in this program, you will do it our way, on the field and off. And I'll be looking for some guys that might want to think about transferring, because that's how tough it's going to be. We're going to start recruiting in two weeks, we're bringing players in, I'm looking for players who have it in their heart that want to bring in good players into our program.

"All in all, now I will say farewell to our seniors. I feel sad for you as you feel bad today, and as always, we appreciate everything you guys have done. This is a sad day. It's a sour, bitter, rotten, disappointing loss so I'm not going to pat everybody on the back and tell everybody it's been wonderful. Because it hasn't been wonderful. I hate this. I hate the way we feel right now. And I hate it more for you than me, because I've been on the mountaintop, boys, and I've been in the valley. It's a lot better on the mountaintop. And that's where we're going."

The season was over, but for one more painful press conference for the head coach. Accompanied by Hulea, whose mournful expression was not what one might have expected from a player who just broke one of the program's longest-standing and most impressive records, Talley attempted to rank the season on his list of personal disappointments. The theme of quarterback play was highlighted early and often during the head coach's meeting with the press.

"I would say of all the seasons that I've had here, this is the most disappointing and the most frustrating," said Talley, "starting with the fact that we lost our quarterback in the first game, and then just couldn't get this team to get better.

"We dealt with so much youth on the team, and I think had we had a growth spurt from our quarterback, we could have done what Delaware did, which is to manage a 6-5 year or a 7-4 year. But they had a grizzled quarterback who was leading them, and our guy's a first-year guy really sort of incapable of doing that. He was surrounded by so many deficiencies, and he just wasn't in a mode to be able to overcome a lot of those deficiencies.

"So many times, we kept thinking that Villanova football, the way we play, is back. We thought that at the William and Mary game, and then we went right out the next week and played poorly against Towson. We just haven't been able to get this team over the hump. Probably the best thing that I can say is that the season is over, and we can go back and try to assess the things that we have to do."

A Delaware reporter asked a direct question pertaining to Jankowski's performance over the course of the season. Talley paused for what seemed like a full minute, before answering in a softer, more evenhanded fashion than he had over most of the season's second half.

"Well, he's a first-year player, and I'd like to think that he would have improved more by the end of the season, and I thought he continued to be inconsistent. And in the position that he was in, it was very important for him to play better each week, because this is a team that will rise and fall on its quarterback. We don't have a good enough defense to keep putting them in harm's way, not that many people in our league do. I think his passing at times was brilliant, but at times he misread some things, and he seemed to be around turnovers more than a quarterback can be.

"So if you can look at it, it's a learning year. He's going to have to try to beat Marvin Burroughs out, because Marvin Burroughs is our quarterback and he'll be back this spring. We always open the quarterback job up, but Marvin is the returning starter and will be installed in the spring. And if Frank can beat him out based on all the experience he had, then we'll have two really good ones."

Before Talley and his senior tri-captain were released, Hulea was asked about the hurt he was feeling, and he echoed some of his head coach's sentiments. "It's very difficult, because you set a list of goals, and when you don't attain it it's very hard," said Hulea. "Like Coach Talley said, I feel like maybe a little bit of the wind got taken out of our sails when Marv got hurt, and it doesn't seem like we ever bounced back from that. I'm very confident in Coach T and all the coaches to get these guys together and to be very successful again next year."

For the head coach, his staff, and the teammates that Hulea would leave behind, the wait until next year would prove excruciating and interminable.

15

ENDGAME

In the days that followed Villanova's loss to Delaware, there was no large-scale postmortem in the local papers about what had gone wrong for the Wildcats in 2005. There were no calls for the head coach's job on the message boards, or covert on-campus meetings between administrators and boosters to discuss the future of the program. The season that had begun on a quiet morning in early April ended in exactly the same manner—with little fanfare.

And that was the upside of the program's relatively low profile, that Talley, his staff, and his players could put the whole episode behind them and move on. The next two months would for the most part be devoted to recruiting, one of the head coach's biggest strengths and chief passions. But anyone who was of a mind to reflect on the circumstances that had led the program to its worst season in a decade could have made an awfully long list.

The leadership from the players was sketchy at times, and that didn't necessarily just mean the three captains, who were indeed earnest in their efforts to inspire from game one through game eleven. But there appeared to be an inherent lack of leadership within the younger classes, who seemed to be waiting to have inspiration delivered to them, rather than seeking to contribute to the leadership structure.

And this was without a doubt a young team, particularly within the two areas where youth hurts a football team most: the offensive and defensive lines. In the fourth quarter of the Richmond game, there had been five true or redshirt freshmen on the O-line at the same time, a hopeless situation for Sam Venuto's offense. On the D-line, where Darrell Adams battled injuries and Russell McKittrick failed to last the season on the roster, undersized true freshmen Damian Kelley and Greg Miller, as well as redshirt freshman Dave Dalessandro, received much more playing time than Mark Reardon would have ever considered ideal heading into the year. Adams's injuries, as well as the inconsistency of the D-line as a whole, had a trickle-down effect for the rest of the defense.

The running game was mostly nonexistent, finishing last in the Atlantic 10 and a distant number 108 in all of I-AA in rushing offense. The state of the line was a factor in that statistic, as was the hot-and-cold play of Moe Gibson, not to mention that the team was forced to throw much more than it ran because of all the large deficits it encountered.

Then, of course, there was the issue of the quarterback. Frank Jankowski had not played well. He had become just the third quarterback in Villanova history to throw for 3,000 yards in a season, joining Brett Gordon and Chris Boden, and had also finished second in the Atlantic 10 in completions. But those were difficult numbers to which to assign much meaning when countered with his 17 interceptions, 7 lost fumbles, and just 18 touchdown passes.

And though Jankowski was but one of eleven players on the field when he compiled those numbers, being the quarterback meant that he owned all of them. The picks that were deflected off of the slippery hands of receivers were his. The fumbles that came as a result of blindside hits brought about by missed blocking assignments were his. The consistent inability of the offense to find the end zone during its frequent trips to the red zone had to be laid at his feet, too. Such is life at the quarterback position, where you either fail or you succeed, with little room for explanation in between. No matter how even his most ardent supporter might try to spin it, the reality was that Jankowski had failed.

And Talley, beginning with the Rhode Island loss, had not been afraid to address that failure publicly, an approach that did not sit well with Jankowski or his family. The quarterback had not defended himself in the press during the season, nor had he really had a forum to, and he had not directly confronted Talley either. But Jankowski and his head coach had barely spoken during the second half of the season, and more than a month following the Delaware loss, after the students had gone home for winter break, the quarterback determined that he no longer wished to be a part of Talley's program. Jankowski's father called Talley two days before New Year's and set up a meeting for the following afternoon. Talley said he would call Venuto to involve him in the meeting. Don't bother, Jankowski's father told the head coach, we only want to talk to you.

In a meeting that lasted less than half an hour, and one that both parties described as being less than confrontational, Jankowski told Talley that he would remain at Villanova, but would focus solely on baseball. Though they didn't get into specifics with the coach, as Jankowski and his father sat in the blue leather chairs across from Talley's desk, they expressed dissatisfaction with the way the quarterback had been characterized in the press.

"They really wanted mainly to say that Frank was going to concentrate on baseball," remembered Talley, "But I think the exact words were that the extended family and the nuclear family were unhappy about my postgame comments about Frank's play, and that that had them upset.

"I went back and looked at everything I said. I chatted with Dean, he went back and looked [the comments] up and felt like there wasn't anything I said that I hadn't said before, and [I was] a little surprised about why they would take it so to heart. I didn't feel anything I said was damaging or hurtful to Frank, and had said the same about basically every quarterback that had ever played here.

"One of the things I've prided myself in is sort of telling it like it is, and speaking the truth, and being clear with everybody so that there's no misconceptions. If we coached a bad game or we played a bad game, that's on me. But you can't throw three interceptions in a game and expect to win, and things like that come up [in the press]. You're going to allude to that. And I'd probably say that again."

The Jankowski family saw it differently, feeling that Talley's public words had gone beyond acceptable postgame analysis. In an interview with the author conducted months after the football season was completed, Jankowski countered any notion that he was some kind of shrinking violet incapable of handling criticism.

"I've been screamed at much worse than Andy Talley has ever screamed at me," said Jankowski. "But my coaches have never degraded me in front of my teammates and in front of the public in a manner which is not justified. That was not coaching. The point was making me the scapegoat. I can handle when people don't pat me on the back or people point out the negatives. But the public pointing of the finger and scapegoating was uncalled for and unacceptable."

Jankowski felt that Talley's unsupportive comments during the second half of the season undermined his leadership abilities. And even though he didn't read the papers, he knew that many of his teammates did. "You were around players all day and then you find out later from one of your buddies that your coach totally downsized you in the media the day before," remembered Jankowski, "and then you realize every other player knows. That cuts the legs out from under a leader. I don't know how you think you're going to be successful as a football team if the coach is constantly pointing the finger at the quarterback to the public."

But what of those twenty-four turnovers? Even if Talley's statements were harsh, and there were conflicting arguments on that issue, wasn't there some truth in them? "I can't recall one loss and honestly blame it on myself," argued Jankowski. "Somebody blindsides you because a block was whiffed, and the ball comes out. How is that your fault? Like Rhode Island, there were two times in that game where we missed assignments and the guy totally came free off the edge and there was a fumble.

"Look at the JMU game. I get hit from behind, my back gets hit, the ball goes straight up in the air in the middle of the field. It's not like I threw that ball. The guy picks it off, so what happens? The other quarterback goes in. It was like they were looking for an excuse.

"Things happen because they're caused, and obviously, yeah, you can make better decisions. You can always work on your decision-making. That's a given in quarterbacking. But the thing is, things have to be put into context, and not just make somebody the scapegoat, to take the easy way out. And that's definitely what happened. You can't point the finger at the offensive line, you can't point it at the quarterback, you can't point it at the running back, you can't point it at the wide receivers.

"I don't see one turnover that cost us the game, and I have every game film. All of a sudden the only thing that's wrong with the offense is the fact that I'm not seeing what needs to get done, and that's obviously not the facts. You can't ever just put things on one person. How can it all be one person's fault?"

Talley was looking for a little more accountability out of his quarterback, and also contended that his miscues were not the only piece of the puzzle that led to the postgame criticisms. "What's important is for a quarterback to be realistic," said the head coach. "There are going to be a few tipped balls that are going to happen, which are really never the quarterback's fault. And there are going to be some blindside hits, where maybe as you were throwing the ball, it got bobbled up, and maybe a linebacker caught it 15 yards down the field. But I think what you need to do is be realistic about the decision making . . . I don't think anybody here was that concerned about tipped balls and lack of protection. I think where we were concerned was his ability to read coverage and throw the ball in the right spot. That's what he was struggling with."

Talley expected his quarterbacks to take over, to bring the team back from deficits when needed, irrespective of the circumstances, and Jankowski, save for the Penn game, never did that.

"The West Coast offense that everybody runs now puts so much emphasis on the quarterback spot," said Talley, "and the quarterback is the guy who carries a college football team and has such a great effect on the defense. The ghosts of [former Villanova quarterbacks] Tom Colombo, Brett Gordon, Chris Boden, Kirk Schulz are always there. Those are big shoes to fill, and there is a lot of pressure in that position."

But Jankowski felt those expectations may have been overinflated for a quarterback who was inexperienced and for a team that hadn't been picked to do much in the first place. "Last time I checked, we were preseason picked four out of [six] in the [Atlantic 10] South, compared to the season before when we were picked number one," said Jankowski. "As a team, we were very young across the board. Those guys are great quarterbacks . . . I have the utmost respect for them, but they never played on this team, and I never played on their team."

And as for the notion that things would have been better with Burroughs at quarterback, Jankowski wasn't buying that either. "Marv's a great quarterback, but the thing is, Marv had such a great year as a sophomore, and we went 6-5. We didn't play a [I-A] team, he started all eleven games, and we were picked to be number one. I got it done as well as anybody else could have in with the situation I was in, with this year's coach, with this year's schedule, with this year's players."

Jankowski's perspective was that he had not been supported dating back to the beginning of his collegiate career, and that that approach held even when he was forced, due to the injury to Burroughs, to become the starting quarterback. The erosion of his relationship with Talley was indicative of that lack of support, argued Jankowski.

"It was definitely worsening, you could tell by the way he was approaching me," said Jankowski of the relationship. "There was an uneasiness between us. One time we even had a meeting [because of] what he said, he even talked about it. After the Rhode Island game, it was so bad, he had to call me into his office to tell me about it, and he said that he was upset because the Westbrook jersey retirement didn't go that well. And yeah, that's a tough thing, but why I am I singled out?

"After Penn, it gradually got worse. Even when we won, there was still a way to point the finger at me for why we didn't win in the past. Quarterbacks do get the most fame and the most notoriety, but at the same time, you don't just throw somebody under the bus. That's just not right, and that's what happened.

"You can perceive the way people feel about you. If the quarterback's not feeling support from the coaches, there's no way he can lead to his capabilities. It's not what they did, it's what they didn't do. They didn't really get behind me and try to get something rolling. I didn't feel like I was really being supported."

Talley bristled at that characterization. "That statement would completely baffle me, because why would any coaching staff in their right mind, with really the only one quarterback that you could win with, not get one hundred percent behind that quarterback? And I think that was obviously his perception, which is sad, because it's so far from the backing he was receiving. He was the man, he knew he had the quarterback spot without question. To me that's a little bit of paranoia that maybe built up through the course of the season on his part. With that kind of thinking, it's obvious to see why he wasn't successful."

In the end, Talley wished he had sat down and had a heart-to-heart with his starting quarterback sooner. "In hindsight, I would have liked for him to come in and say, 'Coach, those comments really bothered me,' so that we could have cleared the air, and I could have explained to him my side of it. But instead, he obviously kept that inside, and his parents kept it inside. I would have even liked a phone call from the father, and I would have responded to it and said, 'Well, let me explain myself, and hey, jeez, maybe you're right, at this point in his career I need to be less open about what's going on.' I think we could have avoided some of those things that obviously upset him down the line. I never knew there was a problem with him because he was an upbeat kid.

"Sometimes I make mistakes," conceded Talley. "Sometimes I say things I shouldn't say, we all do. You'd like to take them back. But when people let things fester, and don't bring it out in the open . . . that's the biggest problem we have in the world today, lack of communication. This kid presents such a great image, that we just assumed he was having a good time, that even though we weren't winning as much, he was finally playing and enjoying himself and was going to grow from the experience."

The one thing coach and player could agree upon in the endgame was that his play would have improved as he matured. Said Talley, "I really think had he stayed with us he'd have had a very good opportunity to be an excellent quarterback over the next two years. Because he's a very strong competitor, he's a very confident guy, he's a very good athlete, he had really good skills, and I think once his decision-making improved, with experience, he was going to be very good in this league."

Jankowski concurred. "I know I could have won a championship here. I know it. That was my first time ever with the first-string, ever playing. I was a sophomore. I still had two more years. Who says I don't go out and win the national title, or who says us as a team don't go to the semifinals, like Brett Gordon did?"

Ultimately, it was Jankowski who made that determination, though he claimed that in the end his hand was forced. "I know how this program works now after being here for three years. I know I was not going to be given a shot, and I also know that if he really wanted me to compete against Marv [in 2006], he would have told me. He wouldn't have just implied it.

"The program is very clean. I never got beat up or mistreated physically. Nothing was ever done like that. It's not like Andy Talley or Sam Venuto treated me horribly. The point of the matter is they never gave me the opportunity to compete, and when after circumstances that were beyond anybody I did get the chance to play, they definitely did not support me, and it was an effort not to support me. And I'll stand by that to anyone."

For those attempting to view the situation objectively, it was hard to know what to make of the circumstances surrounding Jankowski's departure. Talley may have gone too far in his public criticism, and it was true that the situation likely would have improved had Jankowski or his family aired their feelings during the season. It was also true that there was no way you could blame Jankowski for every turnover, but there was no doubt that as a quarterback, he needed to accept more responsibility for those errors than he seemed willing to assume. Jankowski was not surrounded by an impenetrable offensive line or a dominant running back, but it was reasonable to expect more from an offense that included J. J. Outlaw and John Dieser, two of the better receivers in school history, and Matt Sherry, arguably the best tight end ever to wear a Villanova uniform. And the unsupportive picture of Talley that Jankowski painted was difficult to reconcile with the image of the coach that a sizeable majority of his current and former players seemed to share, which was one of a devoted leader and guide who cared as much about the person as he did about the football player.

Whatever side of the argument you fell on, the whole situation was downright lamentable. Jankowski's exit wasn't the only departure the program saw in the offseason. Linebackers coach Sean Spencer accepted a job as the defensive line coach at Atlantic 10 rival Hofstra, moving to Long Island in an effort to be closer to his daughter in Connecticut. Defensive line coach Brendan Daly accepted an assistant job with the NFL Minnesota Vikings. Former D-line coach Clint Wiley returned to campus after a one-year hiatus to take over Spencer's former position, and cornerbacks coach Billy Crocker settled into Daly's former spot.

Also promoted was Justus Galac, the graduate assistant who was still taking biannual radiation shots for the cancer that he had refused to have treated in order to play football during his senior year of college. Galac assumed duties as Villanova's strength and conditioning coach, replacing Reggie Barton, who went back home to Idaho to attend to his ill father and work the family farm. Following Barton out the door was the other graduate assistant, Mike Kraft.

Two other people who would begin picking up NFL paychecks were Darrell Adams and J. J. Outlaw. Neither was drafted, but both were signed as free agents, Adams with the Jets and Outlaw with his father's former team, the Eagles. Neither would make the active NFL roster in 2006, but both were sent to polish their skills in NFL Europe in the spring of 2007, allowing their dreams of stardom to endure.

As he himself had predicted, Brian Hulea was not picked up by any professional team, and in the summer, after receiving his master's degree in education at Villanova, he began looking for a job as a teacher and coach. Hulea's mother had completely recovered from her cancer, to the great relief of the entire Hulea family.

Russell McKittrick was long gone by the time his former roommate received his advanced degree, and though Talley held his place open on the roster, McKittrick wouldn't be back. Soon after returning to Oregon, McKittrick had a falling out with his parents and stopped receiving psychological treatment, heading back to California to be with his girlfriend. McKittrick eventually discovered that while he had been at Villanova, the girlfriend who had led to him jeopardizing his college football career had been cheating on him since he arrived on the Main Line. By the spring of 2006, McKittrick was still in California, working construction, and his by now ex-girlfriend had joined the Coast Guard. The player told the author he planned to finish school elsewhere, but that his football career was over.

"If I was to go back to Villanova I would have had to go up to Oregon, see the shrink, take medication and all that stuff, and I didn't want to do that," said McKittrick. "But I think [the coaching staff] handled me more than fairly. They gave me a lot of chances.

"I love Coach T, I think he's a player's coach. I think he really cares about his players and our well-being. It was me, really. I should have got rid of the girl as soon as I came to Villanova."

Meanwhile, Dave Dalessandro was among the players honored when the team had its banquet in mid-January, winning the Rev. Bernard Lazor, OSA, Award, as the team's top rookie. His parents, who had more than a year before sat in Talley's office and listened to the head coach tell them that he was sending their son home, looked on proudly as Dalessandro accepted his award.

"I always thank Coach Talley when I see him because I could have been another bust, just a bum," said Dalessandro. "But luckily Coach T really helped me out. He's a good friend now. And I owe a lot to him."

It was situations like Dalessandro's that kept Talley, who had now won 142 games at Villanova since resurrecting the program in 1984, from being driven to distraction over difficulties like those regarding Jankowski and McKittrick.

"When I walk out of here, when it's all said and done, I'll be able to walk to a mirror and look at myself and say I left this place a better place than it was when I came here," said Talley. "And that I think is very important. And you do that one day at a time, one kid at a time."

In addition to his interaction with his players, Talley would also be reporting to a new president on the Main Line. Replacing the retiring Father Dobbin in the president's chair would be Rev. Peter M. Donohue, OSA, an associate professor at the university who had also served as the longtime chair of the drama department. The fifty-three-year-old Augustinian was visible and well regarded on campus, and Talley liked him, though there was no immediate determination of what his selection would mean as far as football at Villanova was concerned. Most figured that, at least in the short-term, Donohue would maintain the status quo in regard to the sport.

Dobbin, the number one fan of the Villanova men's basketball team, was sent off with a bang, as Jay Wright presided over the Wildcats' most successful season since Dobbin had come on the job in 1988. The Cats went 25-4 and were ranked in the national top five for most of the season, earning a No. 1 seed in the NCAA Tournament for the first time in school history. The local media was all over the team's run beginning in about December, when the NFL Eagles' fall from grace, aided in large part by an injury to Donovan McNabb and the separation of Terrell Owens from the roster, was nearly complete. The Cats led the *Daily News* sports section for much of the month of March, and the team's success and resultant heightened profile gave the university a PR boost that would be felt for years to come, a boost that was impossible to quantify in dollars and cents. Villanova would just miss on an opportunity to reach the Final Four for the first time since 1985, losing to eventual national champion Florida in the round of eight.

As the NCAA continued to make money hand over fist via the men's basketball championship, stakeholders in I-AA football explored ideas to improve on the dysfunctional model of both their tournament and the perception of their level of play. In late April 2006, noting the minor-league stigma attached to the I-AA label, an advisory group made up of I-AA presidents recommended that the NCAA Division I Board of Directors change the names of I-A and I-AA. The favored monikers were "Division I Bowl Classification" and "Division I Playoff Classification," designations that were tweaked to "Football Bowl Subdivision" and "Football Championship Subdivision" before being formally pushed through during the summer. The money-losing I-AA playoffs were given a shot in the arm in the spring as well, when $450,000 earmarked for tournament enhancements was added to the Division I budget. The increase in resources would allow playoff teams to add more members to their travel party, an effort to add to the "big game" experience that had often been absent in I-AA playoff contests. Atlantic 10 members Richmond and New Hampshire, both of which made the NCAA quarterfinals in 2005, were among those hoping to benefit from the enhancement as they attempted to get back to the playoffs in '06.

Those efforts were a step in the right direction, though they probably meant little as far as Villanova was concerned. No matter what the level was known as, most Villanovans would still regard the football program's national position as being a notch below the big time, and there was no doubt that the program's status as a money-loser would not be altered by the enhancements. The same went for the local media's views of the program, which were unlikely to be shifted greatly or yield any greater coverage of Villanova football unless the team either started dominating its competition or moved up and began playing at the sport's highest level.

Despite those realities, Talley, his staff, and his players would just have to keep on fighting the good fight as they prepared for 2006, and they would do so while trying to salvage something positive from their dismal 2005 campaign. Metaphors equating sports with life had become cliché to the nth degree, and the cynical could have easily looked at Villanova's 4-7 '05 season and summed it up thus: it was unsuccessful, and now over, case closed. Indeed, for programs that heralded winning and bottom-line thinking above all else, that black-and-white view would have been apt.

But at Villanova, there was poignancy in a 4-7 season, and there were some bona fide life lessons to be exhumed from the embers of disappointment. Talley was ultra-competitive—he wanted to win football games, and wanted to win them badly. Of that there should have been no doubt. He knew that football's coaching graveyard was littered with men like him who had preached team-as-family, emphasized the big picture, and operated their programs in a clean, forthright, aboveboard fashion at all times. He knew that had he done all those things and not won during his time at Villanova, he would have no job, and thus no pupils to mould or lessons to teach.

Still, in a way, for a man who had started his professional career wanting to be both a coach and teacher, a poor season offered the ability to prepare his ninety-or-so students for the cruelties of the real world in a way that an 11-0 championship run or a trip deep into the playoffs never could. In that case, the point was:

Life can be difficult, and it can be thankless.

You may associate hard work with virtue all you want, but don't expect it to entitle you to success.

The people you count on in life, like teammates who didn't last the season, will sometimes let you down.

And especially regarding life as a football player in I-AA, and particularly at Villanova, you can't expect to have the importance of your existence or what you're working to achieve validated by outsiders.

Talley often reminded his players that, when it came to his success on the Main Line, he had been to the mountaintop and had spent time in the valley. The 2005 season had not been among the peaks, to be sure. But the head coach knew, and he hoped that all of his players and staff would at some point understand, that the hurt was an important part of that big picture he was constantly trying to keep in their view.

And that perhaps to fully appreciate the view on the mountaintop requires a long, painful stay in the deepest valleys.

A FINAL NOTE

The genesis of the idea for this book came a few days before Super Bowl XXXIX in Jacksonville. That Super Bowl, pitting the New England Patriots and Philadelphia Eagles, was to be the first I covered and was supposed to represent the top of the food chain for a reporter.

And while I was grateful to be there, the experience was initially a hollow one for me. I had made the giant leap from covering I-AA college football to the NFL during the previous summer, and there was no denying as I drove through the streets of Jacksonville that the Super Bowl was every bit as much about commerce and media frenzy as it was about football or football players.

My experience covering I-AA had been totally different, in that I felt like I was reporting about people and the game of football in one of its best and purest forms. My employer, The Sports Network, had sponsored the Walter Payton Award, the I-AA equivalent to the Heisman Trophy, since 1987, and it was in the company's interests to devote a great deal of coverage to I-AA, much more than any other media outlet ever had or likely ever will. They sent me all over the country beginning with the 2000 season through 2003, visiting great out-of-the-way places like Missoula, Montana, Natchitoches, Louisiana (it's pronounced Nack-a-dish, for reasons that remain mysterious to me), and Statesboro, Georgia, writing columns and features and meeting lots of wonderful and dedicated players, coaches, college administrators, and fans. I-AA schools were generally so pleased at any little attention that they really appreciated my presence, very much unlike in the NFL, where thousands of people do exactly what I do and most of the players, coaches, and owners wish there were a lot fewer of us turning over rocks and writing stories.

Jacksonville and the Super Bowl experience made me feel homesick for I-AA, so I came up with an idea that would help me reconnect with that world while shining a light on a level of football that received precious little attention. I wanted to explore some of the challenges these programs faced just to remain afloat, and how they were generally ignored, misunderstood, and stigmatized by most sports fans. I wanted to look at the money that was being spent by programs and whether those dollars could be justified. I wanted to look at the inherent inferiority complex that came with being a member of college football's lower class.

Since I knew I wasn't going to be able to quit my day job to research and write this book, I initially focused on three I-AA schools that were near to my home in suburban Philadelphia.

The most successful nearby program was the University of Delaware, which had won the 2003 national title and represented the top of the heap in I-AA. But Delaware drew an average of twenty thousand fans, had a statewide following, and was financially solvent, which meant it didn't come close to representing the average I-AA member. Plus, I was pretty sure that neither the Blue Hens head coach, K. C. Keeler, nor the athletic director, Edgar Johnson, would be very comfortable affording the type of access I was going to need to write this book.

Another program I thought about exploring was Lehigh University, which was generally a Top 25 I-AA entity. Pete Lembo, then the head coach at Lehigh, was a personal friend and I thought he might be receptive to the project. But Lehigh was atypical of most I-AA programs too, because it played in the sort-of-scholarship world of the Patriot League, and also received quite a bit of media attention in its part of the state of Pennsylvania.

The more I thought about it, the more I figured Villanova to be the perfect candidate for a book of this nature. Villanova had been a generally successful member of I-AA, but its football program had received very little media attention in and around Philadelphia, and the football program had never seemed to me to be very well supported by either its student or alumni base, which meant football was a money-loser for the university. This was a typical I-AA program if ever there was one, and the fact that Villanova was a well-known university from a national standpoint helped sweeten the deal.

Also, significantly, the Wildcats had Andy Talley. Talley had been an absolute dream to cover in the four years I was involved with I-AA. He was probably the least-guarded head coach I had dealt with at that or any other level. He had always been unbelievably giving of his time, he was passionate, he was extremely articulate, and he always seemed to see the big picture beyond football. He also believed in the role of the media and seemed to be at one with an era when coaches and reporters could be friendly for reasons other than the ones that served their own interests.

I thought that a book about the Villanova football program could be worthwhile and important, but even knowing that a lot of people on campus would be supportive, I knew I would have to tread lightly to get the stamp of approval to move ahead.

The first person I presented the idea to was Dean Kenefick, Villanova's assistant athletic director for media relations. I had known Kenefick for almost eight years and he had always treated me great, so I figured he would give me some advice on how to proceed. Kenefick was receptive to the idea, agreed with me that Talley would probably be receptive as well, but my next move was trickier.

Vince Nicastro, Villanova's director of athletics, is someone I also considered a friend. Nicastro trusted me but was hesitant to allow me to write the book because the athletic department had made a blanket policy of not allowing "behind the scenes" access to reporters in regard to other athletic programs, specifically men's basketball. With an assist from Talley, who had already okayed the project, I convinced Nicastro to allow an exception in this case, in that the football program was deserving of a rare piece of stepped-up attention and that my motive in preparing the book was not to uncover all kinds of abuses within the football program (had that been my motive, this book would have been pretty short).

Once I received the go-ahead to start writing, I got to work. And things were going great, until less than two weeks into spring ball, after Villanova had finished a morning practice, I played some pickup basketball near my office with some work colleagues. I went up for a jump shot (which rimmed out, incidentally), landed awkwardly on someone's foot, and subsequently broke my right leg in three places. At that moment, this project could have fallen apart like my fragile tibia. However, due to the yeoman efforts of both Talley and Kenefick, I was able to keep it moving. Talley presented me with a huge scrapbook detailing the first twenty-plus years of Villanova football, which allowed me to continue my research during the six weeks I was laid up following my surgery. Kenefick arranged some vital phone interviews with players, since I was unable to make it to campus to conduct them in person.

By the time August practice rolled around, I was barely limping. The rest is history.

What you hold in your hands is not quite the book I intended to write. I had hoped that things would go much better for the team, because it would have made my job much easier, though I knew the possibility existed that things would go badly. I expected there to be plenty of drama, though I certainly didn't think I would have to dwell as much as I did on the negative elements of the season. In the end, I had to go where the story took me, and I hope that the characters that make up this work, as well as those who invited me to research and write it, respect and understand that.

I knew from the beginning that I would have to present some of the more controversial elements of the history of football at Villanova, though I can admit now that I was a tad naïve about just how polarizing certain pieces of this debate were and still are. I am sure that when this book is released some of the more difficult topics I've explored will be debated and that some of the information I've revealed, particularly in regard to the dropping of football at Villanova in 1981 and the I-A feasibility study in 1997, will be dismissed as being either wildly exaggerated or pure fiction. I don't have any control over that, though people I have previously covered will hopefully acknowledge that I've never pulled a fact out of thin air during my short career and will concede that while writing my first book was not a good time to start doing so.

It should be known that Rev. Edmund J. Dobbin, the president at the time of the I-A study, declined to speak to me up until the week that my manuscript was due to the publisher. It was in the interest of presenting both sides equitably that I (with great hesitation) relayed certain comments to Dobbin that had been made by Tony Randazzo, Bob Mulcahy, and Bob Capone, and afforded him one final chance to respond. It was at that time Dobbin decided to talk with me on the record and offer his views. His perspective was very much appreciated and valued, though his hesitancy about discussing these matters does support the argument of those that would characterize him as having something to hide.

The voice of the athletic director on the job at the time of the I-A study, Gene DeFilippo, is conspicuously absent from my book, though I did attempt to interview him. I made three such attempts through the Boston College athletic department, even forwarding the questions for my would-be interview in an effort to hear his perspective, but DeFilippo declined. Reader can make their own assumptions about what his silence might mean.

I can assure the reader that when I initially contacted Randazzo and Mulcahy, I did so not knowing how they would characterize the I-A study, and I was surprised that they were so direct in regard to their portrayal of the process. I felt that the voice of the chairman of the I-A feasibility committee, Randazzo, as well as that of a sitting Big East athletic director, Mulcahy, would be sufficiently representative of the feelings of the entire committee, and that the fact that both characterized the work of the committee in a similar manner left me 100 percent sure that I was portraying the events accurately.

I felt after talking to people both inside and outside the Villanova athletic department, as well as after conducting interviews with Randazzo and Mulcahy, that the two committee members (apart from Dobbin) who were portrayed to be most vehemently opposed to the I-A move, Robert Birmingham and Mariellen Whelan, were not especially credible sources for information on the I-A study given their close ties to Dobbin. In fact, when I spoke to neutral parties on the Villanova campus about whom I might speak with who might offer unbiased perspectives on the work of the committee, neither the names of Birmingham nor Whelan were offered. The fact that I spoke to neither could be provided as evidence that my account on the matter of the study is unbalanced, though I wholeheartedly believe, through my discussion with Dobbin, that the thoughts of the president presented in this book closely mirror those of both Birmingham and Whelan.

It should also be known that I had no agenda in portraying the findings of the study. In fact, as someone who covered I-AA football for four years, I am of the belief that many of the universities that have moved their programs from I-AA to I-A in the past two decades don't belong at the highest level, and I entered into this project leaning toward the same point of view as it applied to Villanova's discussion of moving up. In evaluating the study and the facts, however, it became clear to me that Villanova had the ability to make the I-A move work based almost solely on the would-be affiliation with the BCS. The capital costs necessary to make the move were indeed significant, but they would have been recouped many times over by the revenue sharing that came with the university's association with the BCS and Big East football. As far as any concerns about the scholarly mission of the school being compromised, I think the folks at fine academic institutions like Boston College, Notre Dame, Vanderbilt, and Duke might argue with the notion that big-time football alters the ability to serve as a first-class academic institution to any great degree. I believe that any argument to the contrary reflects a prejudice against the sport of football and the student-athletes who participate in it, and much more so than any economic factors.

In any event, I hope that the reader has enjoyed what I always intended to be a real story about college football, one that hurts at times but also puts a human face on aspects of a game that, in this era of billion-dollar TV contracts and computer-based formulas to determine champions, seems to become more dehumanized at every turn.